The Second Century

D0825315

The Second Century

Reconnecting Customer and Value Chain through Build-to-Order

Moving beyond Mass and Lean Production in the Auto Industry

Matthias Holweg
Frits K. Pil

The MIT Press
Cambridge, Massachusetts
London, England

© 2004 Massachusetts Institute of Technology

All rights reserved. No part of this book may be reproduced in any form by any electronic or mechanical means (including photocopying, recording, or information storage and retrieval) without permission in writing from the publisher.

MIT Press books are available at special quantity discounts for business or sales promotions. For information, please email special_sales@mitpress.mit.edu or write to Special Sales Department, The MIT Press, 5 Cambridge Center, Cambridge, MA 02142.

Set in Palatino by The MIT Press. Printed and bound in the United States of America.

Library of Congress Cataloging-in-Publication Data

Holweg, Matthias.
The second century : reconnecting customer and value chain through build-to-order / Matthias Holweg, Frits K. Pil.
p. cm.
Includes bibliographical references and index.
ISBN-13: 978-0-262-08332-4 (hc. : alk. paper)—978-0-262-58262-9 (pbk. : alk. paper)
ISBN-10: 0-262-08332-9 (hc. : alk. paper)—0-262-58262-7 (pbk. : alk. paper)
1. Automobiles—Marketing. 2. Consumer satisfaction. 3. Automobile industry and trade. 4. Automobile industry and trade—United States. I. Title: 2nd century. II. Pil, Frits K. III. Title.
HD9710.A2H65   2004
629.222'068'8—dc22   2003066824

10 9 8 7 6 5 4 3 2

To my parents Dorothea and Joachim, and my sister Wiebke. —MH

To my wife Tricia, and our children Ellen and Karl. —FKP

Contents

Acknowledgments

Our research and writing in the auto industry spans many years, and it is hard to list by name all the colleagues, friends, family, and mentors who have helped us in so many ways. Our research has been funded and supported by both the International Motor Vehicle Program (IMVP) and the 3DayCar Programme. In particular we would like to thank IMVP's co-directors, John Paul MacDuffie and Fred Moavenzadeh, and Peter Hines at Cardiff Business School for their continued mentorship and support. John Paul and Peter were also our advisors in our Ph.D. days, and we value their ongoing help, advice, and friendship. The earlier leaders of IMVP, Jim Womack, Dan Jones, Dan Roos, Joel Clark, and Charlie Fine, selflessly shared their wisdom with us. Dan Jones and Dan Roos, the "two Dans," have provided us with invaluable help since our early years as students and novice researchers.

The Sloan Foundation had the vision, many years ago, to support industry research efforts across the United States, and we have benefited tremendously from that vision. Its funding has greatly facilitated our individual research and writing efforts, and we are particularly grateful to Gail Pesyna for her continuing support.

Our colleagues on the International Motor Vehicle Program are simply great. We were fortunate to receive tremendous help from our Japanese colleagues Takahiro Fujimoto, Kentaro Nobeoka, Koichi Shimokawa, and Akira Takeichi. They have helped us on all fronts in our research, including taking the leading role in Japanese data collection. We have enjoyed learning from them at IMVP meetings, conferences, and plant visits. Wujin Chu has played a similar role for us in Korea, facilitating data collection and access and engaging with us in substantive ways on research discussions. We also received help with assembly plant data from researchers in other parts of the world, including Greg Bamber, José Ferro, Russell Lansbury, Kannan Sethuraman, and Nazli Wasti. We

enjoyed stimulating and engaging research discussions with Mari Sako
in Europe and Susan Helper in the United States. We cannot neglect to
mention many additional IMVP friends who have greatly influenced
our thinking: Arnaldo Camuffo, Andy Graves, Ki-Chan Kim, and
Giuseppe Volpato. Donna Carty, IMVP's program manager, has always
been there for us with a helping hand.

Our findings with respect to Europe are largely based on research conducted as part of the 3DayCar Programme, a joint initiative of the Lean
Enterprise Research Centre at Cardiff Business School (led by Peter
Hines), the School of Management at the University of Bath (led by
Andy Graves), and the International Car Distribution Programme (led by
John Whiteman and Malcolm Harbour). We particularly would like to
thank Simon Elias at Cardiff for kindly granting us access to his customer and fleet buyer survey data, and Geoff Williams of ICDP for his
tremendous insights and for his advice on distribution aspects of the
industry. Also, we would like to thank Mickey Howard, Joe Miemczyk,
Nick Rich, David Simons, and Ben Waller for their most helpful support,
and the inspiring discussions during our research days on the 3DayCar
Programme.

The data regarding the financial aspects was kindly contributed by
Max Warburton, a former colleague of IMVP and research analyst with
Goldman Sachs. We also would like to acknowledge the ongoing support
of J.D. Power and Associates. Over the years, we have also had wonder-
ful exchanges and relationships with many other researchers, including
numerous friends at the GERPISA network in Europe. Takahiro
Fujimoto has played a key role in introducing us to many of these
researchers over the years. His leadership in the field of automotive
research and theory continues to be an inspiration to us.

Our colleagues at the Katz Graduate School of Business and the
Learning Research Development Center (University of Pittsburgh), at
MIT's Center for Technology, Policy and Industrial Development, at the
Lean Enterprise Research Centre and Logistics Systems Dynamics
Group at Cardiff Business School, and at the Judge Institute of
Management at the University of Cambridge have been a constant
source of inspiring discussions and friendship. Sara Bragg, Matt
Dunegan, Sondra Kanhofer, and Shirlie Lovell have provided ongoing
administrative support at these institutions, and Jack Aug, Su Chung,
Patsy Guzzi, and Pat Vargas have helped us manage the financial side of
our research.

Nancy Talbert provided us with invaluable editorial help as we wrote the book. Her rapid and detailed reading and her insightful comments were critical to keeping us motivated and writing. We are extremely grateful to her, and we look forward to working with her in the future.

John Covell and Paul Bethge at The MIT Press helped turn our vision of a book into reality. Thanks also to David Light of the *MIT Sloan Management Review* for his encouragement when we first set out to synthesize our learning on build-to-order.

This book would not have been possible without the tremendous assistance we have received from our friends and sponsors in industry, unions, and government. While it is not possible to list each of you, your help has been invaluable—let us know when we can return the favor.

The Second Century

At the Dawn of the Second Automotive Century

As it enters its second century, the auto industry is not a happy place. Layoffs, abysmal profit margins, long waits for popular models, skittish shareholders, dubious investors, soaring development and marketing costs—it suffers just about every plague in Pandora's industrial box.

As they have done since mass production replaced custom crafting in the early 1900s,[1] most auto manufacturers use marginally accurate demand forecasting to build a supply that includes 40–80 days of inventory, which sits in distribution centers and on dealers' lots. Once lots the size of football fields are brimming with loaded models, delighted customers are expected to elbow one another out of the way to get to them.

There is a major flaw in that thinking, of course: What if no one *wants* all the cars on the dealers' lots? This has not been lost on the industry. But instead of fixing the root cause, companies have begun to erode profitability by paying their customers to take the vehicles off their hands—a.k.a. discounting.

Not that mass production is necessarily a bad strategy. It worked well when Henry Ford started out—in a period where demand was unlimited, and companies could count on volume-driven efficiency to lower piece prices. When supply outstripped demand, lowering prices kept volumes up until a company could introduce a new model. Customers generally accepted the way of things.

Today's market is vastly different, and mass production no longer fits. Customers are more demanding, supply is overabundant, and competition is global. Industries that still rely on building to a demand forecast—and far too many do—find themselves with low margins, ample discounting, and a sclerotic value chain that cannot evolve with customers' desires. Worse, there is no easy fix. In Henry Ford's day, when the manufacturer's costs went up, all eyes turned to what the supplier could do to be more efficient. Companies are still attempting to squeeze their suppliers, but the focus on cost is proving disastrous.

As vehicle manufacturers blame the suppliers and push them to reduce costs and shorten order-to-delivery times, the suppliers respond by cutting life-sustaining R&D and by merging in desperation, not in strength. Vehicle manufacturers crank out heaps of cars, amassing inventory to buffer against the poor predictions from the forecasts. Meanwhile, at the local dealer, Mr. Jones reluctantly settles for a white four-door with a sunroof instead of a blue two-door without. Sure, Jones gets a discount for the sunroof, but he doesn't really like white cars and he didn't really want a sunroof. He also doesn't want to wait 2 months to get that two-door, no-frills blue car.

Sadly, Mr. Jones is part of a growing crowd. In Europe, one-fifth of customers drive home cars that are not what they intended to buy; in the United States, half do so. Diehards willing to wade through the billion-plus combinations that car companies offer must delay gratification a month or two *and* pay more than they would if they just took a better-equipped car on the lot.

In other words, companies seem to have forgotten that profitability comes, not from optimizing cost, but from building the right product at the right time.

The Myth of Efficiency and Volume

Car companies realize the difficulties they are facing and are earnestly seeking paths to enlightenment. The recent plethora of combined and hyphenated company names (DaimlerChrysler, BMW-Rover, GM-Fiat) is evidence that many see mergers and acquisitions as the way to Nirvana. Boardrooms echo with "achieve profitability through synergy," "round out our product portfolios," and "devise global strategies." This synergistic journey is fueled by the notion that producing more cars more efficiently yields greater sales volume. Big sales, in turn, put advertising executives in a good mood and enable Investor Relations to claim in the company's annual report that sales are up.

But somewhere in the translation from production efficiency to sales, companies lost sight of the customer. Surely this was unintentional, but it has serious consequences. Marketing expenses are through the roof, and vehicle manufacturers consequently recover less of the development cost per vehicle. Thus, on the one hand this approach racks up numbers, but on the other it eats away at profits. On balance, long-term profitability goes down.

Meanwhile, the push for efficiency and volume has created a disturbing paradox. Factories generate product with as little as 4 hours of incoming inventory, but the typical vehicle manufacturer has a 2-month supply of finished goods sitting in the marketplace (just as manufacturers did in the 1920s). So companies offer variety, and they can produce it efficiently, but somehow the customer never gets it. The result is reminiscent of the "pink flamingo problem." Someone may be selling a pink flamingo, and somewhere someone may want to buy one, but the odds that the two parties will meet are slim. For pink flamingos, there is e-Bay. For cars, the solution is a little more complex.

Under the Hood

To investigate the sources and the degree of dysfunction in the auto industry, we have spent a decade researching it, relying on the generous support of the International Motor Vehicle Program (IMVP) at the Massachusetts Institute of Technology and the 3DayCar Programme at Cardiff Business School. We benchmarked assembly plants in major regions worldwide, and analyzed the broader order-to-delivery value chain by examining data from six European vehicle manufacturers. With the help of our colleagues at the 3DayCar Programme, we also surveyed suppliers and logistics firms, interviewed dealers, and queried customers. Our primary aim was to develop a holistic industry perspective—to look beyond the factory, the dealer, or the design studio—to understand the web of relationships and dynamics that have brought the industry to this point. We thus explore challenges and solutions that are hard to see and understand with a less systemic approach.

Starting with lean production, and continuing the research that led to the 1990 book *The Machine That Changed the World*, we quickly discovered that the challenges the auto industry currently faces are not limited to car and component factories, where lean production has had its biggest impact over the past 15 years. A much broader understanding of "lean," or even a neo-lean model that extends the traditional lean manufacturing model to a system-wide perspective, is needed. Extending the "pull" logic that is at the heart of lean production to the entire value chain and embracing build-to-order strategies requires systemic change, as well as modifications to all aspects of production, design, and logistics. Shifting to such a systemic view is often difficult because it may require sacrificing some local optimization to enhance system-wide performance.

We have aimed at analyzing all major subsystems in the automotive supply chain to provide a comprehensive picture of what building cars to order actually involves.

Productivity Improvements Are Narrowly Focused

In the late 1980s, our IMVP colleagues showed how Japanese firms were significantly more productive than their European and US counterparts, while also attaining superior quality. We find that productivity has increased steadily in all major auto-producing regions over the past decade. The gap between Western and Japanese manufacturers is significantly narrower than it was in the late 1980s and the early 1990s. In fact, all global regions are catching up nicely in terms of labor hours per vehicle. In a number of plants, however, increases in productivity have been achieved through the reengineering of production tasks and processes and through automation. Several companies have neglected necessary changes in work design. Thus, productivity improvements often have come at the expense of flexibility and offer limited quality improvements.

Lack of Customer Responsiveness

Competitive advantage ultimately stems from customer responsiveness—a profitability law that many manufacturers have apparently forgotten. Manufacturing is only a small fraction of the order-to-delivery process, and the rest of that process is not doing so well. Of the waiting time for custom vehicles, fully 80 percent is attributable to bottlenecks in the information flow at the vehicle manufacturer's headquarters—and it is more than a month before an order reaches the factory. The batch-driven legacy IT systems that were supposed to reduce delays actually aggravate them. So much for the promise of "e."

Forecast-Driven Production Still Reigns

That this could be true despite a vastly different market and all our technological advances is monumental evidence that the industry has never stepped out of Henry Ford's shoes, however poor the current fit. In Henry's day, the rules of business dictated high volumes at low cost. As Ford shipped vehicles to dealers, he kept the plant churning out more, figuring that 60 days of finished product was just about the right inventory between factory and customer. The economies of scale, he reasoned, would make bigger factories even more cost effective, which meant buying the biggest presses available to stamp out huge volumes of parts. Efficiently making a large number of vehicles and selling them from dealer stock became the legacy of mass production.

Eventually, however, customers began wanting choice, not just "any color as long as it's black." Henry soon realized that, even at $200 per vehicle, he could not maintain sales of the Model T. Consumers were buying 3- and 4-year-old used cars rather than new Model Ts because they perceived that the used cars had more features and thus were a better value. Ford sales dropped from over 1 million in 1923 to 1926 to 393,000 and 482,000 in 1927 and 1928. The market had moved on.

Unfortunately, 100 years later we seem unable to grasp the significance of this pattern. Companies continue to use the forecast-based model, adopting a philosophy of "build them anyway, and ultimately they will sell." And the focus continues to be on price as the ultimate driver of sales. Lean production has altered the way we go about *manufacturing* cars, but the way we are *selling* cars and thinking about customers' needs has changed little since the days of Henry Ford and Alfred P. Sloan.

Modern Markets

Customers enjoy low prices, but they also desire choice, even at the lower end of the market. In all markets, not just that for automobiles, lower prices cannot compensate for dull designs, low brand appeal, and a lack of technical innovation. And they certainly cannot compensate for a poor customer-to-product match.

If our research underlines anything, it is that customers must get back into the equation. Building vehicles to forecast must give way to building them to order. Responsiveness must be woven into the entire value chain, not just pushed on select parts. Properly implemented, build-to-order not only reduces costly finished inventory and eliminates the need for many types of incentives, it also ensures that vehicle manufacturers can sell the options that customers want—an important source of profits.

Marooned on Islands of Excellence

Most vehicle manufacturers agree that in theory build-to-order is a good solution, and many are tentatively launching pilot projects in small, localized settings to reduce order-to-delivery time so that they *can* build more cars to order. But because these projects are competing in a forecast-driven system, they often are doomed from the start, and any learning dissolves quickly.

Companies take the same narrow view when they create islands of excellence that actually make build-to-order harder to implement across the entire value chain. Assembly plants build lots of cars efficiently to forecast. They have been rated on efficiency for years. Suggesting that they could trade off some of that efficiency to build cars that customers want when customers want them is heretical.

In part, we can thank the Japanese for our stubborn refusal to abandon these islands. In the 1980s, Western automakers wanted to best Japanese production for fear that Japanese companies' superior productivity and quality would result in market-share loss. Western manufacturers launched "lean production" programs to wring the last bit of inefficiency and waste from their manufacturing processes to match Japanese companies.

Today, all but two major Japanese vehicle manufacturers are controlled by US or European companies. Unfortunately, the single-minded focus on factory optimization continues. And so does the failure to deeply understand what it means to be lean.

In its conception, lean production had a strong emphasis on "pull"—to produce only when an item was needed. "Pull" in this sense means the pull of a customer order on the entire value chain, not just the pull within a factory or from suppliers. Yet say "lean" to most companies and they think "waste reduction," mainly on the shop floor. Just-in-time delivery between suppliers and assemblers is an example of how companies have implemented pull. However impressive, it is too often decoupled from the customer, or market pull. Factories hence efficiently create months of finished goods inventory, but that inventory has little to do with the actual customer demand. Thus, it is not surprising that fewer than 10 percent of all vehicles are built to order in the United States, and fewer than 50 percent in Europe. With few exceptions, stock levels are between 1 and 2 months, and manufacturers with order-to-delivery times of less than 3 weeks for cars are unheard of.

The Rocky Path to Responsiveness

To change the system, the industry must evolve its production system to match the market. We often hear that the industry is too cyclical and the demand too variable to sustain build-to-order, yet we have found that the variation is largely artificial—more related to performance measures, goals, and incentives than to demand. Indeed, odd as it may seem, true demand often fluctuates less than what is forecast.

Responsiveness is not an easy road, however; it mandates flexibility in process, product, and volume. Some companies achieve excellence in one area, but none has mastered all three. Specific changes are needed to attain the flexibilities that enable a transition to build-to-order. Companies must rid themselves of certain preconceptions, accepting, for example, that metrics such as person-hours per vehicle and market share bear little relationship to long-term competitiveness and profitability. The path is difficult, but the payoff is high. Building cars that customers want not only has the long-term potential of returning the industry to profitability; it can also break the current cycles of boom and bust by eradicating artificial variability and demand swings.

At the start of the twentieth century, the United States paved the way to the mass-production era. A half-century later, Japan showed the world how to "achieve more with less" and changed the way the industry thought about waste in the factory and in the supply chain. Another half-century later, the auto industry is learning that lean factories alone are not enough to attain profitability or to sustain independence. Acknowledging that the customer must be the ultimate starting point of any value stream is not hard. Altering a comprehensive system including designers, factories, suppliers, dealers, and logistics firms to enhance responsiveness is much more difficult. Some companies have made great strides in creating lean factories. Others have been very successful in attaining volume flexibility, or in creating flexible product designs. But all face significant challenges in making the comprehensive system-wide transition to customer responsiveness.

In this neo-lean world, the European producers are the farthest along, but it is still an open race. Our research reveals that many companies are taking the needed first steps toward greater responsiveness. We will systematically discuss all the changes that are needed to move beyond lean factories and toward a responsive system.

In the twentieth century, production efficiency and minimization of unit cost were believed to be the core drivers of competitive advantage. As we enter the second automotive century, the winners will not be those firms that search for larger and larger scale, or those that run efficient factories, or those that squeeze the last drop of profitability from their suppliers. The winners will be those that build products as if customers mattered.

I   Disassembling the "Order-to-Delivery" Process

In the market of the future—if not the market of today—the company that can get the car the customer ordered to them fastest will be front runners.

—Kosuke Ikebuchi (Senior Managing Director, Toyota Motor Company), in "More than just a production method: The Toyota Manufacturing System," *World Automotive Manufacturing*, October 13, 1999

1   Old Habits Die Hard

If talking about build-to-order could make it happen, many companies would already be building truckloads of custom cars. Indeed, many manufacturers have affirmed strategies to reduce costly finished inventory by shortening order-to-delivery time and building vehicles to customer order.[1] Something has obviously happened to dampen their enthusiasm. The variety of attempts and the scattered strategies reflect a rather half-hearted attitude, and the results often are more accidental than planned. Even at those manufacturers that are the furthest along, build-to-order strategies are not consistent across brands and models, and even vary within model production cycles. Companies tend to reserve build-to-order for luxury models and to use forecast-based production for most other products. Furthermore, build-to-order percentages are much higher at the start of a model's cycle than at the end.

Why haven't companies made the transition? Part of the problem is that no one seems clearly motivated. In the larger scheme of sales sourcing—determining how the customer's order is actually fulfilled—build-to-order is only one possibility, and owing to current long waits it is not a popular one. As table 1.1 shows, true build-to-order requests—the ones the company receives *before* building the car (new orders from a customer or orders already in the system amended to customer specifications)—do not typically amount to a significant percentage of sales sources. The high percentages for Germany and for Toyota in Japan are outliers rather than the norm.

Both sales from central stock and sales from dealer stock are build-to-forecast sales—the customer selects a vehicle from existing stock. The vehicle can come either directly from the stock at the dealer the customer visits, from another dealer, or from stock held at distribution centers awaiting dealer orders. To identify a suitable vehicle from the stock at a distribution center or at another dealership, dealers access the vehicle

Table 1.1
Sales sourcing in major volume markets, 1999–2000.*

	Europe	UK	Germany	US	Japan (Toyota)
Cars built to customer order	48%	32%	62%	6%	60%[a]
Sales from central stock (distribution centers) or transfer between dealers	14%	51%	8%	5%	6%
Sales from dealer stock	38%	17%	30%	89%	34%

*Sources: G. Williams, Progress towards Customer Pull Distribution, research paper 4/2000, International Car Distribution Programme, Solihull; H. Shioji, "The order entry system in Japan," International Symposium on Logistics, Morioka, Japan, July 2000; Office for the Study of Automotive Transportation, University of Michigan Transportation Research Institute, Delphi Study X, 2001.
a. Recent interviews at Toyota suggest that the current build-to-order level for Toyota in Japan is more like 50% across all sales channels.

manufacturer's stock-locator system. Once a dealer finds a vehicle, the distribution center transfers the product to the dealership. If the vehicle is at another dealership, the transport incurs an extra fee, since it is usually a single car on the truck. Ultimately this inefficient delivery mode translates into higher logistics cost, which all customers absorb. In the United Kingdom, this transfer cost is an estimated $180 for each delivery. The transfer from distribution centers is generally cheaper because the center can schedule more cars per truck.

Table 1.1 shows how radically three high-volume regions—Europe, Japan (Toyota), and the United States—differed in 1999 and 2000. We isolated Germany and the United Kingdom to show how even within a region, markets can differ significantly. We used Toyota to represent Japan. Even though it is considered the benchmark in the auto sector, it achieves only 60 percent build-to-order. This relatively high ratio is specific to the Japanese domestic market: all Japanese firms, including Toyota, are largely building to forecast in Europe and the United States.[2]

Much as in Europe, there is great diversity in the progress and effort Japanese manufacturers are making towards build-to-order in Japan. On one end of the spectrum are Honda and Subaru, which historically have made virtually all their cars to forecast. Honda bases its production entirely on forecast. Plants in Japan handle high levels of variety, but production is batched. Under *kanban* (a pull system with suppliers), all material is delivered by suppliers in the forecast batches, and this makes creating the pull required in a build-to-order system extremely difficult to attain. Toyota and Nissan, in contrast, have openly declared their intention to reduce order-to-delivery lead times and implement build-to-order. Toyota, known for *kaizen* (continuous improvement), has applied this strategy to its build-to-order efforts. Toyota initiated "daily ordering" in 1999, the objective being to reach an order-to-delivery target of 14 days. Currently, Toyota achieves an average of 23 days across all sales channels.[3] Nissan's build-to-order efforts in Japan are already well advanced. In 1991 Nissan implemented a new order entry system, called ANSWER,[4] that allowed dealers to schedule daily orders into the production schedule 6 days before production. (This was called "D-6 scheduling.") The number of days was reduced to 4 in 2001 with the launch of ANSWER II. Nissan's underlying philosophy is *douki-seisan*, which can be translated as "'the origin of everything is the customer." After trials in Japan, *douki-seisan* was announced on a global basis in 1997. With a 30-day order-to-delivery lead time (the target is 15 days), Nissan still lags behind Toyota. However, it has made tremendous progress in using build-to-order to cut inventory, and it holds only 20 days of inventory in Japan—half Toyota's average stock.[5]

The US market is a clear outlier, with most cars sold from dealer stock. In the United States, instant gratification rules. Customers have been trained to go to a dealer, find a car that roughly matches their needs and wishes, haggle for a good price, and drive away with a car the same day. Car buying is akin to grocery shopping: go in, take what is on the shelves even if it's not exactly what you want (after all, something is better than nothing), and drive home. Indeed, the average supermarket shopper hardly ever finds all the goods that are on his shopping list and commonly buys several items that aren't on it.[6] Apparently, car shopping is conducted in a similar spirit. At the other end of the gratification spectrum is Germany. The German market follows a tradition of long waits for custom cars,[7] so it is no surprise that it has the highest build-to-order content in Europe.

Toyota's build-to-order percentage is high in part because all its suppliers, retailers, and customers are conveniently co-located. That, coupled with overseas exports to provide a stable production base, makes it easier to implement build-to-order. This geographic concentration of value-chain stakeholders is common in Japan. The experience of other Japanese manufacturers shifting to build-to-order is similar. Nissan, for example, has been able to attain a 50 percent build-to-order rate on fairly short notice in the Japanese market.

In the United Kingdom, 19 percent of customers did not receive the exact specification they asked for, which relates to the high percentage of vehicles bought from existing stock. In Europe, on average, 20 percent of customers compromised on their vehicle's specifications, according to dealer perceptions. Despite Germany's high use of build-to-order, 24 percent of German customers felt the same way. These numbers strongly imply that no single market leads in proactively altering its processes to increase building to order. The high percentage in Germany is more of a cultural anomaly, as is the low percentage in the United States. Toyota's high percentage is due to its geographic concentration of supporting elements and exports.

A closer look at the built-to-forecast percentages also shows how aspects of the forecast distribution model affect the implementation of build-to-order. The trend in the United Kingdom is particularly revealing. When the technology for stock-locator systems first became available in the late 1980s, Ford and some other companies pioneered them in the United Kingdom, initially with great success. As figure 1.1 shows, in 1992, 45 percent of new vehicles were sales from dealer transfers. Soon, however, manufacturers realized that each sale from a stock-locator system came with a $180 transportation-to-dealer cost. As logistics costs skyrocketed and eroded profit margins, vehicle manufacturers backed away from stock locators and turned to distribution centers. By 1999, the 45 percent had dwindled to 15 percent.

But although distribution-center sales increased, build-to-order failed to take off. Part of the reason was that reliance on distribution centers introduced an additional objective: remove stock from the dealer and fulfill orders with less overall stock. Consequently, by the end of the 1990s sales from dealer stock had also decreased dramatically. Despite shifts in where product originates, the fundamental problem remains: all but one-third of the product is built to forecast demand rather than actual demand, and is shuttled around post factory to ultimately match up with a customer.

Figure 1.2 shows how the forecast-driven strategies set up two vicious cycles. Stock levels in the marketplace disconnect the entire value chain from the customer, which in turn frees factories to address a stable, long-term forecast without worrying about individual customer requirements.

No one will debate that the push strategy is tempting, but it is also a trap. An industry that supplies customized high-volume products ends up pushing finished goods into the market to get the revenue to offset bulk production and design costs.

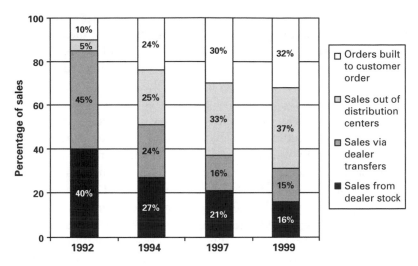

Figure 1.1
Sales sourcing in UK volume car market, 1992–1999. Sources: G. Williams, European New Car Supply and Stocking Systems, ICDP, 1998; Williams, Progress towards Customer Pull Distribution, ICDP, 2000.

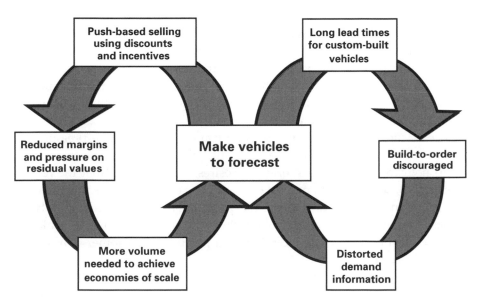

Figure 1.2
The vicious cycles of make-to-forecast. Source: M. Holweg and F. Pil, "Successful build-to-order strategies start with the customer," *Sloan Management Review* 43 (2001), no. 1: 74–83.

The focus turns to efficiency on the shop floor to get the unit cost down. The motivation to optimize the whole system from the customer to suppliers is lost in a frenzy of build, sell, and build more. Vehicles that must be built to a specific order are so unusual that the order-fulfillment lead times increase. The longer the wait, the less willing customers become to go through the gauntlet of getting exactly what they want.

In a push-driven world, customers have three basic choices: wait for a custom-built vehicle, settle for a vehicle in stock that isn't exactly what they wanted, or go to another brand with a similar configuration and better availability. The go-to-another-brand option translates to a lost sales ratio—total customers divided by the percentage of customers who bought elsewhere because they didn't get what they wanted in time. In 1999, this ratio for the United States was an estimated 36 percent.[8] In the United Kingdom, lost sales dropped from 10 percent in 1994 to 6 percent in 1999, and in the same period Germany's lost sales went from 11 percent to 3 percent. In France, the ratio stayed constant at 5 percent.[9] These numbers clearly imply that companies are altering their distribution systems to retain the customer.

Any lost sale represents lost revenue. Yet there is a larger issue. The longer it takes to provide customized vehicles, the more customers are actually discouraged to request a car built to their specifications. The manufacturer gets farther and farther from the customers, relying on sales forecasts that are based on artificial measures. For example, suppose a forecast contains X number of red cars. Now customers actually like blue cars, but dealers induce them to buy red cars with 0 percent financing, better trade-in offers, free upgrades, discounts, and other sales tactics. Eventually customers reluctantly give in to the pressure. Those evaluating the sales and generating the manufacturer's forecast do not capture customers' original desires; they see only that the red cars sold, so they again put red cars, perhaps even more this time, into the production program. Since the production program is generally based on historic sales information, the cycle is self-fulfilling. It breaks only when no amount of incentives will persuade a customer to buy a neon-pink car.

Incentives also end up increasing the cost of the sale because the manufacturer is essentially paying a customer to reduce its inventory. The more discounts are needed, the lower the per-vehicle profit becomes. The lower the profit, the less cost the manufacturer can recover on each sale, so it increases volume to recover cost through economies of scale. Higher volume then forces the manufacturer to push even more vehicles into the market, using still more incentives, and the vicious cycle gets more vicious.

A less well known failing of the push strategy is that it depresses the market for used cars. As manufacturers boost vehicle sales through fantastic discounts and incentives, the prices for used and nearly new cars plummet. This downward spiral not only lowers the residual values for specific vehicle lines; it also erodes the entire value perception of a brand. Such loss in perceived value greatly affects the purchase decision. Volkswagen, Mercedes, and Porsche capitalize on this relationship by touting the competition's loss of brand value in their marketing campaigns.

Plummeting residual values also have serious ramifications for financing companies. Leasing firms, for example, generally predetermine the price at which the vehicle will be bought back years later. In 2000, when market demand was less than expected in both the United Kingdom and the United States, leasing companies suddenly found drastic discrepancies between their book value and the actual prices they could achieve for their formerly leased vehicles. For example, a loaded 1997 Ford Expedition XLT with a sticker price of $36,580 was expected to be worth $25,606 after a 3-year lease. Instead, it fetched only $16,500 at auctions in 2000, and the bank or auto maker had to cover the $9,106 difference.[10] Two years later the situation was no different. The average auction price of an off-lease Taurus, which in October 2000 was $10,750, fell to $8,650 in March 2002. Other models fared no better—during the same period, the average auction price of a used Toyota Camry went from $11,475 to $10,250.[11]

In short, the forecast-driven model has dramatic costs, some of which are visible at the point of sale and some of which do not wreak their damage until many years later. The vicious cycle of build-to-forecast is hard to break out of. We will examine the order-to-delivery model associated with the vicious cycle of build-to-forecast, and from there will turn to the changes that are needed to introduce a build-to-order system in which cars are built as if customers mattered.

The patterns outlined thus far show that a transition to build-to-order is far more challenging than many companies had envisioned, perhaps in part because they lacked a deep understanding of how each stage of the order-to-delivery process affects build-to-order. In fact, it is worth pausing a moment here to clarify exactly what we mean by "order-to-delivery." Despite what some people think, order-to-delivery is *not* build-to-order. "Order-to-delivery" has two distinct meanings: (1) the process from the time the customer or dealer places the order until the vehicle is delivered to the customer or dealer and (2) the time this process takes. Thus, order-to-delivery and build-to-order stand in simple relation to one another: a manufacturer's order-to-delivery (process) time must be short enough to inspire customers to wait for their vehicles to be built to order. If the potential order-to-delivery time falls outside the customer's waiting tolerance, the customer can move to another manufacturer with better availability or shorter order-to-delivery time. When manufacturers talk about "reducing order-to-delivery," they generally mean shortening the process time so that they can build more vehicles to order and not lose customers to other brands with faster availability.

Another misunderstood term is "value chain." In fact, from this point on, we will begin using a term that is more representative of where value originates: "value grid." "Chain" implies that relationships and units within organizations contribute to profitability in a linear fashion. Nothing could be further from reality—despite what finance and strategy folks would have us believe. Relationships have complex interdependencies and overlaps that affect profits in far-from-straightforward ways. Equipment suppliers, for example, may have customers other than auto manufacturers. Even within a manufacturer, some activities (e.g., the development of fuel cells) can occur in parallel with other value chains. This is true of other industries too. In the wireless telecommunications industry, for example, Nokia is collaborating with other handset producers to maintain a sufficiently large user base of its software. That way, Nokia hopes to fend off Microsoft, which threatens to capture the value in the handset business much as it has done in the personal computer business. In contrast, Microsoft has penetrated the handset industry laterally, and views the handset operating software as a way of enhancing and reinforcing its core business in operating software for computers.

A prerequisite to understanding the order-to-delivery process and build-to-order capability is to have some measure of what is realistic. To satisfy this requirement, we evaluated the generic systems and benchmarked the order-to-delivery processes for six vehicle manufacturers—two European-owned and two US-owned vehicle manufacturers operating in Europe and two European divisions of Japanese car producers. Most of the research done in the past 20 years has focused on assembly operations, on the integration of component suppliers, and on distribution logistics. Relatively little is known on how the entire order-to-delivery process actually works, yet without viewing the entire process no company can identify and remove the obstacles to a build-to-order transition.

Benchmarking order-to-delivery capability is tricky. We mapped the full circle of information flow, from order entry at the dealers through national sales organizations, production planning and scheduling functions at the vehicle manufacturer, and the material or physical flow from the suppliers through the assembly plants and back through the distribution channels to the vehicle's delivery to the dealer.[12] Our focus was on system capability[13]—the minimal system-related throughput time for a custom-built vehicle—rather than on average lead times for specific orders.[14] In using system capability, we assume that each subsystem provides the fastest currently feasible throughput, with no rework or other delays. Averages, on the other hand, typically include delays of various kinds—e.g., vehicles held in queues if the supply of an option many customers are requesting is limited, or if quality problems occur in a single order. By focusing on the critical path (the best possible time), we are accurately defining the best response of the current systems to a vehicle order. Most actual orders will take longer than this theoretically achievable time, but system capability portrays the manufacturer's and the supplier's basic ability to support build-to-order. Approaches based on actual average performance cannot provide this, since they would be distorted severely by the demand-supply scenario for a particular model.

Finally, in our benchmarking, we defined "delivery" as delivery to the dealer, excluding dealer preparation. Our research shows that customers rarely go immediately to the dealership to pick up their vehicles, but prefer to wait until the weekend, so it would be pointless to add the time the dealer takes to hand over the vehicle to the customer.

Figure 1.3 is a greatly simplified diagram of a typical order-to-delivery process. Of course the order-to-delivery process is more complex than any one diagram can convey, comprising dealers, national sales companies, head offices, assembly plants, tiers of component suppliers, and logistics companies in an arrangement that differs across manufacturers. Our goal in drawing the process map was to capture the underlying logic across order-to-delivery processes, which is surprisingly similar across manufacturers. From this map, we identified four basic stages in order-to-delivery, which we use as a basis for deriving order-to-delivery process times. These steps are order entry, production scheduling and sequencing, vehicle production, and vehicle distribution. We also

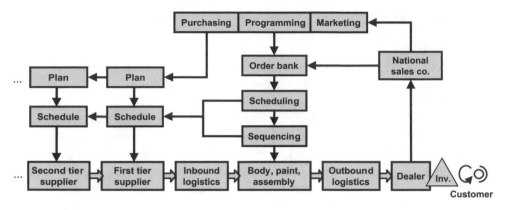

Figure 1.3
Map of typical order-to-delivery process.

identified four linked processes that are critical to understanding order-to-delivery: sales forecasting, production programming, supplier scheduling, and inbound logistics.[15] Thus, the order-to-delivery process includes the following stages and processes:

• *Sales forecasting* aggregates all dealers', national sales companies', and importers' forecasts and uses them as a basis for regional sales forecasts, which in turn become input for production programming.

• *Production programming* maps a consolidation of forecast market demand onto available production capacity to yield a framework that defines how many vehicles will be built in each factory, the vehicles' specifications, and the markets to which they will be delivered.

• *Order entry* is the stage in which orders are checked and entered into an order bank to await production scheduling.

• *Production scheduling and sequencing* fits orders from the order banks into production schedules, according to the production program. Once scheduled for a particular plant, these orders are used to develop the sequence of cars to be built on the scheduled date.

• *Supplier scheduling* is the process by which suppliers receive forecasts at various times, actual schedules, and daily call-offs—all of which can vary dramatically.

• *Inbound logistics* is the process by which logistics service providers (often third parties) collect parts from suppliers, consolidate them, and deliver them to the assembly plants at the required time.

• *Vehicle production* is the process of physically welding and painting the body and assembling the vehicle, including all testing and rework.

• *Vehicle distribution* is the stage at which the plant ships the finished vehicle to the dealer (or in rare cases, directly to the customer).

These eight processes and stages represent the building blocks most manufacturers rely on to manage the order-to-delivery process. The activities within each stage provide useful insights into the benefits and limitations of the current information and material flows in the supply chain.

Although customers would like to believe that their vehicles spend weeks being carefully crafted, the shocking truth is that most of the delay occurs before the vehicle ever gets to the assembly line. The actual production process in the assembly factories takes less than 2 days. The initial stages of order-to-delivery thus represent considerable opportunity for companies to deliver a product more quickly and efficiently.

Sales Forecasting

In this initial stage, the national sales company asks dealers to supply their annual volume forecast several months before the end of the calendar year. This forecast serves as a baseline that the national sales company revises either monthly or bimonthly. The national sales company's regional staff then visits the dealers and reviews the actual numbers in relation to the forecast. Although the forecast process does not directly interfere with order fulfillment, in most cases it commits the parties to predicted volumes. Moreover, changes are not always balanced. Dealers tell us that the national sales company often raises the initial volume forecast if sales are exceeding the forecast, but it rarely lowers the forecasts if sales are down and inventory is piling up.

Sales forecasting thus involves the manufacturer's sales department, national sales companies (which can be either independent companies, such as importers, or subsidiaries of the vehicle manufacturer in various countries), and dealers. The demand forecasts become the basis for production programming.

The volume commitment can rest with the dealers or with the national sales company. When the dealers are responsible, they must often supply orders in line with their forecast volume up to 90 days ahead of production. They must identify major features such as model and engine early, but they can defer the decision on options, such as radio and air conditioning. The primary reason for committing the dealer to sales volume is to perpetuate a wholesale-driven push system. Predictably, this comes with a high level of sales from stock and a heavy reliance on discounting.

Production Programming

The production programming stage begins with the first programming meeting to review regional sales predictions and production issues with the aim of finalizing production volumes. This process is a compromise between production capacity and each market's sales requests, taking into account forward sales and stock-level requirements. As such, the forecasts typically contain healthy doses of wishful thinking and optimism. One strategic planner at a first-tier supplier jokingly noted that if you add all the predicted sales in the UK market, you get 130 percent of actual new-vehicle sales!

The production program sets the production parameters for the next period on volume, model, and trim level. It also allocates to markets major items (such as engines) or constraint options (such as air conditioning, heated windscreens, or popular engines—e.g., diesels in Europe). Finally, it allocates product in short supply across the manufacturer's national and regional markets according to the vehicle's profitability and pricing, regional competitive pressure, and the power of regional sales organizations.

The programming meeting is thus not only an operational decision point on future vehicle production, but also a central and strategic steering instrument. The finance department is present, since the differing return per vehicle makes defining a profitable program essential. The financial strategy is typically to push volume into the markets where the average revenue is higher, even if demand is low and the push adds wait time for other customers.

In the short term, and with the current accounting system, volume push makes sense. The vehicle manufacturer sees profit for the sale of a car once it is signed over to distribution at the factory. The car at that point is allocated to a market, and into the financial responsibility of the national sales company. Certain markets can absorb vehicles with higher sales prices, so the volume push is directed at those markets. Thus, in the short run, quarterly results improve. But the repercussion comes a few months later, when the manufacturer has to subsidize moving the vehicle off the lot or out of the distribution center. Discounting seriously erodes profitability and has other nasty side effects, including loss of brand strength and the low residual values discussed above. Discounts in Europe for aging vehicles are around 4 percent for stock that is 90 days old, and between 6.5 percent (France) and 11.1 percent (United Kingdom) for stock that is 270 days old.[1]

Programming meetings are generally monthly, but stakeholders typically make decisions 3 months in advance and make every effort to adhere to them. The idea is to ensure production stability and balanced assembly lines by giving suppliers some notice of the volume and the product mix they need to produce. Decisions can change 1 month before production at the latest, and typically only because the manufacturer failed to achieve a target or because some new component is imposing unanticipated constraints.

Production planning becomes increasingly detailed as the build period approaches. The manufacturer generally determines volume and model type (sedan or station wagon, for example) about 3 months before production, the details of power train and transmission 2 months before, and final color, trim, and option choices 1 month before. The vehicle manufacturers we studied varied only slightly from these self-imposed time lines.

Consequently, the production program allows for only a few amendments in the month before actually building the car—principally to trim and color, and occasionally to engines and transmissions. Moreover, the main operational boundaries of production volumes and product mix are decided 3 months before actual production and are based on sales forecasts created even earlier.

These process times and their attendant limitations are important because they greatly influence the way order fulfillment plays out and hence are the root of many build-to-order implementation difficulties.

Order Entry

The order-entry stage begins when a salesperson enters a stock order from a dealer or an order from a customer into the system. The order can come directly from the dealership or through the Internet and sometimes even by fax or mail. The national sales company then processes the order and submits it to the manufacturer's headquarters, where a computer checks it for build feasibility and expands it into a list of individual parts. Only then does it go into the order bank and become available for scheduling.

The order-entry process (figure 2.1) is nearly identical for private, retail, and retail fleet orders, except for very large, direct fleet orders, which the national sales company or vehicle manufacturer's head office enters. The vehicle manufacturer is responsible for all steps in order entry except the allocation check, which falls to the national sales company.

Allocation Check

By the time a salesperson enters the order, the order's financial clearance and other formalities should be complete. Often the national sales company follows the order entry with a check to see that the dealer and market have an order *allocation*—that the desired vehicle is available for that dealer and that market. If not, the sales company delays the order artificially until the next allocation period. Some markets might not use their allocation, but few systems permit allocation swapping.

Build-Feasibility Check

The order must obviously conform to the specifications offered for the particular model in the particular market and model year. A central engineering database, which the manufacturer maintains, contains all the needed data. Ford's World Engineering Release System, for example, contains all the information about which specifications are standard and which are offered as options or packages. Thus, if a customer orders an optional antilock brake system (ABS), the build-feasibility check ensures that ABS is available as an option for that vehicle in that market. If the check finds that it is a standard feature, the system rejects the order, and the dealer must make the necessary order correction. Without the build-feasibility check, the dealer would inadvertently be ordering ABS parts twice—once as standard and once as an option.

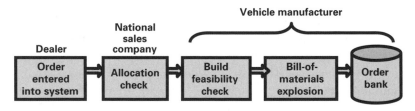

Figure 2.1
Steps in order entry.

The check is particularly useful in tracking specifications in cases of model-year changes, where dealers might place orders for one model year but, because of delays, the factory actually builds the vehicle in the new model year. Consecutive model years typically have significantly different specifications, so the dealer must inform the customer and so on.

Bill-of-Material Conversion

When an order comes to the manufacturer, it is in dealer codes, which define the model, body style, engine type, and options. The manufacturer's system must then convert the order to a bill of materials—a list of all the components the factory needs to build that vehicle. On the surface this stage seems rather straightforward, but even identical orders placed in different countries will have different bills of material. Country-specific equipment alters the technical specifications and hence the parts requirements (left-hand or right-hand drive, standard equipment levels, emission levels, and so on). For the most part, this process is automatic, but someone must update the database so that it can correctly specify the required parts to reflect evolution in national regulations or regional marketing initiatives.

Transfer to Order Bank

The final stage in order entry is to transfer the order as a bill of material to the order bank, where it stays until the system assigns it to a build period in a plant and transfers it into the plant's production schedule.

Although order amendment is not strictly an order-entry step, dealers can choose to amend forecast orders while they are still in the order bank or in scheduling. The actual point of being "too late" to change varies by feature and manufacturer or plant, as table 2.1 shows. Dealers choose from their own forecast orders or any unsold orders in the system—the open-order pipeline—to specify amendments that would fit the vehicle to the customer requirements. ("Unsold" means not yet allocated to any customer.) The open-order pipeline essentially increases the chance of finding the customer's desired vehicle among all stock orders.

However, as the table shows, some order features have little chance of being changed. Model and body style are generally fixed, and most other feature alterations are bound to strict time frames. Power trains, trim levels, and certain options have the longest amendment lead times, while color, wheels, and stereo type have somewhat more flexible time horizons.

Table 2.1
Lead times for order amendment (days before start of production) for five manufacturers.

Manufacturer	Engine	Options[a]	Color	Wheels	Stereo
A	No amendment permitted	No amendment permitted	No amendment permitted	No amendment permitted	Amendment after assembly at dealership
B	60 days	15 days	6 days	6 days	6 days
C	26 days	26 days	19 days	19 days	Information not available
D	26 days body, 42 days, engine	26 days	19 days	19 days	19 days
E	6 weeks	3–6 weeks	3–5 weeks	Amendment after assembly at distribution center	Amendment after assembly at distribution center

a. air conditioning, sunroof, etc.

Thus, although the open-order pipeline lets the factory address some aspects of build-to-order, it is equivalent to patching a system driven by stock orders. This patch is not without risk. If forecast orders remain in the pipeline that do not find a customer in time to be altered to the exact specification, there is a great temptation for the manufacturer to build these vehicles despite the lack of demand. And once these vehicles end up in stock, they pose a high risk of triggering the vicious circles of making to forecast all over again.

In the boxes that follow, we briefly synthesize the delays that are inherent in each basic stage of the order-to-delivery system.

---

average delay from order entry: 3.8 days

Most people believe that, in the digital age, order entry happens online or even in real time. Orders might be entered online, and the allocation and build-feasibility checks might take only about 2 hours, but in fact orders wait overnight (and often longer) to be converted into lists of required parts. The national sales company often batches orders, thereby adding to the delay.

Production Scheduling and Sequencing

As figure 2.2 shows, production scheduling is a complex stage. A scheduling team uses a set of proprietary scheduling algorithms to convert orders in the order bank to feasible plant production schedules. The schedules, in turn, determine the sourcing of all needed parts from suppliers. Production scheduling accounts for almost half the time an order spends in the system. A vehicle can have as many as 15,000 part numbers, representing 2,000–4,000 individual components, so scheduling is not trivial. Although the computational part of scheduling is automated, the process requires considerable trial-and-error planning.

The scheduling process consists of fitting the orders in the order bank first into a weekly and later into a daily build schedule, which a human scheduler converts to a production sequence. As part of weekly scheduling, the scheduler, with some automated assistance, tries to assign orders to each plant according to its available production capacity. To ensure that the scheduling respects the plants' overall mix and capacity constraints, as well as the availability of entities such as the number and

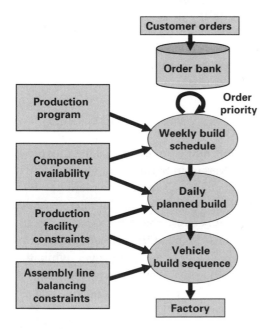

Figure 2.2
Steps in production scheduling.

types of engines available, the scheduler tool defines *control entities* for the algorithm. If the engine supplier can build only 200 V6 engines, for example, the scheduler will insert a control of 200 to limit the number of V6 engines that can be scheduled. Most manufacturers insert controls manually, adjusting them as needed to arrive at a feasible production schedule. The more controls, the less likely the algorithm can arrive at such a feasible schedule.

Once each plant has set weekly schedules, schedulers move on to daily production scheduling, which splits weekly schedules into daily planned builds. The split must take into account a plant's volume and mix restrictions—no more than 60 percent station wagons, no more than 25 percent automatic transmission, and so on. The daily schedule also allows for component restrictions; for example, it cannot schedule for Monday all the V6 engines the supplier can build in a week. Production sequencing converts the daily production schedule into a chain of production orders, also called a "string of pearls." Some plants generate one sequence that includes several production steps—for example, the body shop, paint shop, and assembly (create the metal body shell, paint it, add powertrain and components). Others generate a separate sequence for each production step. The final production sequence that is generated must respect capacities and changeover restrictions in the body lines, rules for batching in painting, and labor constraints on the assembly line to balance each worker's tasks so that the plant can reach an acceptable level of labor efficiency.

Sources of Complexity

The complexity that facility constraints alone can introduce to scheduling is significant. In 2000, for example, Nissan in Sunderland produced two models on two platforms: the Micra and the Primera. The plant had two body shops, two paint shops, and two assembly lines. The Micra and the Primera had separate body shops, but because the volume for the Micra was much higher, Micras would also use some of the Primera paint shop. The Primera paint shop was entirely solvent-based, however, while the Micra paint shop had both water-based and solvent-based colors, so lead times for painting and drying varied. After paint, both models could go on either assembly line, but only right-drive Micras for line 1.[2]

Scheduling plant processes is subject to a range of technical and logistical constraints, most of which relate to the workforce on the trim and final assembly line. A product has so many options that the workers find it difficult to complete the tasks within the allotted time. Putting the roof liner into a station wagon, for example, takes much longer than it does for a hatchback. The plant addresses this discrepancy by alternating products with high and lower labor content, thereby balancing labor on the assembly line. Consequently, the worker has the time to assemble one station wagon but must then assemble at least one hatchback or sedan, and perhaps several, to maximize his efficiency. Although this certainly addresses the efficiency problem, it makes the entire assembly process very rigid and the factory has much more difficulty responding to customers' variable needs and wishes.

In table 2.2, for example, a plant is constrained in the number of three-door vehicles it can make in three of the four production stages (indicated by an X). Similar constraints are also true for five-doors. There is also a low-volume van, so overall the plant roughly makes just under 60 percent three-doors and 40 percent five-doors. For ABS, there are no constraints in body and paint—any car can have it—but in trim and final assembly, the plant can put it in only two-thirds of cars.

The Scheduling Algorithm

The scheduler sets the framework, and the algorithm tries to assemble a schedule based on this framework. If it fails, the scheduler changes the

Table 2.2
Example of constraints in an actual plant. Xs denote production stages in which the plant faces constraints.

Constraint	Body	Paint	Trim	Final assembly	Maximum
Three doors	X		X	X	3 in 5 cars
Five doors	X		X	X	2 in 5 cars
ABS			X	X	2 in 3 cars
Air conditioning			X	X	2 in 3 cars
Automatic transmission			X	X	1 in 13 cars
Special edition	X		X		1 in 10 cars
Diesel			X	X	1 in 2 cars
Electric sunroof	X		X		1 in 4 cars
"GTI" trim	X		X	X	1 in 12 cars
Alarm				X	1 in 5 cars
Lateral airbag			X	X	1 in 13 cars
Turbodiesel engine			X	X	1 in 28 cars

settings, and the computer looks again through all available orders to see if it can come up with a schedule.

The algorithm automatically adheres to plant constraints and order priorities, which the system has previously assigned. Priorities are based on factors such as the dealer's or national sales company's decision to force or hold back single orders, employee and non-employee status (with employee orders often taking priority), and sold orders (which come before stock orders). Generally, the longer the order is in the system, the higher its priority, since theoretically some orders would otherwise stay in the order bank until the end of the product's life cycle.

The scheduling algorithm must have some basis for scheduling, which is usually some period of orders from the order bank. Our research suggests that this buffer should currently be about 5 days for the system to work, which goes a long way toward explaining the almost 9-day order delay associated with the order bank.

The algorithm uses an iterative trial-and-error method, taking into account the constraints that the control entities impose. The entities influence the algorithm to respond to a particular plant or supplier constraint or to satisfy some other requirement. As in the earlier example of the 200 V6 engines, a control entity can be some exact value, or it can set a clear minimum and a clear maximum.

When it encounters an exact-value control entity, the algorithm forces the system to re-select orders until this newly inserted control entity is met. The complexity of interrelations between these entities is tremendous, so schedulers often need to run the algorithm three or four times to find a feasible solution, redefining control entities and swapping individual orders between build days. A standing goal is to minimize the number of controls, since each one distorts the flow of orders coming in from customers.

The scheduler's secondary objective is to maximize the use of any options or components that are in short supply at any time. If, for example, the plant has only so many diesel engines, the scheduler checks the overall number of orders for that engine. If it exceeds the feasible build rate, the scheduler will force the schedule to use all the available engines by creating a minimum-use control entity for that part number. This approach is a significant problem for manufacturers that import high-value items, such as engines and transmissions, because the time to acquire such items is typically up to 6 weeks. Thus, the schedulers face a dilemma: Do we not use these imported items and incur stock-holding cost, or do we use up the available stock and in so doing put an additional constraint on forthcoming schedules?

Resolving the dilemma has interesting ramifications. Suppose all cars with V6 engines come standard with leather seats, only 250 leather seats are available, and a customer wants an I4 engine with leather seats as an option. The scheduler must take into account both the constraint on leather seats and any efforts to use all available V6 engines optimally. That renders it nearly impossible to predict the waiting time for the car with an I4 engine and optional leather. This example illustrates why production scheduling is so unreliable and why dealers end up "padding" delivery dates.[3] Most just want to be on the safe side, but others exploit this scheduling weakness. One manufacturer we studied requires dealers to commit to taking orders they have placed, but allows order amendment. We watched the order flow change in real time as the manufacturer's dealers swapped unavailable diesel engines into orders they didn't need in the hope of delaying their possession of the product. They then monitored the order and swapped a gas engine back in when they found a customer. A related benefit for playing this game is that the customer who gets the "amended" order receives a vehicle much more quickly than if the dealer had waited until the customer came forward before entering the order.

It is no surprise, then, that no one can trust the current supply systems to deliver a vehicle when promised.

Production Lead Times

Table 2.3, taken from our study of 71 plants around the world, shows that plants on average know their target production volume (initial schedule) 77 days in advance. The table also shows that the average plant will not accept any changes in volume past 20 days before production and that it will accept only 21 percent volume change either way at the point the final

Table 2.3
How changes in lead times (measured in days before production date) affect production scheduling.

	Initial schedule	Schedule fixed	Change permitted
Volume	77 days	20 days	21%
Model mix	91 days	13 days	35%
Engine	78 days	14 days	33%

volumes are fixed. Model mix has the longest lead time, 91 days, but on average the plant will accept changes up to 13 days before production starts.

For the customer, these scheduling times translate into roughly an entire month before anyone on the factory floor even starts building the desired car. The obvious question, and one we asked vehicle manufacturers, is "Why build this delay into the system?" The only requirement we see is the 5 or 6 days currently needed to build up enough orders in the order bank to create a feasible schedule. Other than that, scheduling and sequencing could be done in a day. The answer we got over and over was that suppliers need the additional weeks to plan their production.

The suppliers, on the other hand, told us that, although they like having information to complete their planning, they rarely got any data stable enough to do so. Moreover, manufacturers were making changes right up to the point of shipment.

---

average delay from order processing and scheduling: 30.4 days

Order processing and scheduling is the longest part of order fulfillment. The manufacturer must observe order priorities, factory constraints, and labor-balancing issues to create a feasible production schedule on the one hand and give suppliers enough notice on the other. The order spends 8.8 days in the order bank, 15.1 days in scheduling, and 6.5 days in sequencing.

Supplier Scheduling

Given the production schedules, the supplier scheduling subsystem communicates the component and material needs to first-tier and raw-material suppliers. The suppliers receive three basic pieces of information. The first is a long-term forecast—up to 12 months—based on the production program. This is driven entirely by forecasts, but it lets the supplier do at least some long-term capacity planning.

The second piece of information is the weekly supplier schedules, which provide the supplier with 6–10 weeks of planning information derived from weekly production schedules and the order bank. The schedules provide only a rough guideline for the plant's planned production, however, because orders do not yet have an assigned build date. In a few critical cases, the vehicle manufacturer may ensure component availability by guaranteeing to cover the first-tier suppliers' cost to buy raw material.

The last piece of information is more detailed and is given closer to the build date. This "call-off" or "call-in" is based on the daily vehicle production schedule and is usually provided 2–10 days before production starts. Although it is fairly accurate, it does not include the final assembly sequence, which cannot be determined until the vehicle exits the painted-body store, an inventory just before the assembly stage of production. (See figure 3.1.) Thus, the call-off is inaccurate from the broader view of order fulfillment. Moreover, because any unexpected supply constraint can cause further rescheduling and late amendments, a defect at one supplier can have a domino effect on the requirements of other suppliers.

In addition, suppliers that deliver complex modules and bulky systems such as dashboards or seats in the sequence in which vehicles are built (also known as SILS, JIT, and just-in-sequence supply), typically get only 2–8 hours' notice for the final call-off sequence. The sequence for modules and bulky systems is generally the same as that for vehicles entering the assembly line, so strictly speaking the supplier doesn't know what is being ordered until that point.

As we mentioned earlier, suppliers view the information they receive from manufacturers as too variable to be of much use in planning. Schedules do not match previously received forecasts, which in turn do not match the final call-offs. The demand variability is not an accident; it is an unfortunate side effect of the continuous reshuffling of orders from dealer to factory. This reshuffling is inherent in the forecast-based order-to-delivery process. Forecast-based information is gradually updated during scheduling, but the supplier cannot determine the actual requirements until the scheduler assigns the order to a build time (or, in the case of sequenced supply, provides an assembly sequence). Forecasts and schedules are doomed to clash, and even daily requirements are subject to change, since no one knows what is required until the actual assembly sequence is set. And that generally happens only when the vehicle leaves the painted-body store.

A recent trend is for suppliers to co-locate with automobile factories in supplier parks. A supplier typically moves close to the assembly plant when the component requires sequenced-in-line delivery, with a lead time of less than 2 hours. Such components are usually complex and model specific, may have to be configured to individual vehicles, and may be expensive to transport in complete form. Suppliers typically provide modules, seat and interior trim, and external painted parts, such as bumpers. Certainly these suppliers can provide complex subassemblies on short notice, but most parks owe their existence to quite another reason: The manufacturer simply cannot provide reliable call-off information. If the manufacturer knew the actual assembly sequence more than just a few hours before production, these supplier parks might not be needed. Admittedly, it makes sense to co-locate some suppliers, such as those who provide components that are too bulky or sensitive to ship (dashboards and brake pipe systems, for example), but far more suppliers could do business just as effectively elsewhere if they had better planning information.

Inbound Logistics

"Inbound logistics" is the process of moving parts from the supplier's factories to the manufacturer.[4]

Because factories ship out so many parts and components, the cost of inbound logistics can be as high as 10 percent of the plant-based manufacturing costs and thus 1.4 percent of the (pre-distribution) "finished vehicle cost."[5] One way to reduce costs is to make the transporting of components more efficient, but this strategy is often at odds with the requirement for frequent and reliable deliveries. The supplier can send trucks with the required components directly to the manufacturer's plant, for example, which works well as long as each truck uses its

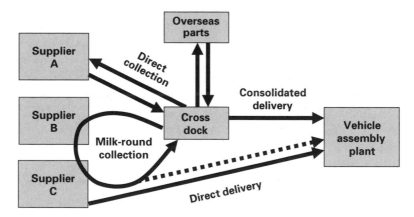

Figure 2.3
Inbound logistics strategies to improve efficiency, including direct collections and deliveries, milk-round collections, and cross-dock consolidation.

capacity to a certain degree and the trucks are large. Obviously, as delivery frequency increases, capacity use decreases, which forces the supplier to use smaller trucks, thereby increasing the cost per shipment.

"Milk-round" collections are efficient for smaller shipment sizes because they offset the inefficiency of small trucks and avoid congestion at the plant's unloading points. In a "milk round," the truck visits more than one supplier to collect components for delivery to the plant or other in-transit points. Collections can involve one or more vehicle manufacturers or even multiple industries, as in news media, components for electronics companies, or even packaged food items.

Another efficiency-enhancing strategy is cross-dock[6] consolidation, which manufacturers generally use when trucks that have picked up components from suppliers are not completely full or when components are to be delivered to several plants. Consolidation points allow the trucks to unload components at a cross dock and then load in a different sequence with parts from other milk rounds. This strategy uses trucks more efficiently and allows more frequent deliveries. Consequently, less stock ends up sitting at the plant.

---

average delay from suppliers and inbound logistics: none

The time for suppliers and inbound logistics companies to receive notice of part requirements is built into order-processing delays and thus the customer does not incur any additional wait time.

Production, Distribution, and the Best We Can Expect

In complex situations, we may rely too heavily on planning and forecasting and underestimate the importance of random factors in the environment. That reliance can also lead to delusions of control.

—Hillel J. Einhorn

As figure 3.1 shows, the production process has three major stages and two between-stage inventory buffers, or stores: the body shop, the body-in-white (BIW) store, the paint shop, the painted-body store (PBS), and the final assembly line. After assembly, the vehicle is moved to a test area for quality control and rework.

At various points in the process, the plant alters the sequence of vehicles it is producing to optimize resource use[1] or to deal with assembly-line-balancing constraints. As we will discuss in chapter 14, manufacturers use various means to stabilize the original schedule in producing the vehicle that finally leaves the factory. Two of these approaches are having large and fully accessible painted-body stores and linking an in-process product to a specific order as late in the production process as is possible.

The average production lead times from the first spot weld to delivery for distribution can vary from 20 to 60 hours. The product spends one-fourth of that time in the body shop and the BIW store, one-half of it in the paint shop and the PBS, and the remaining fourth in assembly and testing. Although many manufacturers try valiantly to maintain the planned production sequence, they must often reshuffle in-process vehicles, which makes the assembly sequence less reliable and often makes it that much harder to predict what will be assembled when.

Vehicle reshuffling has significant consequences for the whole system. First, sequenced supply is practicable only within very limited call-off

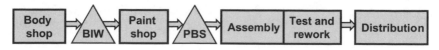

Figure 3.1
Basic vehicle production process.

times. Second, it thwarts any plans to distribute vehicles efficiently—a sore point with logistics service providers, who must determine how to transport the finished product from the factories.

Rework and missing components are other reasons plants reshuffle vehicles. Resequencing here is a stickier problem because individual rework times vary, so no one knows exactly when the vehicle will re-enter production after rework. "Rework" can mean anything from a spot repair to a complete paint re-spray. Furthermore, any vehicle could incur multiple sources of delays, which could add days to its throughput.

Table 3.1 shows an example of actual production throughput for a one-day schedule of 600 orders per day. Almost immediately, vehicle production deviates from the scheduled build time. Although the average lead time is 1.4 day, the vehicle-build-time spread is considerable.

Table 3.2 shows average first-time-OK rates for various regions. This evidence also shows a gap between scheduled and actual build times. The rates in "Body" are averages for on-line and off-line repairs in the body shop (of missed welds, for example). The percentages in "Paint" and "Assembly" are the fraction of vehicles requiring off-line repair in the paint shop and assembly areas, respectively, including vehicles that fail the water, electricity, and dynamic tests. Finally, "combined first-time OK" is the probability that a vehicle will pass through all processes without being taken out of process for rework.

Across regions, the aggregate first-time-OK levels are between 59 and 71 percent. Our research shows that the best plants average 98 percent in body, 85–90 percent in paint, and better than 97 percent in assembly. However, the probability that a vehicle will pass through all processes with no repair rarely exceeds 85 percent. Even Toyota, master of lean production, recently admitted to having first-time-OK rates of about 70 percent in some of its assembly plants.[2] Overall, this highlights the importance of reliability in both component supply and vehicle manufacturing.

Although vehicle production contributes only a minor delay to the overall order-to-delivery process, throughput unreliability adds complexity to both the supply chain and distribution.

Table 3.1
Throughput for a one-day production schedule of 600 orders. The actual position of vehicles in production deviates considerably from the scheduled build date.

Age of order (in relation to date released into production)	Not yet framed	Body shop and BIW store	Paint shop	Painted body store	Assembly	Vehicles off track (rework and missing parts)
Day 0: Orders are released into production[a]	248	202	100	2	25	17
+ 1 day	5	165	149	19	133	77
+ 2 days	1	21	14	3	74	122
+ 3 days		1	5		4	72
+ 4 days		2	5			58
+ 5 days						19
+ 6 days						10
+ 7 days						12
+ 8 days						6
More than +8 days						29

a. Orders released is slightly less than 600, possibly because of financing, special parts, cancellations, etc.

Table 3.2
Average first-time-OK rates.

	Body	Paint	Assembly	Combined[a]
North America	92.2%	83.8%	81.5%	63.0%
Japan	95.5%	86.6%	86.1%	71.2%
Europe	91.8%	86.0%	77.2%	60.9%
New entrant countries[b]	94.8%	82.8%	75.3%	59.1%

a. Likelihood of passing all processes without repair.
b. Argentina, Australia, India, Korea, Mexico, South Africa, Taiwan, Turkey.

---

average delay from vehicle production: 1.4 day

Vehicle production contributes only a minor delay to the order-to-delivery
process because of the many efforts to make production efficient. Process
unreliability is the main reason for delivery delays, posing significant challenges for suppliers and post-production operations.

Vehicle Distribution

Vehicle distribution, or outbound logistics, involves transporting vehicles
from the assembly plant to the dealership or even directly to the final
customer for large fleets. Transport is most commonly via train and
truck, and via ship for exports and short coastal routes. Our focus is on
road transport, which is more popular given the unreliability of and
time required for rail transportation.[3]

Even here, companies use vastly different processes, depending on the
relative location of plants, ports, distribution centers,[4] and customers,
but most use some variation of the outbound routes in figure 3.2. The
main volume routes are from the plant (or port of entry) to market compounds or distribution centers and then to the dealership or customer.
The average cost of transport from the factory to a dealership is £60.[5]

The 65 percent dealer pick-ups include both private and retail fleet
customers (the so-called user-chooser fleet customers). The 25 percent
direct delivery, on the other hand, is usually to a large fleet customer.

Dashed lines in figure 3.2 show less frequent routes, which include
direct deliveries from the plant to the ports for exported vehicles and
deliveries direct to dealers from the factories. Unsold stock at the dealerships can be taken back to distribution centers after a time to increase the
chance of finding a customer. The arrow between the dealers reflects the
vehicles being transferred between dealerships (around 15 percent in the
United Kingdom).

Although manufacturers look to distribution centers to reduce dealer
transfers, these centers come with their own set of transfers. Vehicles are
continuously ferried among regional compounds in response to variations in local demand. One logistics service provider claimed that almost
20 percent of the vehicles from a particular manufacturer had to be
transferred between distribution centers.

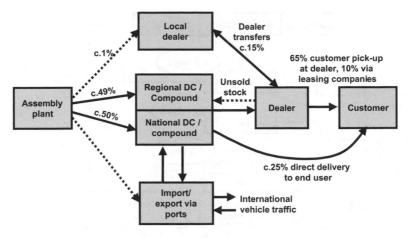

Figure 3.2
Standard routes for transporting vehicles from assembly plant to dealer or customer (UK average). Source: M. Holweg and J. Miemczyk, "Logistics in the three-day car age," *International Journal of Physical Distribution and Logistics Management* 32 (2002), no. 10: 829–850.

Our benchmark for the United Kingdom shows that, on average, a car waits 0.9 day in the factory before being loaded onto a transporter and another 3.8 days en route to the dealer, totaling just under 5 days. Actual movement takes less than 24 hours. Within Europe, a 10-day distribution time is considered good practice. Again, most of this time is spent on planning and load consolidations.

---

average delay from distribution: 4.7 days (United Kingdom); c. 10 days (Europe)

In the United Kingdom, distribution is a minor delay in the order-to-delivery process. Yet the actual driving time rarely exceeds 24 hours, and so the delay could be shorter. For cross-continental shipments, distribution time is substantively more significant.

The Order-to-Delivery Benchmark

Figure 3.3 shows the average delays for a custom vehicle across the six manufacturers we analyzed. Again, we assumed that all subsystems

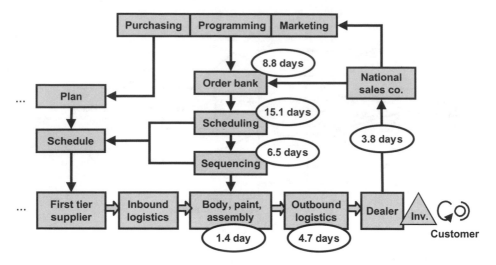

Figure 3.3
Average order-to-delivery times for six manufacturers.

work at optimal throughput and thus minimize throughput time. We found no bias in any one region.[6]

Figure 3.4 gives the delays for each of the basic stages in the order-to-delivery process. The information flow, which comprises order entry (including time in the order bank), scheduling, and sequencing, accounts for 85 percent of the delay. The physical flow—production and vehicle distribution—accounts for only 15 percent. Production is clearly not a significant part, accounting for only 3 percent.

As figures 3.3 and 3.4 clearly show, the information flow causes far and away the most delay in order fulfillment—an amazing 34.2 days. Yet historically the industry has devoted most of its time and energy to the 20–60 hours the product spends in the manufacturing process. No one has put much effort into reducing the 85 percent delay in the information flow, where (apart from paper shuffling) little value is added.

Other analyses also provide insight into the current state of order fulfillment and help define the extent to which the order-to-delivery system could be improved. Demonstrated best practice (DBP) benchmarking,[7] for example, assembles the best features of several systems to create a benchmark for a theoretical operation that comprises the best features of each. The logic behind DBP is that, in theory, if one company can achieve a certain level within one subsystem, then under similar conditions companies with comparable products could achieve the same level of perfor-

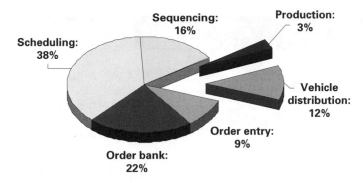

Figure 3.4
Percentage each order-to delivery process stage contributes to overall delay in order-fulfilment process. Source: Holweg and Pil, "Successful build-to-order strategies."

mance within the same subsystem. Hence, the overall DBP of a sample is effectively the best solution currently achievable over the sample, taking the best bits from each one (again, assuming that current systems are performing optimally and that technology conditions are similar).

In an order-to-delivery comparison of the six manufacturers we surveyed (figure 3.5), the worst performer is a company that builds almost exclusively to forecast. The long order bank is the result of markets' sending their orders in 3 months ahead of time—giving an average wait per order of a month and a half. The best performer builds 44 percent to order (not as large a proportion as some of the other manufacturers we looked at). The process is certainly capable of handling more. Between the best and the worst is a huge spread in lead time, even though the underlying order-to-delivery processes are very similar.

The DBP analysis shows that systems are capable of an order-to-delivery time just under 11 days. Of course, being theoretical, the DBP analysis is obviously limited, neglecting such practical considerations as subsystem interactions. Nevertheless, at least in principle, current order-to-delivery systems could support the 10 or 15 days that manufacturers' initiatives envision. Yet no one is even close to hitting these targets.

In Pursuit of the *n*-Day Car

Just about everyone in the automobile industry is talking about how to get a car to the customer sooner. Academics discuss the three-day car, policy makers[8] push a five-day effort, and manufacturers launch 10- and

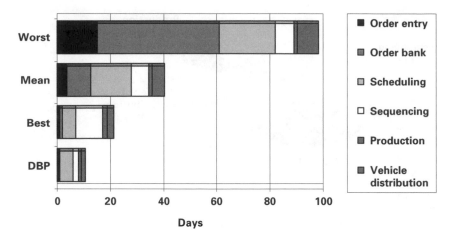

Figure 3.5
Comparison of times for order-to delivery processes in four analytical contexts: worst, mean, best, and "demonstrated best practice" (DBP).

15-day-car initiatives. Few people realize that the idea originated in the Manufacturing for the 21st Century Consortium, a program started in the mid 1980s. The consortium was part of a research project that aimed to identify challenges Japanese manufacturers would have to meet to remain competitive in sectors such as electronics, food, machinery, and motor vehicles. The research team was a mixed group of academics and representatives of major Japanese companies from all industrial sectors, with Nissan representing the motor vehicle sector.

For the motor vehicle sector, the team identified as a major challenge the need to supply vehicles in days, not weeks, after the customer places an order. The ultimate goal, they argued, should be 3 days from order to delivery—an idea that the industry has come to know as "the three-day challenge." This challenge required abandoning the paradigm of mass production in favor of responding more quickly to customer orders through build-to-order. Lead times, the team argued, are too long, and dealer stock is too high. If a custom-built car from the factory had a short lead time and required no dealer stock, the resulting savings would help offset the higher materials cost of a modular-structure, custom-built car.

The three-day challenge was only one of nine challenges the team identified for the motor vehicle sector, which they documented in Manufacturing for the 21st Century Report—The Future of Japanese Manufacturing[9] and which we list in table 3.3. All support the transition

Table 3.3
What researchers in 1989 identified as challenges for the Japanese motor vehicle industry in the 21st century.*

Break dependence on economies of scale.

Create a system to produce vehicles in low volumes at reasonable cost.

Deliver a car with custom features within three days after ordering.

Further downsize the scale of production operations.

Allow the same components to be configured many ways.

Create work stimulating to the people doing it.

Cultivate the automotive "prosumer," a customer who participates in his own order fulfillment. In this case, the prosumer participates in the design of his own vehicle.

Create an ordering system that will instantly check the combination of customer requests for engineering safety and feasibility.

Manage large masses of data and control their flow.

---

*Source: R. Hall, "The challenges of the three-day car," *Target* 9 (1993), no. 2: 21–29.

from make-to-stock/sell-from-stock to making only the products and quantities that customers want.

Many of these challenges have since become topics for provocative conversation in the motor vehicle industry. It is sobering and a little embarrassing to realize that they have been under consideration for nearly 20 years.

However inspiring, the notion of the 3-day (or 5-day or 10-day) car can be misleading. It doesn't mean "Build every vehicle in that time." It means "Be able to do so for customers who want it that quickly"—a service the manufacturer might offer at a premium to those who are not interested in a discount or other incentive in exchange for waiting. Our focus on responsiveness is consistent with that selectivity—"Build the car the customer wants, when the customer wants it." The process must be fast enough to satisfy the most impatient customers; otherwise we end up with a mix of build-to-forecast and sell-from-stock to satisfy the impatient customers and a BTO system for the rest—a combination doomed to failure.

Thus, the n-day car (where n is some number between 3 and 15) requires shortening the order-to-delivery time so that manufacturers can build to order. The best processes we benchmarked suggest that n is closer to 21, which means the industry must radically rethink its current practices if it ever hopes to cut that time in half.

II   Band-Aid Solutions to Stem Red Ink

For every complex problem there is an answer that is clear, simple, and wrong.

—H. L Mencken

While companies have spent more than 10 years "planning to implement build-to-order," their actions have betrayed their real intentions. Most of their deliberate changes have gone to what they *really* consider critical for competitiveness: factory efficiency and large scale. They have relentlessly pursued lean production in their manufacturing activities and volume as a means of driving cost down. Worst of all, they have become dependent on demand forecasts, which have generated vicious cycles that have eroded profitability.

4

Islands of Excellence

Ford Motor Sends Bosses to Factory in Search of Lean
—headline in *Automotive News*, August 19, 2002

In the late 1980s and the early 1990s, the significant gap in labor productivity between Japanese producers and those in the rest of the world sparked disbelief and fear in boardrooms in Australia, South Africa, Korea, Germany, France, and the United States. Since 1990, non-Japanese producers have made tremendous efforts to catch up by instituting programs to push major productivity and quality improvements on the shop floor. Most Western manufacturers have launched some interpretation of lean production incorporating some or many of the ideas pioneered by Japanese manufacturers—Toyota in particular. Ford launched its Ford Production System; Lee Iacocca at Chrysler renamed lean production "agile manufacturing," and Mercedes-Benz and Volkswagen translated *kaizen* as *kontinuierlicher Verbesserungsprozess* (KVP).[1] Regardless of the name, the central tenets of Toyota's practices became the focus of improvement at most major car producers.

These efforts have clearly paid off, as figure 4.1 and table 4.1 show.[2, 3] In 1989, North American plants needed an average 24.9 hours per vehicles, relative to Japan's 16.8 hours. By the mid 1990s, the performance gap had narrowed dramatically and by 2000, the 1989 gap of 8.1 hours had shrunk to little more than 4 hours—16.8 hours in the United States versus 12.3 hours in Japan. It is important to note that there is substantive variation within some of these categories. For example, plants in South Korea do not differ substantially from the average European plants in productivity.

But although the performance gap has shrunk, the regional ranking remains the same as it was in 1989: Japan, followed by the United States,

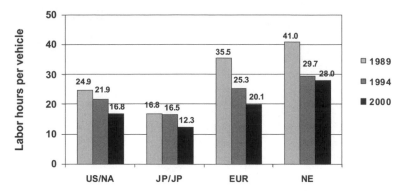

Figure 4.1
Labor hours per vehicle, 1989, 1994, and 2000. All data unmatched and scale-weighted.
US/NA: US-owned factories in North America. JP/JP: Japanese-owned factories in Japan.
Eur: European factories. NE: factories in new-entrant countries, including Argentina,
Australia, Brazil, India, Korea, Mexico, Taiwan, and South Africa. Data for 1989 collected
by J. Krafcik and J. MacDuffie; data for 1994 collected by J. MacDuffie and F. Pil. On the
history of the assembly-plant study, for data sources, and for methodology, see notes 2 and
3 to this chapter.

Table 4.1
Regional distribution of plants for assembly plant data reported in this book. (Some
analyses report on subsets of these data.)

	Round 1 (1989)	Round 2 (1994)	Round 3 (2000)
US/NA	16	25	23
Europe	24	21	14
JP/JP	9	12	8
New entrants	17	22	23
Other	4	8	3
Total plants	70	88	71

Europe, and new entrants. Figure 4.2, which splits productivity across
labor types, clearly shows that the regional differences are attributable to
direct labor—the work involved in welding, painting, and assembling
the vehicle.[4] Indirect labor, such as material handling, inventory
management, and the salaried work of supervisors and managers,
contributes little to the variation in regional performance.

Automation may partially explain regional variations in the efficiency of direct labor. As table 4.2 shows, various direct-labor activities
use automation to different degrees. Automation is consistently prevalent in the welding and paint shop, for example, but has barely entered

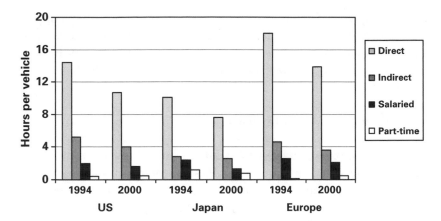

Figure 4.2
Productivity breakdown across labor types in US, Japan, and Europe in 1994 and 2000. Data for 1994 collected by J. MacDuffie and F. Pil. All data unmatched and scale-weighted. On the history of the assembly-plant study, for data sources, and for methodology, see notes 2 and 3 to this chapter.

Table 4.2
Automation by region and plant area (all figures weighted by volume).*

	US	Japan	Europe	New entrants
Percentage of all direct production steps that are automated	41.0%	39.6%	36.1%	27.7%
Welding area	94.0%	92.5%	79.6%	65.2%
Paint shop	58.7%	56.0%	52.1%	31.9%
Assembly area	1.5%	2.1%	3.0%	2.8%
Robotic index (robots per vehicle per hour)	5.0	6.8	5.2	5.6
Body shop welding flexibility[a]	84.2%	86.3%	83.5%	94.3%

*Early versions of these metrics were developed by J. Krafcik (A Comparative Analysis of Assembly Automation, International Motor Vehicle Program, MIT, 1989). For a detailed discussion of automation from the 1980s through the mid 1990s, see J. MacDuffie and F. Pil, "From fixed to flexible," in *Transforming Automobile Assembly*, ed. K. Shimokawa et al. (Springer-Verlag, 1997).
a. Percentage of welds by worker or robot, as opposed to inflexible "hard" automation.

the assembly area. Though the differences across regions do not appear huge, we have weighted these numbers by plant scale. Looking at averages would show significantly lower automation levels for the new entrants, where a number of very-low-volume plants have little automation.

Automation in the Assembly Area

In the plant's more manual assembly area, automating tasks is extremely expensive and poses two problems. First, automation often requires a stop-go process, which runs contrary to assembly's continuous flow. Second, the assembly line's manual segments are "up" virtually 100 percent of the time, but even the best automated equipment has up times of only 97–99 percent, which introduces another discontinuity. Manufacturers have attempted to address these problems in various ways, such as rerouting the assembly line and redesigning processes so that all automated activities can be grouped in automation "islands" where maintenance workers can watch the equipment. But predictably, these approaches introduce new costs, like maintenance, that offset any savings on the direct-labor front. They also tend to fragment the work related to automated activities. Consequently, the remaining work becomes so mind numbing that few individuals can stay sane performing it at all, let alone performing it to meet quality expectations.

Toyota has been experimenting with in-line automated activities as a means of engaging direct workers and reducing line discontinuities, but these activities still affect only a fraction of assembly tasks.

Labor-saving automation in assembly generally centers around assist tools, those that help workers perform their tasks more efficiently and with less strain but do not attempt to replace the workers. Assist tools include lifters for seats, dashboards, and instrument panels; retractors on bolters; and the familiar cart that hooks into the conveyance system to carry tools and small components. Assist tools are generally inexpensive and designed by production and maintenance workers in close collaboration. We found that when production workers were not involved in tool design, the final tool was often over-engineered, hopelessly expensive, and not well received by production workers.

Collaboration is also necessary in designing assembly processes. Top-down reengineering of assembly processes results in some improvements in direct labor; however, productivity differences persist if production workers are not actively involved.

Labor: Distinguishing Cost from Efficiency

The implication of current manufacturing processes is that fundamental differences in productivity stem from the manual areas of the factories, mainly assembly. Regardless, as figure 4.3 shows, all regions made significant improvements in the efficiency of direct labor from 1994 to 2000. The gap between Japan and the rest of the world is closing.

We could stop on that happy note and simply acknowledge that plants across the globe are more productive than they used to be. However, we would be remiss to depart the subject of productivity without answering this question: To what extent do efficiency differences contribute to competitive advantage?

Figure 4.4 shows the cost of productivity for various regions. Suddenly the picture is not as clear. Higher wages in Japan blur their overall competitive advantage. Likewise, higher wages in the United States result in very high per-vehicle expenditures on labor despite decent efficiency. It must be noted that the numbers do not consider benefit costs, and that they underestimate the salaried component of production. As a result of this, and because we are only looking at a set of core activities all assembly plants undertake, the numbers significantly underestimate the total labor cost per vehicle, and should be viewed as

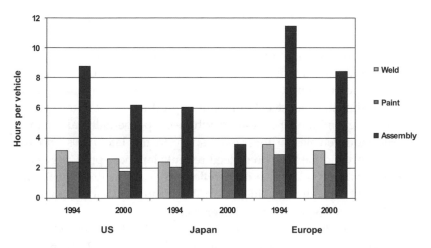

Figure 4.3
Breakdown of direct-labor productivity by area in US, Japan, and Europe in 1994 and 2000. Data for 1994 collected by J. MacDuffie and F. Pil. On the history of the assembly-plant study, for data sources, and for methodology, see notes 2 and 3 to this chapter.

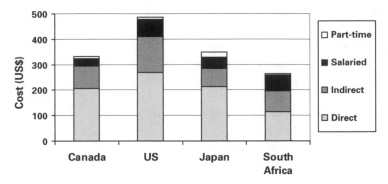

Figure 4.4
Cost of labor hours (with Europe excluded because of tremendous cross-national wage variation). Not scale-weighted; no adjustment for absenteeism; benefits excluded; work week set at 40 hours; adjusted for vehicle characteristics and break times. Salaried share is underestimated for all (based on average engineer and supervisor wage). Part-time worker cost estimated using average production worker's wage. As a result, numbers are indicative of differences but reflect only a portion of the labor cost.

generally indicative of differences—rather than definitive. We have included the cost indicators to show the risks of focusing solely on labor efficiency. Yet labor hours per vehicle is the very metric that manufacturers pursue, often to the detriment of the value grid.

The Quality Quest

Beyond labor productivity, quality is the metric receiving the most attention as manufacturers strive to emulate and attain the performance of their Japanese counterparts. While European and US manufacturers denigrated the "look and feel" of Japanese products, they found it hard to ignore the grumbling of customers who were perpetually taking their Western-made vehicles to the repair shop. In the late 1980s and the 1990s, not only did the Big Three bleed red ink; Japanese products dominated J.D. Power's list of the most problem-free cars. In 1991, the Saturn was the only US-produced vehicle to rank decently on that list, attaining quality levels no US producer had ever reached.

Eventually quality did improve—from several defects per vehicle in the late 1980s to one flaw per vehicle in 1990. In 1993, 48 models achieved zero defects.[5] In the late 1990s, J.D. Power changed its data-collection tool to better capture the quality challenges that producers continued to face.

Vehicle manufacturers also improved their ability to produce products of acceptable quality, but progress was not always steady. Figure
4.5 shows quality changes across regions using defects that originated in
the assembly plant as a measure of quality.[6] Japanese companies in
Japan (in our notation, JP/JP) showed steady but small improvements
relative to European manufacturers, which started at a much higher
defect rate but have since nearly matched Japan's quality levels.
Japanese firms building cars in North America (JP/NA) are backtracking
to some extent, most likely because of the addition of considerable plant
capacity in the United States. Overall, however, US manufacturers are
lagging, with quality levels only slightly better than those of new
entrants that sell products in the United States.

Efficiency and Quality: Strange Bedfellows

To understand how superior quality affected efficiency, we correlated
the quality and productivity levels for each plant across all regions.
Some plants map nicely onto a good-to-poor productivity and quality
continuum—not surprising, since lean production generally means
superior productivity and quality and (old-style) mass production typically means poor efficiency and quality. For many more plants, however,
the mapping was quite a bit messier. As figure 4.6 shows, mapping

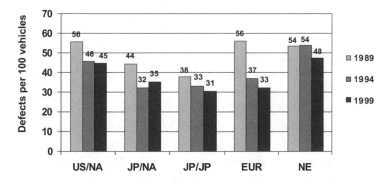

Figure 4.5
Quality across regions, 1989, 1994, and 1999. Regions include domestic US (US/NA),
Japanese plants in US (JP/NA), Japanese plants in Japan (JP/JP), European plants (Eur),
and plants in new-entrant nations (NE). Only reflects major defects originating in assembly plant, scale-weighted. Matched on time-series questions. Calculations based on J. D.
Power and Associates quality data. On the history of the measures, and on the methodology, see note 5 to this chapter.

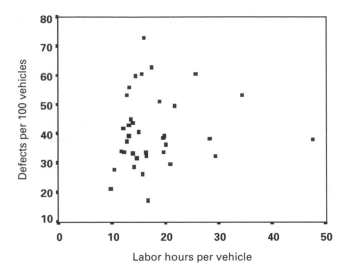

Figure 4.6
Relating productivity and quality. The plot reflects only major defects originating in assembly plants, matched on time-series questions.

plants on quality in relation to productivity looks more like a funnel than a direct linear relationship. On the one side were, predictably, lean plants that had mastered quality and productivity, but the remaining plants seemed to fall into multiple categories: plants that showed good quality but at the expense of productivity, plants that were productive but had very high defect levels, and a few plants that attained neither productivity nor quality.

After reviewing the data in more depth, we noted an interesting development. Many plants in the United States that use top-down efforts, focusing on cost and head-count reduction in assembly to improve productivity, are doing so at the expense of product quality.

This finding again raises the question "Does labor efficiency really drive corporate performance to any significant extent?" Nissan's Sunderland plant in the United Kingdom has been hailed by some as the most productive and efficient plant in Europe, while in Ryton (formerly Chrysler Europe's manufacturing operation, also in the United Kingdom) Peugeot 206s are built much less efficiently. Yet Peugeot is very profitable, while Nissan has struggled to be so. Thus, although labor productivity is important, it is clearly only one of many factors that influence corporate performance.

Once more, Henry Ford's legacy explains this efficiency focus. Henry built his business model around the notion of high volume at low cost. As he shipped vehicles to dealers, he also kept the plant turning out more at the same rate, regardless of how many cars were already in the market. The industry has followed this strategic agenda for decades. And why not? The focus on assembly plant efficiency and production volume means that cost per vehicle from the factory becomes the number-one performance measure. To satisfy it, the manufacturer merely keeps the factories running at stable full capacity and high volumes. Cost per unit decreases—not just in the factory, but also from the supplier because the cost of piece prices for components decreases. Less expensive vehicles result in larger sales, resulting in a virtuous cycle of higher volumes and lower unit costs.

The beauty of this is that production costs per vehicle are predictable. The manufacturer already knows the fixed costs of running a factory, the cost of the workforce, and the overhead cost. All that's left to get a cost per vehicle from the factory gate is to determine how many vehicles the fixed costs will be spread across. What could be more attractive to financial planners? They can offer vehicles at a certain retail price, with a clear understanding of the differential to the actual production cost. The finance department simply monitors the profit and ensures that the company recovers the overhead and development costs.

The overarching mission of the distribution system, the national sales companies, and the dealerships then becomes to get rid of the product. The more product in the market, the potentially greater their reward. In fact, the message is that *more is better for everyone.* Some would even go so far as to say that more is better for the customer because it keeps the price down. Yet in a sophisticated market of fashion products and brand profiles, to what extent does price really influence demand? More to the point, to what extent is volume *hurting* the value grid?

Shop-Floor Myopia

With all the emphasis on volume, inventory is inevitable, and reducing it has become a major goal for many suppliers and manufacturers. Inventory not only masks problems on the shop floor; it also raises quality questions, because it gets shuffled around or simply rusts waiting to be used. Inventory reduction is a cornerstone of the Toyota Production System. Around the world, manufacturers use just-in-time strategies to address inventory levels both within the plant and between first-tier suppliers. The best-performing plants receive several deliveries from their suppliers in windows of a few hours—even less in Japan, where suppliers are much closer to the assembly plants.

In the mid 1990s, companies began extending just-in-time efforts to achieve sequenced supply. The aim of this strategy is to closely integrate a supplier's production through synchronized small batches and to have the supplier manufacture the components in the sequence used to assemble vehicles. In parallel with the move to sequenced supply was an increased outsourcing of modules and systems. The inherent complexity and variety of these units meant that suppliers had to build each module or system specifically for a vehicle on the assembly track—that is, the components would be built in the same sequence as vehicles on the assembly track.

When line-side inventory is low, the components can be stored closer to where they ultimately need to be and thus curtail the shuffling around that can degrade efficiency and quality. However, the smaller the container or the closer to a single-piece supply, the more effort is required to order, handle, and manage the material. Therefore, the optimal line-side stock for larger components is generally an hour or two of material.

We found that average plant stock levels for eight key parts—wheels, wire harnesses, steering wheels, tires, instrument clusters, headlights, interior carpet sets, and batteries—are consistently under two days, and in many instances can be measured in hours. The exception is the new-entrant countries, where infrequent shipments and long distances for certain parts increase stock levels slightly. The low plant inventories are due largely to the push approach to vehicle production, which enables the manufacturer to buffer assembly factories from any demand variations in the market. Factories are thus decoupled from distribution and retail, freeing manufacturers to create islands of manufacturing excellence that distance themselves from the huge inventory of finished vehicles in distribution centers.

This decoupling becomes evident in an inventory profile across the supply chain, such as that in figure 4.7. That figure clearly shows that the manufacturing process is lean. Relative to the initial benchmarks more than 10 years ago, stock levels inside the plants, both line-side and in the on-site warehouses, have gone down drastically. Also, because of the increased integration of suppliers from just-in-time and sequenced deliveries, the stock levels within first-tier suppliers show much lower profiles for assembly and finished goods. We also found that the more complex the component, the lower the inventory of finished goods within the supplier.

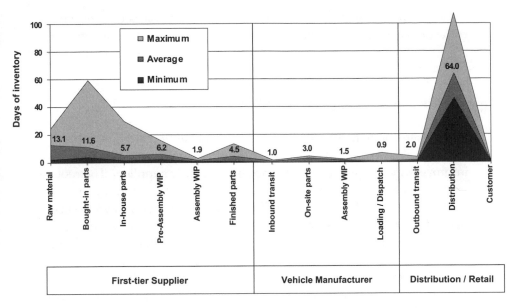

Figure 4.7
Inventory profile across UK auto supply chain, with average stock levels at each stage given numerically. The profile is an aggregate of the benchmark of the six vehicle manufacturers, our surveys of suppliers and logistics operations, and ICDP distribution data (Williams, Progress towards Customer Pull Distribution).

Nevertheless, suppliers tend to hold a buffer—on average, 4.5 days of finished components—to cope with demand fluctuations and last-minute changes to demand forecasts. First-tier suppliers carry, on average, 21.9 days of stock, driven mainly by large inventories of raw materials (13.1 days) and bought-out parts (11.6 days). The size of the inventory is due in part to the squeeze between the manufacturer's requirements and the unresponsiveness of batch-oriented suppliers of raw materials. Manufacturers want first-tier suppliers to assemble and deliver smaller quantities of components. Suppliers of raw materials (e.g. steel and resin), on the other hand, favor large bulk-driven schedules, not frequent small deliveries.[7] Hence the squeeze, which makes larger inventories inevitable.

The profile highlights the islands of excellence at the assembly plants and the inbound supply chain. Most manufacturers spend tremendous efforts to shorten the manufacturing process by minutes, only to have the finished car sit for months in the marketplace. Clearly, assembly-plant efficiency has come at the expense of the overall supply-chain performance as inventory accumulates at the most expensive point in the supply chain.

Profiles like these are more evidence that the emphasis on efficiency comes at the expense of responsiveness. They also show that this emphasis is a sure recipe for a hyper-cyclical market and less-than-optimal profitability.

The Challenge of Supplier Integration

The implementation of lean production did not stop at the boundaries of the assembly plant. Manufacturers soon realized that they could improve only so much if they did not involve their suppliers. The roots of the Toyota Production System date to the 1950s within Japan, yet Toyota waited until the 1970s to roll out this just-in-time system to suppliers. In fact, the manuals it gave its first-tier suppliers at that time were probably the first official documents about the system, and it took another 10 years for the first publications to appear in English.[8]

In 1990, the boundaries of an assembly plant were clear: the plant started at the inbound warehouse and generally ended at a railhead or a truck-loading bay. Today these boundaries are far less clear. Suppliers, often co-located, have taken over considerable chunks of the assembly operation. Supplier parks and even supplier staff working inside the assembly plant are becoming common. Now no one is quite sure where vehicle assembly starts and component assembly ends. This makes it much harder to identify constraints and improvement opportunities.

Co-Location Troubles

Close supplier integration seems idyllic, but it has its own problems. For example, seven major modules of the "Smart" (a small car built in Hambach, France) come from on-site suppliers. The exception is the engine, which DaimlerChrysler's Berlin engine plant builds and ships to Hambach daily.[9] The total content of purchased parts for the Smart is about 85 percent, versus 60–70 percent for most other vehicles.

Academic literature generally hails the Smart production approach as the prime example of how to use modularity. Our impression while visiting the factory, though, was that Smart management would like to reduce supplier power by bringing more assembly tasks back in house. Also, the supplier managers unofficially hinted that despite their obvious commitment and close integration, they were treated in much the same way as more traditional suppliers: an arm's-length relationship.

The Hambach factory also faces an interesting labor challenge. Because employees of the manufacturer and employees of suppliers work on the same site, they quickly discovered the wage differentials between the companies. This led not only to labor migration from the suppliers to the manufacturer, but also to outright dissatisfaction among the workers. In November 1999, the Smart assembly factory (dubbed Smartville) saw its first strike over hourly rates and lost 900 cars' worth of production in the process. (Ironically, the actual difference in compensation was not that dramatic after taking into account the bonuses paid out at suppliers.)

The labor challenges Hambach faced are common when suppliers are co-located. We found that, at least in Europe, co-located suppliers find it extremely difficult to attract skilled engineering and maintenance employees.

The Pressure of Cost Reductions

Supplier integration enables cost reductions, but they come in different forms. Ford and GM ask for annual cost reductions, generally 3–5 percent per year. It falls on the supplier to figure out how to cut costs.

Quality and Warranty Concerns

Integrated suppliers are also becoming increasingly embedded into quality and warranty. Ford will share warranty savings with suppliers that have a direct influence on improving quality.[10] Chrysler, starting with 2004 vehicles, will require suppliers to sign explicit agreements about the cost of recalls and warranty work.[11]

Reduction in Numbers

Predictably, supplier integration has led to fewer suppliers. Vehicle manufacturers have "cut the tail" on their purchases and consolidated the purchasing volumes of low-value components. Consolidating the supply base has also reduced the number of first-tier suppliers. Estimates predict that suppliers will go from 8,000 in 2002 to 2,000 in 2010.

The increased sourcing of systems and modules from large system suppliers has effectively relegated many previously first-tier suppliers to second tier.[12] As table 4.3 shows, regional variation in the number of supplier supplying individual assembly plant is significant. We did not include South Africa in the table, because it mixes pre-selected component

Table 4.3
Numbers of suppliers in 2000. "New entrants" excludes South Africa and Argentina.

JP/JP	206
Europe	341
US/NA	376
New entrants	201

kits supplied from overseas sister plants or supply centers with local supply—a rather unusual practice. New entrant plants as well as North American plants exhibit continued efforts to reduce the number of suppliers they rely upon. For example, American plants in North America, which averaged about 500 suppliers in the mid 1990s, have reduced that number dramatically. Interestingly, reductions are not limited to vehicle manufacturer's first-tier suppliers. In fact, the remaining first-tier suppliers are cutting some of their second-tier suppliers. Valeo, for example, is aiming to cut its supplier base from 4,500 to 3,000, having already cut it by 20 percent in 2001.[13]

Buying the Setting Sun

In the 1980s, the Japanese were poised to rule the global auto market. Their efficiency and quality attainments on the manufacturing front became legendary, as they captured market share both through imports and local transplant production. When Japanese imports reached 1.68 million in the early 1980s, the United States negotiated voluntary restraint agreements.

Nearly 10 years later, the Japanese market share was still a threat. The top-selling car in the United States was the Honda Accord, with a 4.5 percent market share—1.1 percent more than the second-place Ford Taurus. Of the top ten vehicles, four were Japanese (Honda Accord and Civic, Toyota Camry and Corolla). Douglas Fraser, president of the United Auto Workers, declared: "The Japanese are not exporting cars to the United States. They are exporting unemployment." Henry Ford II called Japanese imports an "economic Pearl Harbor."[14]

The fear in the United States and in many other Western countries became a near panic with the publication of *The Machine That Changed the World*, which showed that some Japanese factories were twice as productive as their Western counterparts.[15] The competitive advantage from lean manufacturing was significant, and the knowledge was worth a lot.

Table 4.4
Foreign ownership of Japanese vehicle manufacturers in 2001.*

Fuji Heavy Industries (Subaru)	20% owned by GM
Honda Motor Company	None
Isuzu Motors	49% owned by GM
Mazda Motor Corporation	33.4% owned by Ford
Mitsubishi Motors Corporation	37% owned by DaimlerChrysler
Nissan Diesel Motor Co	22.5% owned by Renault
Nissan Motor Co.	36.8% owned by Renault
Suzuki Motor Corporation	20% owned by GM
Toyota Motor Company	None

*Source: Japan Automobile Manufacturers Association.

In 1994, for example, Samsung spent $3 billion on its car operations, relying mainly on Nissan's knowledge of manufacturing products and technology. Today, the balance of power is very different. In 2000, Renault paid $512 million to take over Samsung's entire car operation.[16] Western manufacturers either are controlling or have taken over all the major Japanese manufacturers except Toyota and Honda. Table 4.4 shows the ownership structure of the Japanese manufacturers. By Japanese law, 33.4 percent gives the owner controlling interest in a company.

Honda sent a clear message that its future expansion will not be based on a merger with another manufacturer. In a three-year business plan characterized by "spirited independence," the company said it would increase production in a number of countries, including China, Indonesia, Taiwan, the Philippines, and the United States, but keep production capacity in Japan flat.[17]

Toyota has been profitable through most of its history. It has explored strategic moves like New United Motor Manufacturing Inc. (NUMMI), a venture it undertook with GM in 1984 to produce Chevrolets and Toyotas. For the most part, however, Toyota, like Honda, has avoided mergers with Western firms. Instead it has relied on its superiority in manufacturing and in product-design speed[18] to maintain continuous growth.

That Western manufacturers have taken over so much of the Japanese auto operations illustrates their strong belief that manufacturing efficiency is the pathway to growth and profitability. It is true that Western firms have benefited tremendously from Japanese efficiency lessons, but it is also true that efficiency and volume are not panaceas for flagging profits.

5

It is not often that the chief executive of a large corporation himself discovers visible overproduction by a physical check of the inventory. But automobiles are big, units easy to count.

—Alfred P. Sloan, *My Years with General Motors* (Doubleday, 1963), p. 131.

Those who believe that volume and efficiency drive profitability have only to look at the industry's current state. Factory efficiency is at an all-time high, while industry-wide profitability is poor at best. Still, the industry stubbornly insists that scale is the only way to survive, and its resistance to moving beyond scale is creating a variety of problems.

Fallout from Merger Mania

The most popular routes to scale involve mergers, alliances, joint ventures, and the like, lending a kind of desperation to what once was a dignified business decision. Mergers have become less like carefully considered partnerships and more like the hasty union of passengers going for the last lifeboat. David Cole, then director of the Center for Automotive Research, expressed this survival mentality succinctly: "No one is big enough, smart enough or rich enough to go it alone any more."[1]

Figure 5.1 shows many of the current complex interactions and links between manufacturers, as well as significant joint ventures such as NUMMI. Some argue that all these alliances, mergers, and joint ventures have blurred companies' national characters: Is Ford's Jaguar still British? What about Sweden's Volvo? Is Nissan now French? For some firms, such as Opel and Ford in Germany, this blurring seems to work to advantage. In the 1930s, both companies were undeniable American

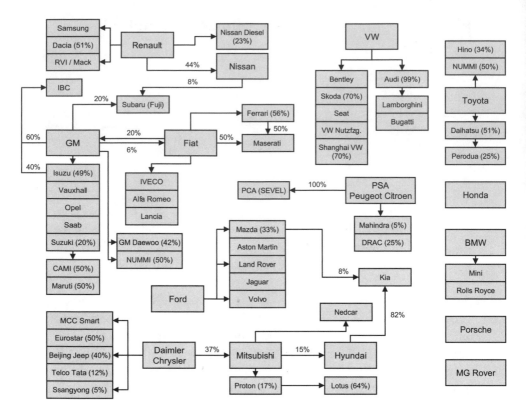

Figure 5.1
Financial structure of global auto industry. Updated from P. Wells and P. Nieuwenhuis, *The Automotive Industry* (British Telecommunications, 2001) and from *Japan's Automobile Manufacturers* (Japan's Automobile Manufacturers Association, 2002).

transplants, but they have since adopted local identities, and most consumers now view them that way.

Mergers come in all shapes and sizes. At one extreme is the unified corporation; at the other, an opportunistic tie-in. The Daimler-Chrysler merger is an example of the first extreme. In 1998, Jürgen Schrempp announced with great fanfare that this would be the world's largest industrial merger. The $92 billion merger between Daimler-Benz and Chrysler would "change the face of the industry," he claimed. In 2002, Schrempp, now DaimlerChrysler's chairman, was more circumspect: "I am a very cautious man. So I am saying it's early days, but it is going well."[2] Adjustments have been necessary in everything from language and culture to technology. Meetings are held in English, for example, and German speakers initially feared that they would lose some influence in the meetings because they could not express their views as well in a foreign language. Technology-wise, there was a clash between Chrysler's front-wheel-drive and Mercedes' rear-wheel-drive architectures. Frustrated Mercedes engineers argued that Chrysler was 10–15 years behind the Mercedes technology.

Ultimately, few doubt that, at least managerially, the merger resulted in Daimler dominance rather than a true partnership of equals. One party offered this wry observation: "DaimlerChrysler is very proud to announce it has revisited the name of the merged enterprise. In the spirit of equity, managers decided it was important that the new name integrate the identities of both organizations. Therefore, it is herewith decided that the new name will combine the first syllable of Daimler with the second syllable of Chrysler. . . ."

DaimlerChrysler is partly a volume story because Daimler-Benz wanted access to Chrysler's superior ability to negotiate with suppliers and figured that adding in Daimler-Benz would increase bought-in volumes from individual suppliers while simultaneously providing opportunities to share platforms and components on some products.

Some companies, including Land Rover and Rolls-Royce Motor Cars, have nearly drowned in the acquisition wave. The long-struggling Rover Group first went to British Aerospace and then added Honda to the mix in 1979. After several joint projects, including the Rover 200/400, the Honda Civic, and the Rover 600, the company was bought by BMW in 1994. In 2000, after 5 years of consecutive losses—despite BMW's investment of $4.72 billion—the Quandts (BMW's owning family) were no longer willing to subsidize Rover, which was losing £2 million per day.[3] A short time later, "the English Patient" (as the German press called Rover) was evicted from the Bavarian Empire along with most of its board members. With the sale of Land Rover to Ford in 2000 for £2 billion, Rover employees suddenly found themselves under both Ford and BMW, and many felt they belonged to neither. There was so much tension in the air that even a visitor could feel it. No one really knew whom it was safe to talk to and who now was the "competition."

Rolls-Royce's story has just as many twists, but it has a happier ending. In 1998 after an exuberant bidding war between Volkswagen's Ferdinand Piëch and BMW's Bernd Pischetsrieder, VW succeeded in buying the Rolls-Royce and Bentley factory in Crewe, England, for £470 million. Yet the Rolls-Royce name belonged to Rolls-Royce Aero

Engines, with whom BMW had other ventures, and Pischetsrieder obtained the Rolls-Royce brand name for only £40 million. Piëch now had the Crewe factory, but he also had a product without the brand name. BMW and VW subsequently reached a gentlemen's agreement, and the Rolls-Royce brand went from VW to BMW in January 2003. Rolls-Royce automobiles are now being built at BMW's new factory in Goodwood, England. On August 30, 2002, the last Crewe-built Rolls-Royce rolled off the production line, which had been the home of Rolls-Royce and Bentley Motor Cars since 1946.

The DaimlerChrysler, Land Rover, and Rolls-Royce alliances occurred primarily because the companies wanted greater efficiency, higher volume, and a complementary brand portfolio. Indeed, most alliances have specific efficiency goals that relate to the pursuit of volume. The GM-Fiat alliance aimed to share platforms and purchasing. In 2000, the cumulative purchasing turnover of their joint purchasing unit bought in €33 billion.[4] In 2002, though, after GM had devalued its stake by 91 percent from $2.4 billion to a mere $220 million, the alliance took an interesting turn. When Fiat reported projected losses in 2002 of $1.16 billion, some speculated that GM would merge Fiat and Opel and thus control both troubled companies without injecting any more capital.

So, although many companies are satisfied with the volume benefits of a merger, true gains seem elusive. More to the point, companies do not have to go through all this to be profitable. Mergers come with their own set of problems that companies can avoid by taking other routes to profitability. The wave of mergers has done little to reduce industry over-capacity or enhance responsiveness. Reflecting a sentiment often felt but rarely articulated by participants in the various alliances, Osamu Suzuki said his company's joint venture with GM had become a "fishbone in his throat"—with capacity utilization in their joint plant at only 40 percent of its 200,000 units.[5]

Supplier Consolidation

In 1990, the automotive supply market (direct to OEM and aftermarket) was $496 billion, with 30,000 companies. In 1998, the market had grown to an estimated $932 billion from only 8,000 companies. Suppliers have been consolidating, and forecasts suggest that by 2010 only 150–175 suppliers will able to provide large modules and systems. The remaining suppliers will then be second-tier suppliers.[6]

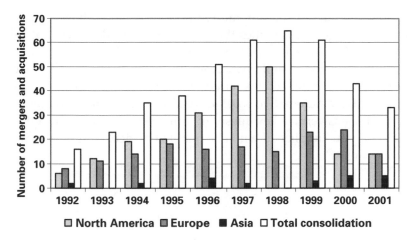

Figure 5.2
Supplier mergers and acquisitions, 1992–2001. Source of data: SDC Platinum Database, Thomson Financial, 2001.

Figure 5.2 shows supplier consolidation patterns since 1992. "Total consolidation," the sum of the mergers in all markets, has been decreasing since 1998. Most of the moves since then have been larger companies acquiring smaller ones.

Regardless of whether the acquisition was horizontal or vertical, the result has been a healthy exchange of both physical and intellectual capital. The purchase of specialty divisions is also a relatively common vehicle for capital exchange, an example being American Axle and Manufacturing's purchase of GM's Axle and Propeller divisions in March 1994.

In general, the horizontal acquisition of physical capital seems to have one of two objectives: expand production in the acquiring firm's existing market or expand the acquiring firm's market into new territories. Since 1992, the German parts manufacturer Robert Bosch has initiated 12 mergers and acquisitions worldwide, with the aim of expanding its brakes business—five in Japan, two each in China and the United States, and one each in Germany, Holland, and Korea.

Supplier consolidation has interesting implications for the balance of power in the system. Whereas previously the relationship between the vehicle manufacturer and supplier was more like Goliath and David, today some of the top suppliers are in the same league or even exceed the turnover of their smaller vehicle manufacturer customers.

The low margins in the automotive supply business have forced some OEMs to convert activities that were once considered central to vehicle manufacturing into independent organizations. Delphi and Visteon are examples. Similarly, automotive supply operations that were once part of larger conglomerates are spun off, and concerns are similar: "As TRW Automotive is being readied for sale, the auto industry awaits the answer to a key question: Will TRW emerge as a healthy $10 billion-a-year supplier, or will it be hobbled by debt shifted from its corporate parent?"[8]

Shifting the Metal

"Would you tell me," said Alice, a little timidly, "why you are painting those roses?"

Five and Seven said nothing, but looked at Two. Two began in a low voice, "Why the fact is, you see, Miss, this here ought to have been a RED rose-tree, and we put a WHITE one in by mistake; and if the Queen was to find it out, we should all have our heads cut off, you know."

—from *Alice in Wonderland,* by Lewis Carroll

In Henry Ford's day, price was the primary determinant in car buying because cars were nothing more than a basic means to enhance mobility. Today, a customer interested in buying an S-class Mercedes will not be persuaded to drive a Fiat Punto, even if the dealer halves the Punto's suggested retail price. Customization, brand image, and status, not to mention personal taste, influence the decision to buy far more than simply getting from point A to point B at the least cost.

In this kind of market, customer pull should be the focus, yet a forecast-driven system has no regard for individual preferences.

It's Not What You Wanted, but . . .

In the mid 1970s, nearly 45 percent of those who had bought British cars claimed that the color of the car they bought was not their first choice; only 30 percent of those buying imports made that claim.[1] By the early 1990s, in the United Kingdom, more than half of all customers were accepting a car that differed from what they had planned to buy. In 1997, this percentage had shrunk to 23 percent, but it has changed only slightly since. It was 19 percent in 1999.[2]

Thus, although they have made some progress, car companies are still doing a poor job of producing cars that customers want. In a recent speech, Tony Koblinski, GM's order-to-delivery director, admitted to meeting the right specification only 60 percent of the time, a percentage we believe is typical for the US market.[3] Alternative specifications take a long time to produce, and with attention on moving inventory, everyone looks, not at what customers want, but at what it will take to coerce them to select a vehicle from stock.

Our survey of 1,033 customers from the United Kingdom in 2000 and 2001 revealed some interesting patterns.[4] More specialist buyers took an alternative specification (26.8 percent) than volume buyers (21.8 percent). Specialist brands were more likely to be built to order, yet even here the customer was compromising. It took so long to build a custom car that even the most patient got fed up and bought their Jaguars and Mercedes from stock, although they'd much prefer to have that Nav-System.

Customers under the age of 25 were more than 1.5 times more likely to pick an alternative specification than those over 25, and women were marginally more inclined to buy than men.

Figure 6.1 shows the response when we asked customers to describe what about the original specification had changed. Color or paint type was clearly the most often accepted change, followed by interior option. In the United States, the picture is similar. Executives at vehicle manufacturers told us that their research shows color, engine size, and radio type are of the most concern to car buyers. Customers hence are not

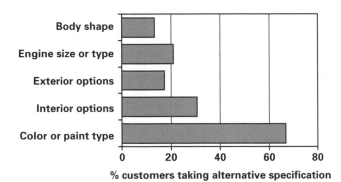

Figure 6.1
Percentage of customers accepting alternative specifications for each feature. Figure based on survey of 1,033 customers in UK in 2000 and 2001 (Elias, New Car Buyer Behavior, 3DayCar Research Report, Cardiff, 2002).

making trivial sacrifices; they are compromising on items they care about.

The Lead-Time Battle

ICDP research[5] shows that the average order-to-delivery time for volume cars in Europe in 1999 is 48 days for a volume car, 76 days for a Japanese car, and 43 days for a specialist vehicle. As figure 6.2 shows, order-to-delivery times decreased somewhat between 1994 and 1999,[6] but they are far from the 10–15 days manufacturers often mention as their objective.

How Long Will Customers Wait?

Certainly a reduced order-to-delivery time in itself is a source of competitive advantage, but understanding customer expectations about order-to-delivery times is equally important—something manufacturers do not completely understand. This confusion becomes clearer when we look at the lead-time risk, which is the potential that the delivery time will exceed customers' expectations and cause them to buy from other brands with better availability. Knowing just how long customers will wait gives manufacturers the insight they need to select the most appropriate order-fulfillment approach. The result is fewer lost sales and far lower lead-time risk.

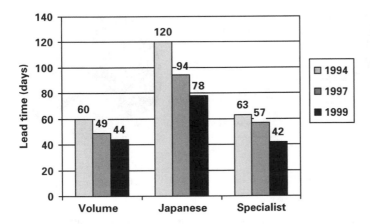

Figure 6.2
Average order-to-delivery times in Europe, 1994, 1997, and 1999. Source: Williams, Progress towards Customer Pull Distribution.

We asked customers how long *ideally* it should take from placing their order to getting their new cars. Figure 6.3 shows their responses, which are somewhat surprising: 41 percent indicated that they would wait 2 weeks or longer. This clearly contradicts the perception that customers would always want their cars "tomorrow." Most require at least a few days between order and purchase, since a vehicle purchase often involves significant planning: sell the old car, arrange insurance, get new license plates, and so on.

Of course, the ideal time varies across customer types, and this is a relationship that manufacturers could leverage to create stable order flows—something no one has yet done. Our research also shows that dealers misjudge their customers' preparedness to wait: though only 6 percent of UK customers said they would wait more than 4 weeks, the dealers claimed fully 39 percent would wait that long.

Even in the United States, where manufacturers traditionally sell vehicles from dealer stock, a 2001 survey[7] showed that nearly 75 percent of consumers would rather wait and have the vehicle they want instead of settling for one now from the dealer's lot; 62 percent were willing to order the car to get it in their preferred color; most, however, were not willing to wait more than 3 weeks.

In the United States, GM admitted to order-to-delivery times for custom orders of 50–70 days, with "fast" lead times closer to 40 days in

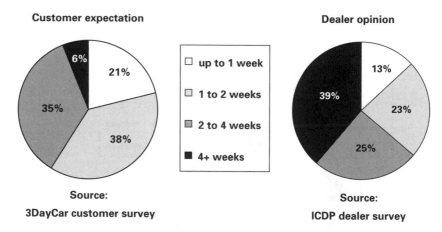

Figure 6.3
Results of asking customers "How long *ideally* should it take to get your car after ordering it?" and asking dealers "How long are your customers willing to wait?" Customer data from Elias, New Vehicle Buyer Behaviour, 2002; dealer data from Williams, Progress towards Customer Pull Distribution.

2000. Delivery dates are so uncertain that no one could make any promises.[8] Even at Toyota, Jim Bolte, general manager of IT Systems for Toyota North America, said: "Let's face it. Everyone is working on this issue." Adding that Toyota's current order-to-delivery time in North America was 77 days,[9] Bolte went on to say "We think we can take the entire process—A to Z—to 12 to 16 days." This is interesting, since Toyota's efforts at the Solara plant in Cambridge, Ontario, sparked the initial interest in North America to reduce order-to-delivery times.[10] In 1999, Toyota claimed that it could build a vehicle 5 days after receiving the order at its Ontario factory. Manufacturers in Detroit quickly dismissed the idea. ("They would need helicopters to fly cars around the country.") As it turned out, the claim was a misinterpretation. What Toyota meant was that the factory could *build* a vehicle in 5 days after the order had been received at the factory. The vehicle would still have to be distributed to the dealership, which bumped the order-to-delivery time to 10–15 days—still a dramatic improvement over the current US average. Consumer research in Japan gives a very similar picture: 80 percent of Japanese buyers for almost all makes would find a two-week delivery window for a built-to-order car acceptable.[11] Toyota and Nissan currently achieve order-to-delivery lead times of 23 and 30 days, respectively. Toyota has the objective of reducing this further to 14 days; Nissan aims for a 15-day order-to-delivery lead time in Japan.

As we described earlier, customers vary in their sensitivity to order-to-delivery time. US customers have been educated to expect instant gratification—go to the dealer, pick a car, get the financing (or have it already), and drive the car off the lot. German customers, on the other hand, have gotten used to expecting just the opposite, so they order and wait. In the rest of Europe, cultural sensitivities are not as easy to pin down.

As table 6.1 shows, age is another factor: 84 percent of customers under 25 want a car in 2 weeks or less, versus 54 percent of customers between 25 and 35 and 58 percent of those over 55. This trend is also reflected in the average ideal wait times. Of the customers we interviewed, almost 40 percent said order-to-delivery time was very important. Buyers under 25, a group many vehicle manufacturers are targeting, were far more likely to rate it important. Although they were also more inclined to take an alternative specification, this only indicates that they felt they couldn't get what they wanted quickly enough, so they took what was available.

Table 6.1
Waiting tolerance by age group.*

Age group	Average ideal OTD[a] time	Impatient customers[b] as percentage of age group
< 25	10.5 days	84%
25–35	19.7 days	54%
36–55	20.1 days	62%
>55	18.6 days	58%

*Source: S. Elias, "Research highlights," 3DayCar Sponsors Conference, Ardencote Manor, UK, December 2001.
a. Order-to-delivery.
b. Defined as those who wanted the vehicle within 2 weeks.

We also found that buyers of volume cars tend to want their cars more quickly, relative to buyers of specialist cars. Alfa Romeo and Volkswagen buyers are notable exceptions. Apparently, buyers see a relationship between quality and time: a quality or specialist car, they reason, will take longer to make and deliver than a volume car. Such beliefs are likely based on the idea that craftsmanship does and should take time. Manufacturers have exploited these beliefs to some degree, using the notion of exclusivity to make waiting a virtue. A quality product takes time to build, our product is so good that everyone wants one, and so on.

Expectations vary across brands. Although the divide between volume and specialist manufacturers is largely natural, some conditioning is taking place. Ford buyers, for example, expect the shortest order-to-delivery time, possibly because of previous experience with the brand. The dealers push stock and so are more inclined to get the customer a deal. The customer tells his friends, who expect the same treatment, and so on. This is brand education. Of course it may actually be that the Ford brand attracts impatient consumers, such as young motorists who want cheap and cheerful entry-level cars.

Despite the flippancy of our last statement, the correlation between Ford and youth is not as far-fetched as it sounds. Younger buyers are particularly demanding in their expectations: With 84 percent in the impatient group, people under the age of 25 were far and away the leading fans of short delivery times. The next closest age bracket was 25–35, at 54 percent. (See table 6.1.) Younger buyers are also far more likely to use the Internet in their buying process. It is hard to say if their Internet reliance is due to youthful impatience or simply the comfort level of technology use in this generation. Regardless, this group is easily in the vanguard of the instantly gratified consumer, whose expectations give us some idea of where buyer behavior is heading over the next 10 years.

Institutional Buyers

The discussion about customer profiles almost always centers on the private consumer, but considerable volumes also go to fleet buyers —institutional buyers that purchase vehicles for company fleets as part of a large corporation, government, or rental car company. The fleet sales volumes can be significant for certain models, commonly large sedans and compact cars. Also, in some countries, such as the United Kingdom, tax laws favor company cars, so the fleet market is around 40 percent of all vehicle sales.

In 2001, we surveyed 317 fleet buyers, generally the fleet managers of large companies, including 11 rental car firms. Most kept their fleet cars for 36 months or less than 100,000 miles. Buyers tend not to lock the users into a model within a brand or even to a brand. They let their employees specify the vehicle.

Because fleet buyers purchase in volume, we expected price to drive their buying behavior, and the availability of the vehicles and particular specifications to be a secondary concern. As table 6.2 shows, waiting tolerance was high; 88 percent of fleet buyers, however, stated that build-to-order was as relevant for the fleet market as it was for private customers. As the table shows, fleet buyers tend to be much more patient than, for example, young private buyers.

Their expectations stand in stark contrast to when they actually received their vehicles. Only 3 percent of the vehicles were received in

Table 6.2
Fleet buyers' waiting tolerance.*

Ideal OTD time	Percentage of buyers
< 1 week	0
1–2 weeks	8
2–3 weeks	17
3–4 weeks	46
> 4 weeks	29

*Source: S. Elias, "Research highlights," 3DayCar Sponsors Conference, Ardencote Manor, UK, December 2001.

Table 6.3
Percentages of cars delivered in Europe after date promised.*

	Volume manufacturers	Japanese manufacturers	Specialist manufacturers
1994	21	14	13
1997	24	15	10
1999	19	18	9

*Source: G. Williams, "Customer aspects of vehicle supply," ICDP Annual Conference, St Paul de Vence, France, October 1999.

less than 2 weeks, 13 percent in 2 weeks to a month, 44 percent in 1–2 months, and for 34 percent more than 2 months.

The Cost of Broken Promises

It is one thing to wait for a car before its promised delivery date; it is quite another to wait for a car *after* that date. Indeed, our interviews and survey show that customers perceive an unreliable delivery date as *worse* than a longer order-to-delivery time. This is not a good thing when so many vehicles still arrive late to the dealers. In Europe, current deliveries are late between 9 percent and 19 percent of the time for specialist and volume cars, respectively, as table 6.3 shows. In the United States, GM gets the car to the dealer late fully 30 percent of the time.[12] Thus, in addition to the struggle to get a custom car in a reasonable time, the customer must face the possibility that the promised delivery date is less than reliable.

Reliable delivery is an important component of build-to-order. A build-to-order system that provides unreliable delivery dates cannot earn the trust of dealers and customers and is doomed to fail from the start. The message is clear: Make delivery-date reliability the first priority, followed by a reduction in order-to-delivery time.

III

The Case for Build-to-Order

The fun has gone out of what should be the most exciting industry on the planet.

—Thomas Stallkamp, speech at Global Leadership Conference, White Sulphur Springs, West Virginia, October 2002, quoted in *Automotive News,* October 28

The clear message so far is that manufacturers can either (a) sell as many cars as can be sold with the liberal use of incentives and stock holding or (b) sell fewer cars at a higher prices by meeting customers' needs.

What is the cost of continuing on path a? Could things get any worse? The state of the industry is abysmal. Manufacturers try to keep up volume; suppliers try to avoid bankruptcy. Manufacturers and suppliers engage in mergers in the hope that the resulting alliances will give them the critical mass for survival. Profit-and-loss cycles wreak havoc not only on investors but also on employees, the supply base, and the economy in general. (Other concerns include the benefit and pension obligations the Big Three, particularly GM, will face over the coming years. See G. Lapidus et al., Automobiles—United States, Research Report: May 31, Goldman Sachs, New York, 2001.) While these cycles do relate to business cycles, the industry seems to learn nothing from one cycle to the next. Capacity is built during each upturn, but is not eliminated when times are leaner. "The problem," Goldman Sachs aptly observed, "is they're sizing demand to meet capacity rather than sizing capacity to meet demand. The Big Three operate at the same capacity utilization today in a 17-million light vehicle market as they did 5 years ago in a 15-million market, but it costs them an extra $1,500 per vehicle in incentives. The situation is not sustainable." (ibid. and update of April 9, 2002, Goldman Sachs, New York)

Even during "normal" years, firms make little effort to manage and smooth sales volumes. Not only do the volumes fluctuate dramatically, but rigidities at the factory level mean that some factories are run over capacity, while others must cut shifts or shut down lines.

The arguments for build-to-order are compelling. The benefits the industry claims it gets from building to forecast do not generate profit, and the volume and efficiency that the industry points to as solutions to cost efficiency are actually obstacles to greater gain. Although selling lower volumes at higher prices does not automatically guarantee greater profits, it is clear that incentivized sales to generate volume are rarely the pathway to superior financial performance.

Ripping the Lid off the Revenue Box

It isn't that they cannot see the solution. It is that they cannot see the problem.

—G. K. Chesterton, *The Scandal of Father Brown* (1935)

In the preceding chapters, we have strongly implied that the profits from a forecast-based business model are tenuous at best. In this chapter, we dig more deeply into the motor vehicle industry's cost structure, which even seasoned insiders regard as a labyrinth of direct, indirect, overhead, labor, R&D, and distribution costs. In understanding this structure, we can better see why building to forecast cannot be profitable in the long term.

Figure 7.1 shows part of the revenue stream for an average European mid-size (C-segment) car. The Smart car, for example, as we mentioned earlier, is assembled from seven key modules supplied by co-located suppliers, so the percentage of bought-in parts is significantly higher—about 85 percent of the product cost, excluding product development and overhead.

For most other manufacturers, the percentage is more like 60–70 percent. Also, specialist manufacturers, such as BMW and Mercedes, will have significantly higher product-development content than generic volume cars because they rely less on suppliers for design assistance and emphasize technological preeminence.

In other words, no single example can capture every twist in the cost-structure maze. But if we do not provide at least some context, an analysis of that structure and of BTO benefits will be vague at best.

As figure 7.1 shows, the main costs relate to the materials and components purchased, and this is largely true for any vehicle. Typically, components make up 60 percent of the retail price, either made in house

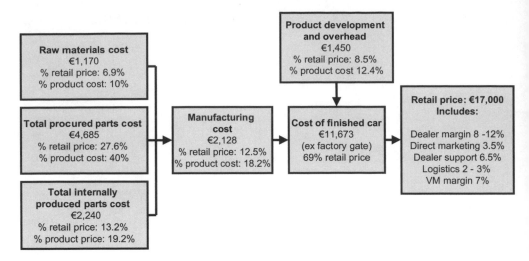

Figure 7.1
Generic industry cost structure for European mid-size car. Distribution data averaged from interviews at vehicle manufacturers; other data from Max Warburton of Goldman Sachs.

or sourced from suppliers. This explains the emphasis on integrating the supply chain. Customers seldom realize that the cost of manufacturing a vehicle is less than one-fifth of what they pay for it. The rest is taken up by parts and material and by sales and distribution (logistics costs, dealer and vehicle manufacturer margins, marketing).

Unfortunately, the pressure to attain volume sales causes many structural irregularities that no flowchart, generic or otherwise, can capture. UK dealers, for example, are subsidizing their new-vehicle sales by giving them to customers at zero or even negative margins in the hope of capturing after-sales revenue from maintenance and servicing, which can be considerable. Some dealers bluntly admitted that they saw no money in selling new cars, but new-car sales represented a path to profits in used-car sales and servicing.

Used-car sales are also a motivation to cut corners on selling new cars. In the United States, new-vehicle sales account for 59 percent of the average dealer's revenue, used-vehicle sales for 29 percent. The gross margin on new cars is only 6 percent—about half the margin for used cars.[1] The low margins are sometimes a deliberate strategy to earn revenue. Manufacturers often review sales volume monthly or quarterly and reward high sales with volume bonuses. The dealer then uses this reward to offset any money it lost on a sale.

The 2.8-Million-Car Pileup

As we described in chapter 6, demand forecasting results in an over-supply of desired products or (worse) an undersupply of desired products with an oversupply of undesirable variants. Savings from lean manufacturing are then eaten up by the costs of managing and storing inventory when (surprise) no one can find a customer for the oddly equipped product. Of the average 17 million vehicles sold in the United States each year, about 2.8 million new vehicles are held in inventory (approximately 60 days' worth). Very conservatively, this translates to an annual interest expense of more than $2.5 billion, or $150 per vehicle sold. Put another way: *Every customer who buys a vehicle pays an extra $150 simply because the manufacturer buffers production at its factories.* And the $150 doesn't even include the cost of logistics, handling, storage, and insurance, for which the average US dealer has to spend another $468 per vehicle.[2]

Goldman Sachs estimates that a BTO strategy would save manufacturers $1,200 per vehicle because it would wipe out these phantom costs, which also include dealer discounting to entice customers and lost sales from customers who go elsewhere to get the vehicle they really want.[3]

The large inventory is another throwback to mass production. When we mentioned at the start of this book that the industry is having trouble shedding Henry Ford's legacy, we weren't kidding. Henry believed that 60 days was just the right amount of inventory at his dealers, and 80 years later, manufacturers still believe that, and some are going even higher. At the end of 1999, inventory had risen to 3.5 million vehicles. Multiply that by an average sales price of $21,000 and you get a whopping $73.5 billion to accommodate those extra vehicles that lean manufacturing made oh so efficiently. As hard as it might be to overlook this inventory, current accounting practices muddy the true cost of this stockpile.[4] Furthermore, secondary cost such as increased warranty expenditures are generally measured, but hardly ever linked to the fact that the vehicle had been sitting in stock for months.[5]

Figure 7.2 shows stock levels across years and seasons. The spikes in winter and the lows in summer months support the idea that the factory pushes vehicles into the market year round. In summer, when cars actually sell, stock goes down. In winter, when they do not sell as well, stock goes up.

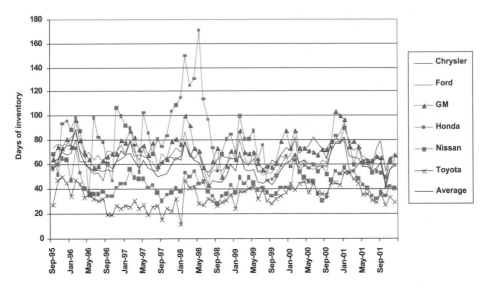

Figure 7.2
Stock levels of new vehicles in US, 1995–2001.

The situation is not much different in Europe. In 2001, European car manufacturers sold 17 million cars and light trucks across Western Europe for a total of €133 billion. Inventory cost for 8 weeks at a rate of 11 percent totaled about €2.25 billion. Had inventory levels been reduced to 2 weeks, the cost would have dropped to €563 million—a saving of €1.68 billion.[6] Ford's COO, Nick Scheele, estimated that in Europe the savings in inventory alone after implementing BTO would be as much as €99 per vehicle in 2002,[7] assuming only 2 weeks less market inventory. Commenting on Renault's goal of 3 weeks order-to-delivery (OTD) time, Scheele said: "If they [Renault] can manage, great for them, but Ford is still very far from such an ambitious target."[8]

Some manufacturers, particularly in Europe, are moving in the right direction. Figure 7.3 shows that inventory objectives in the United Kingdom shrank from 1994 to 1999. In 1999, the ten UK manufacturers with the largest sales volume had an average new-car inventory of 64 days, with the lowest at 46 days and the most at 108 days. Specialist manufacturers held far less inventory, with an average of 25 days and a low of 19 days.[9] Doubtless the lower specialist inventory is due to the manufacturers' reliance on BTO. Other areas showed similar patterns. European stock levels for volume, Japanese (UK-produced), and specialist cars were 57, 72, and 40 days, respectively.[10] The Japanese inventory

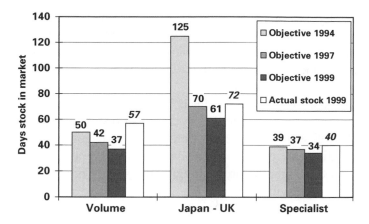

Figure 7.3
New vehicle stock objectives in UK in 1994, 1997, and 1999 and actual stock levels in 1999. "Japan-UK": Japanese models produced in UK. Source: Williams, Progress towards Customer Pull Distribution.

levels are the highest, even though plants like Nissan Sunderland are some of the most productive in Europe.

In the United Kingdom, distribution centers have caused stock levels to fall sharply. Geoff Williams of ICDP told us that between 1992 and 1997, when distribution centers became popular in the United Kingdom, stock objectives decreased by an estimated 33 percent, and actual stocks fell an average of 25 percent. However, from 1997 to 1999, although manufacturers had further reduced their stock objectives,[11] actual stock levels did not decline on par, and still remain considerably above objective.

Obviously, fully stocking the market has serious cost penalties to the national sales companies, which own and run the distribution centers, to the manufacturer, which must establish and maintain central inventory holding areas, and to the dealers, which must lease the land, secure the premises, maintain the storage area, and pay exorbitant insurance prices.

Also, additional shipping adds to the overall logistics cost. Cars in storage at one side of the country might be shipped to a dealership on the other side when a dealer there matches the vehicle to one of its customers. Whether the vehicle is in a dealer lot or in a distribution center, the logistics cost is hefty. One UK manufacturer that manages new-car stock through regional distribution centers told us that it ships 20 percent of its vehicles between centers to accommodate customers in different parts of the country. Swapping between distribution centers is cheaper than the dealer transfers (which, as was mentioned earlier, typically run about $180), since the national sales company can arrange to transport several vehicles on one large truck. Still, the cost ranges from $50 to $75 per vehicle, depending on the distance.

Arrangements to cover the cost of dealer transfers can get intricate. When dealer A locates a car in dealer B's stock, dealer B still owns it and has not paid the full sticker price for it. Thus, dealer A negotiates with dealer B about the sales price, and the two dealers come to some arrangement about splitting the profit margin and cost for the transfer. The customer ends up paying for it all.

A Sale at Any Cost

We have already said that manufacturers are paying customers to buy their cars in the form of discounts and attractive financing. Vehicle manufacturer spend $470 beyond this in advertising on average per vehicle,[12] and dealers spend a further $507 per sale in advertising,[13] for a total of almost $1,000.

Discounts come in four flavors: reward for a bulk purchase, compensation for accepting the car the customer didn't really want at first, incentives to clear out aging stock, and special editions. As the term implies, bulk purchases are volume purchases sold directly to the customer, including rental cars, company fleets, and government uses. The alternative specification discount is obvious. Joe wants a green car; the lot has a tan one. The dealer offers Joe a lower price if he'll just take the tan car as is. The aim of aging-stock discounts, which are often provided by the manufacturer, is to clear slow-moving stock at either the dealer or a central stocking location. Generally aging stock is 6 months or older, and discounts take the form of advertising, promotions, and direct incentives for the dealers, such as volume-related bonuses. Finally, special editions push old models by giving them a facelift— essentially offering some options free and tacking "special edition" onto the model name.

Table 7.1 presents the average discounts we observed in the United Kingdom in 2000. Private retail customers are a smaller fraction of the market because UK tax laws favor providing a vehicle as part of employee compensation.

Both the manufacturer and dealer try to avoid giving discounts to private retail customers, yet in the current system discounts are essential to

Table 7.1
Volume and average discounts in UK, 1999–2000.

Customer type	Volume	Discounts
Private retail	40%	0–10%
Retail fleet	20%	10–20%
Direct fleet	25%	30–40%
Demonstrators, showroom cars	5%	—
Employees	10%	15–20%

sales success. Of all the UK customers we surveyed who took an alternative specification, 46 percent surveyed received some discount. Benefits varied considerably across brands, and the variation did not always correlate with the perceived brand strength. Jaguar and Volkswagen, for example, have strong brand images in the United Kingdom, yet their customers were more likely to receive benefits. The significant differences across brands could be due to the variance in options offered, and problems getting the right car to the customer on time. Volkswagen has notoriously long delivery times in the United Kingdom, for example. Some brands offer as standard features that other brands consider optional, and all brands have different packages.

Figure 7.4 shows the nature of the benefits offered: discounts were the most popular, followed by vehicle upgrades. We also found that volume buyers were more likely to get a financing deal, while specialist buyers were more likely to get a better trade-in price and an upgrade offer.[14]

Manufacturers disagree on whether incentives are good or bad, sometimes sharply. "Compared with lower production," Rick Wagoner of GM argued, "we make more money [offering high incentives]."[15] Porsche's CEO Wendelin Wiedeking, on the other hand, publicly told Fred Schwab, president of Porsche Cars North America, "We will reduce production before starting discounts."[16]

GM's stance is far from unusual. Throughout the automotive industry's history, incentives have attempted to keep volumes up. Zero-percent financing dates to 1916, when most manufacturers, unable to compete with Ford on price and perceived value, introduced purchases on credit as a way to lure customers into their showrooms. By 1919, 65 percent of Ford sales were on credit. Customers who could not afford a car now had a way to buy it. History offers some wisdom for proponents of incentives. In its first year, the General Motors Acceptance Corporation (GMAC) had to write off $2 million in bad loans. Despite

Figure 7.4
Types of benefits received. Source: Elias, New Vehicle Buyer Behaviour.

these setbacks, the industry had discovered a compatible sales partner for mass production, and by 1924, credit purchases had become the norm, with more than three-fourths of all purchases made via installments.[17]

In October 2002, GM gave an average incentive of $3,855 per vehicle. Toyota and Honda, who generally offer lower incentives, were subsidizing vehicle purchases $729 and $1,140, respectively.[18] Incentives are unusual at Toyota and Honda, which tend to use them when the industry is facing its greatest challenges, thus effectively making downturns that much more painful. In the United States in January 2001, Chrysler's incentives increased to $2,600 per vehicle from $1,200 in 1998, a jump due mainly to overstocking.[19] This is not specific to the United States. In the UK market, the variable marketing costs can be as high as £2,500 per vehicle, but are generally in the £400–£600 range.[20]

Incentives may entice customers to buy, but they have some nasty side effects:

• Customers grow to expect them. CNW Marketing research found that US buyers take it for granted that they can get at least $3,000 off list price when buying a new vehicle.[21] Brand image and residual values erode. If Jim can get a car $3,000 lower this year, he is not likely to settle for the same car at a higher price. He is more likely to walk next door to the showroom that has that price. It becomes all about the cost, not the brand features.

• Dealers get accustomed to using them. Giancarlo Boschetti, Fiat's CEO in 2002, said Fiat's dealer network was not efficient. Sales of Alfa Romeo,

Lancia, and Fiat cars within the group relied too heavily on discounts to rental agencies and to buyers of barely used demo cars.[22] This is actually a bit unfair. The problem with incentives is far greater than the distribution system. It is the result of years of forecast-based push systems that create high market stock levels, which in turn *require* incentives. The dealers are only filling their role as the system dictates.

• Prices become uncertain. The more uncertain the price, the less a manufacturer can sustain profitable sales, and the more severe the customer dissatisfaction. Most buyers do not enjoy haggling, nor do they like not knowing if they made a good deal. The sticker price has been around since 1958 to protect the customer from dealers that would charge more. Incentives have destroyed this transparency, and we are back to square one.[23] Recommended retail prices in the current push system—other than perhaps new-model prices—are a farce. Most people agree that, except in buying select "hot" products, only the gullible or feeble-minded pay the sticker price.

• Market share shrinks. From 1996 to 2000, while the marketing costs per vehicle of the Big Three increased by 87 percent (to an average $2,900 per car sold), their combined market share dropped by more than four percentage points, representing $15 billion in lost revenue for 2000 alone.

• Residual values on off-lease vehicles fall. As incentives shift market demand to new vehicles, demand for used cars falls. The amount the manufacturer can get for the off-lease vehicles is less than what it anticipated and used to build its lease-pricing model. From July 2001 to July 2002, average wholesale auction prices dropped 6 percent[24]—a change attributable primarily to the increased incentives needed to keep major new-car inventories moving.

Out of Options

Stock holding and incentives are fairly obvious sources of cost penalties in using a forecast-based push system. The third major cost penalty—lost profits from selling a sub-optimal mix—is more subtle. Stock vehicles have less chance of hitting the exact combination of options that customers want. Either the customer does not want an option that is fitted to a stock vehicle and hence doesn't pay the full price for it, or the car doesn't have an option that the customer would have paid for. In both cases, the manufacturer, and to some extent the customer loses, and profitability goes down. Renault has unofficially confirmed this relationship, finding that actual customer orders showed a far richer and hence more profitable option mix than the stock orders the dealer pre-specified.[25]

Not selling options is a major loss of revenue, since selling a loaded model is much more profitable than selling a base version. Figure 7.5 shows the price range from the base to top model for six vehicles in the United States, the United Kingdom, and Germany. The length of each bar should leave no doubt that manufacturers take a hit on profits when they do not sell options. The base model and the top model of the Ford Focus have the same body, but the top model costs 132 percent more. The top-of-the-line BMW in Germany is more than three times the price of the base model.

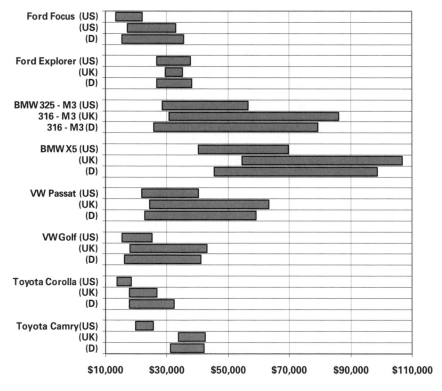

Figure 7.5
Model price bands by country for six vehicles.

This is major revenue. Making the underlying base car is almost as expensive as making the top model. Yes, the power train is more expensive, but a 4-cylinder engine costs around $600 to produce; a V8 costs $1,800. The customer pays a lot more than $1,200 for a top model with the V8 option.

Figure 7.5 also shows that the price for the same car varies drastically across markets, the price in the US market being the lowest. The Toyota Camry, for example, is considered a mid-size car in the United States but an upper-middle-class car in Europe. The top BMW X5 is about $37,000 cheaper in the United States than in the United Kingdom.

8   Closing Arguments

All great truths begin as blasphemies.
—George Bernard Shaw

Some in the industry feel obliged to point out that Ford, General Motors, and DaimlerChrysler on average outperformed many of their suppliers in the 1990s. In view of the suppliers' performance, that is hardly a noteworthy achievement. The average operating margin (profits divided by revenue) is 1.9 percent for auto suppliers, and 4.8 percent for the rest of the Fortune 500 companies.[1] Any financial index paints the same dismal picture. The Standard & Poor's 500 shows the simple average after-tax margin for suppliers to have been declining since 1995—from 6 percent to less than 1 percent in the first quarter of 2002. Larry Yost, CEO of ArvinMeritor, had this to say:

The Big Three's profits have been deteriorating, but it's not just them. It's also we suppliers. Our returns being down affects value creation. For most of us, the weighted average cost to capital is about 9 percent. The return on invested capital would average somewhere around 6 to 8 percent. If the weighted average cost to capital is below 8 percent, we are destroying economic value.[2]

Vehicle manufacturers have fared only slightly better. Goldman Sachs estimates that Ford's average pre-tax operating margin over the past 30 years is 2.4 percent. Ford has experienced significant cyclical variability around that average, ranging from a negative 9.9 percent in 1980 to a positive 9.2 percent in 1999. Capacity use explains 80 percent of the margin variability, indicating that there has been almost no change in the basic economics of making cars and the profit per unit of capacity.[3]

Ford's cyclical variability is not unique. Indeed, except for perhaps Toyota, vehicle manufacturers pocket money faster than a gambler betting at the table of a blind blackjack dealer, but they lose it just as quickly in leaner times. (See figure 8.1.[4]) If any of the auto producers had been able to keep even half of the money it accumulated during each upswing, we would be forced to conclude that building to forecast works, and we would not be writing this book.

The Supplier Squeeze

In times of financial trouble, the power structure in a supply chain comes into play, and the manufacturer exercises its power. In the grocery industry, powerful retailers such as Wal-Mart meet equally powerful suppliers (e.g., Coca-Cola). In the auto industry, the scenario for all but the largest suppliers meeting manufacturers is more akin to a corner drugstore taking on Procter and Gamble. The manufacturers dictate all the terms, generally a take-it-or-take-off proposal. Annual price reductions of 3–5 percent, in some cases even 10 percent, are common.

Consider the following news excerpt:

. . . with recession cutting into auto sales, Ford drastically cut inventories, changed its schedule of payments to suppliers from 60 to 90 days, and unilaterally reduced prices for raw materials and components. Dealers were forced to accept larger shipments of cars than they ordered, paid for by borrowing from local banks.

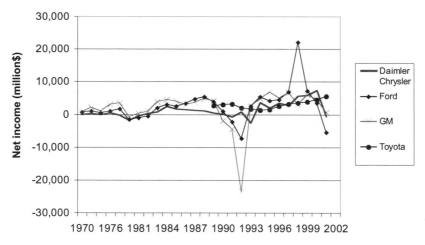

Figure 8.1
Net income for vehicle manufacturers. Source: *Automotive News Yearbook*, 2002.

This could have been in the *Detroit News* yesterday, followed by a "here they go again" reaction from most suppliers. In reality, it dates back to the 1920s.[5]

Recently, Metaldyne Corporation CEO Tim Leuliette said: "The Big Three cannot return to their past glory by having the supply community financially subsidize their inability to address their own problems." A General Motors vice-president, asked to comment on Leuliette's remark, said: "Oh, was that the guy who went crazy in Traverse City?"[6] Broken contracts, incessant demands for lower prices, unpaid bills for tooling, ruthless purchasing people are issues at the core of the fractured and contentious relationship between many suppliers and the Big Three.[7]

Even here we find cycles. In the early 1990s, Chrysler was the darling of suppliers, in part because it had no other hope of refreshing its product line. Recently, Nick Scheele, COO of Ford, urged employees in an e-mail message to treat suppliers better: "If we are not our suppliers' customer of choice, they will dedicate their best people, invest their best resources, and offer the newest technology to our competitors. . . ."[8] From June 2001 to June 2002, however, the prices vehicle parts declined 0.2 percent. That was the sixth year of a steady decrease.[9]

Manufacturers are still squeezing their suppliers, leaving them with less to spend on the research and development of new parts or to invest in manufacturing efficiency, let alone shoulder product development, warranty, and tooling costs.

"In the current automotive environment," one supplier commented, "what the customer is willing to pay is less important than what your competitor is willing to charge." Suppliers, desperate for a leg up, offered design services and accepted novel pay systems, among other concessions. Pay-on-production, which Ford once heralded as a major pillar of its efforts to reduce supply-chain costs, is no longer a strategy for many components, because Ford found that it contributed little to savings. Further, some firms (including Ford) are reclaiming design, in part to offset price increases from outsourcing design. David Thursfield, executive vice-president at Ford, notes that Ford let the cost of its roof rack for the Focus balloon to $39, although $14 is more typical for such components.[10]

The burden of capital investments is increasing so much so that suppliers are relocating to lower-wage countries, such as Mexico and Eastern Europe.[11] This makes the overall manufacturing system less responsive.

Among the manufacturers working to address relationships with suppliers, Toyota is the leader. Toyota called for price reductions in 2002, but its aim was to reach them through joint efforts and shared cost savings. To reduce the cost of parts, it has suppliers produce dual-sourced parts, cooperating on parts purchases. The company is looking for reductions of as much as 30 percent over the next 3 years, but plans to time price reductions to coincide with model introductions.[12]

The Job-Creation Payoff

Besides "Squeeze the Supplier," manufacturers are adept at playing "Get the Subsidy," a game that involves pitting governments against one another to acquire free land, training, and infrastructure. In the United States, as of 2003, local and state subsidies for new facilities generally exceed $100,000 for every job created. In 1993, Mercedes received $253 million from the state of Alabama as a subsidy for a 1,500-worker plant; in 2003, Hyundai received $234 million from the same state as a subsidy for its new 2,000-employee plant.

Employment creation sits well with voters. The jobs associated with automobile manufacturing are doubly alluring because every superbly paid job at the manufacturing plants generates multiple jobs at suppliers and in other sectors in the region. Of course, the subsidy elicits no guarantee that the created jobs will last. In the late 1970s, the state of Pennsylvania spent $100 million to encourage the establishment of a Volkswagen plant, which shut down 10 years later.[13]

Similar subsidies are prevalent overseas. Volkswagen received more than $70 million to build its Dresden plant, which will employ about 800. In England, rarely a month passes that manufacturers aren't begging for and receiving government handouts. In many developing and newly industrialized countries, blocking imports is an equally effective way to subsidize the auto sector.

Despite chronic over-capacity, the lure of government incentives is hard to resist. Manufacturers often fall into a herd mentality, setting up operations where others have done so. Figure 8.2 shows the dramatic growth in production capacity in Brazil, for example. General Motors is not alone in its renewed enthusiasm for Brazil. Ford, Fiat, and Volkswagen dominate the local industry, but Renault, Hyundai, and Asia Motors also considered a move there. Mercedes, which previously produced trucks and buses, has started assembling passenger cars in Brazil, and Toyota has expressed similar interest in entering Brazil's

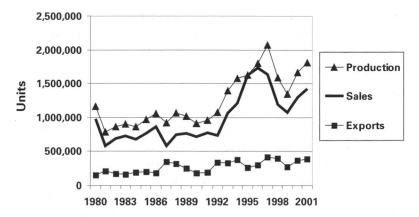

Figure 8.2
Brazil's auto production, sales, and exports.

passenger-car market.[14] It is hard to justify all this newly built capacity, even with the promise of greater free trade in Latin America. Indeed, as figure 8.2 shows, exports have changed little, with most of the variability stemming from the local Brazilian market.

Significantly lower wages are among the attractions of producing overseas. With production worker wages in the United States hovering around $30 per hour, the appeal (particularly for suppliers) of working with producers in developing or newly industrialized countries is easy to understand. Nonetheless, exchange rates can vary dramatically from year to year, which causes wages to halve or double at will. Fiat knows only too well the risks associated with setting up camp in an emerging market. The company invested $650 million in its plant in Cordoba, Argentina, which has the capacity to build 800 cars per day, but it sold only 13,568 cars in all of 2001.[15]

Time for Change

These closing arguments should cause even the recalcitrant to recognize the importance of adopting build-to-order and reconnecting the customer and the value chain:

• Manufacturers provide the right car more quickly, which improves customer service and minimizes redundant stock.

• Manufacturers and dealers no longer finance inventory, since the fields of cars have disappeared. Discounts are no longer needed to move inventory or compensate for alternative specifications. The dealer can sell all the desired options in each vehicle and the individual sale will yield more profit.

These benefits are difficult to quantify, however, because discussing build-to-order savings relative to the forecast-based production model is an apples-to-oranges proposition. The build-to-order model provides cost-reduction opportunities that extend beyond reduced inventories in the market, lower incentives, and fewer discounts. The model also does something that forecast-based production cannot. It creates more opportunities to sell profitable options, for example.

Predictably, these differences complicate any discussion. We refuse to be yet another player in the "me, too" game in which everyone strives to have the greatest estimate of savings from a build-to-order strategy. Any cost savings from build-to-order will vary by manufacturer and by market, and the numbers quoted are often based on unstated assumptions that seem to get more convoluted the more you try to define them. Thus, in the rest of the book, we omit the *what*—and discuss *where* these savings will occur and *why*.

On the other hand, it is tempting to at least peek at what others allege are build-to-order savings. Table 8.1 gives an overview of the findings from three recent efforts. None of the numbers are likely to be reproduced, and we are not certain that these estimates reflect the costs associated with build-to-order. Nonetheless, the consensus is that build-to-order has significant savings potential for the automotive industry in all major markets.

Potential savings through a build-to-order strategy are often mixed with savings from other improvements. Build-to-order has a range of associated benefits, such as opportunities to leverage e-commerce, but we consider these to be secondary—impressive, but not direct benefits. The result of the debate within the automotive industry, held years ago, was that huge savings in transactions would be achieved through business-to-business e-commerce. Even though exchanges like COVISINT fell somewhat short of expectations when the e-bubble burst, the estimated transactions of $1,300 billion worldwide in various tiers of the light-vehicle supply chains[16] still represents a mind-boggling potential.

Regrettably, the benefits of build-to-order have eluded manufacturers, most likely because they have channeled too much energy into the more visible parts of the value grid, such as manufacturing plants, while ignoring system-wide opportunities. Meanwhile, islands of excellence

Table 8.1
Predicted savings through build-to-order and related measures.

Source*	Market region	Predicted savings	Savings achieved
Goldman Sachs	North America	$60 billion total savings in North America $3,650 total savings per vehicle	$1,531 through build-to-order $1,048 through online sales $1,064 through supply chain and purchasing improvements
ICDP	Europe	€11 billion one-off savings for the entire European Automotive industry €4 billion annual savings c. 10% vehicle cost savings possible	Inventory reduction Increased unit profitability through enhanced product mix Distribution system reform
Roland Berger	All	$1,200 per vehicle (North America) $639 per vehicle (Europe) $540 per vehicle (Japan)	New vehicle inventory savings Purchasing: transaction cost savings through B2B Product development cost reduction Manufacturing cost reduction

*G. Lapidus, eAutomotive: Gentlemen, Start Your Search Engines,"Goldman Sachs, New York, 2000; ICDP, Fulfilling the Promise, Solihull, 2000; Roland Berger, *Automotive e-Commerce* (Roland Berger, 2000).

are drowned in a sea of misinformation and waste. Companies flog themselves and others to increase scale, forgetting that "bigger" is not more nimble, efficient, insightful, or profitable. Indeed, no one is really certain what economies of scale beyond 1.5–2 million vehicles per year have to offer.

In its frenzy for efficiency, the industry has forgotten the advantages of flexibility. Manufacturers have become blind to true demand and to the value that derives from being responsive to customers' needs.

IV Three Dimensions of Responsiveness: Process, Product, and Volume

Well Mister I want a yellow convertible, four-door de Ville
With a Continental spare, and a wide chrome wheel
I want power steerin' and power brakes
I want a powerful motor with a jet off-take.
I want air conditionin'. I want automatic heat.
I want a full Murphy bed in my back seat.
I want short-wave radio. I want TV and a phone.
You know I gotta talk to my baby when I'm ridin' alone.

—Chuck Berry, "No Money Down"

Fortunately, despite its downward spiral, the industry hasn't yet flat-lined. If companies can break the cycle of boom and bust and can forgo islands of excellence in favor of system-wide optimization and customer-centricity, they will not only come out of their moribund state, they will experience renewed vigor. On the other hand, it is likely that firms persisting with a shift-the-metal philosophy will continue to generate returns no better than those offered on a passport savings account.

Admittedly, the three-day car is not exactly on the horizon. The current order-fulfillment process has too many knots to respond quickly to variation in demand. Vehicle supply systems worldwide have been forecast-driven for too long, and the systems driving the corporate value grid and mindset have been built around it.

Nonetheless, the value grid has much room for improvement. If the focus moves from forecast volume to real customer demand, processes must also become more flexible. The current goals are far too rigid and the focus on volume runs counter to a build-to-order system's fundamental objectives.

But process flexibility is only one dimension. As we mentioned in our introductory chapter, a build-to-order system demands flexibility along *three* dimensions—all three—to succeed. Process flexibility is perhaps the hardest to achieve, because a process twists through the entire value grid, affecting order entry, production, suppliers, and logistics. *Product flexibility*, which brings customization closer to the customer, is also critical. At the heart of product flexibility is the ability to offer customers many product variations yet keep production simple.

Finally, *volume flexibility* enables companies to pace production to market demands. Within this dimension is the company's ability to structure its factories to efficiently accommodate a range of demand—from low-volume variants to popular option mixes to fleet orders to seasonal variations.

9   Process Flexibility and Customer Demand

There is only one boss—the customer. And he can fire everybody in the company from the chairman on down, simply by spending his money somewhere else.

—Sam Walton

Although companies were eager to improve their processes, usually in the factories, they seemed unable to make customers' needs the basis of those changes. Consequently, the industry is dotted with efficient factories and saddled with highly rigid order fulfillment. Remember Joe from chapter 7? Part of the reason he had to settle for a tan car instead of a green one is process inflexibility. Joe's green car simply could not be translated into decisions and operating mandates. In the current forecast-driven model, most companies cannot modify schedules or amend order flows in any reasonable time.

This lack of responsiveness should be no surprise. Process flexibility necessarily cuts across all parts of the value grid, which means manufacturers, suppliers, and distributors—the ones who get along so famously right now—must work together. If the climate in the supply chain is characterized by short-term cost-reduction initiatives, forget it. Process flexibility is achievable only with consensus, trusting relationships, and shared benefits.

Because its effects are far-reaching, process flexibility itself has three prerequisites. First, customers' needs must drive the entire value grid. Second, production and demand must be directly linked, with actual demand triggering production. Third, the production system must be flexible enough to cope with the variety and lead-time requirements of the customers, which means that multiple players, including suppliers and logistics managers, must collaborate.

Many in the industry feel that automation is the key. Information technology, they reason, can be made to straighten any process kinks. Unfortunately, the tasks in process flexibility require far more than IT can deliver. In fact, as the delays in order to delivery attest, IT is more of a problem than a solution.

Rather than look for a quick fix to provide flexible and responsive processes, companies must focus on customer demand and how it can drive the rest of the value grid.

Information Technology: Help or Hype?

If you are like us, you have probably read a slew of management books, each of which features a chapter on the fabulous enabling power of information technology. We would love to wow you with our story of IT, but we're a bit more cynical. Although we believe that IT in theory can certainly enable a build-to-order system at some point, it is more of an inhibitor right now. IT has good intentions, but attempts to update legacy systems that have borne years of patching remind us of what happens when technology implementation fails to keep pace with technology's evolution. And more important, what happens when expectations about what technology can do are far greater than its actual abilities.

The problems listed below stem from the complexity and heterogeneity of the IT infrastructure. IT systems have grown organically, with each department developing its own proprietary solutions. Integration came much later, and people are still sorting out ways to make dispersed systems on a range of hardware and software platforms into a "seamless" unit that operates smoothly within a local-area or a wide-area network.

Complexity and Batching

As figure 9.1 shows, the sheer complexity of an IT system inside any vehicle manufacturer precludes a seamless anything. This example, although disguised, is a diagram of an actual system landscape. The order bank, which is critical, not only links markets and factory systems; it also interacts with finance and leasing systems and technical systems, such as the engineering databases, to check if certain build combinations are feasible, for example. It further ties into material and supplier systems to control the component and material flows.

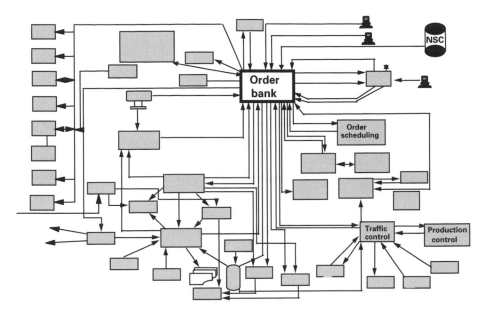

Figure 9.1
Diagram of actual IT landscape at vehicle manufacturer. Boxes represent different IT systems, often in different departments or business units.

Moreover, complexity often stems from multiple systems in a single location. IT managers reported a single factory that used 150 different computer systems!

This complexity has a high price in errors and lost time. Many systems still operate in batch mode, rather than in real time. The materials-planning systems record all transactions through the day, but they update the databases only once a day in an overnight run. This batching practice dates to less efficient times, when the run time for a single update was several hours, making real-time operation infeasible.

Order banks also operate in batch mode, which means that the order waits, on average, a day at each batch operation. Consequently, an order's lead time can be several days, since one batch system must hand it off to another, which hands it off to yet another. As we said in chapter 3, the order needs more than 30 days to make its way from submission at the dealer to the factory. On average, 3–5 days of this time are lost in handing over an order from system to system.[1]

Heterogeneity

Many individual systems have roots in the early days of computing. They are patchworks of modules and upgrades, but the underlying programs are still clunking away oblivious to technological advances. The legacy system might be in Basic or Fortran, but the new additions are in C++ and Visual Basic or even SAP's ABAP4.

The conglomeration of programming languages and platforms would not in itself be a problem, but linking something to this beast is a huge challenge. Updating one part has a domino effect in the rest of the system, which not only multiplies the effort needed, but also the time and cost of the upgrade project. It doesn't help that some of the system was programmed about 20 years ago.

Reality Check

Thus, IT can hardly be viewed as a driver of change. Rather, upgrades are costly and slow. The IT budget of General Motors is estimated at $3.5 billion, for example, and the company took more than 10 years to replace its materials-handling systems with the global MGO system.[2] Most manufacturers have similar delays. Anecdotes from BMW's Munich headquarters tell us that IT managers had serious concerns about whether all their systems would handle the Y2K problem, since no one could test all of them.

The thought that IT can solve all supply-chain illnesses is engaging, and it is certainly a good selling point for many enterprise software vendors, but the sad truth is that hurdles are formidable, and IT itself is often responsible for a significant component of the delay in order fulfillment.

The Truth about Variability

The first step in analyzing demand is understanding the difference between real demand (i.e., what the customer wants) and demand that is artificially induced by organizational decisions. In other words, build-to-order means that manufacturers must stop blindly fishing for customers using a complicated net of incentives and begin looking at demand from all angles, with their eyes wide open.

This shift is not easy for most companies. People tell us that customer demand signals are unstable, demand is too variable, and therefore they *need* market inventory. It is *true* that variation abounds and tends to get worse the farther the demand signal proceeds upstream in the chain. It is *not true* that this is all related to *customer* demand. Most of these demand swings are artificially created as orders move along the value grid. The swing gets amplified and results in the well-known "bullwhip effect," so called because the distortion gets larger with each link in the ordering process.[3] The bullwhip effect is the result of complex systems that cannot follow the demand signal, long lead times, large production batches that add to that time, a lack of demand visibility, and other uncertainties (including price fluctuations) that throw distributors and dealers into a panic. To further add to this, dealers tend to exaggerate their ordering for constraint products, but still feel safe knowing that a buffer is between them and the chaos.

Figure 9.2 gives a classic example of demand amplification from an automotive supplier of a piece of optional electronic equipment. The incoming demand pattern (VM call-off) is from the vehicle manufacturer, which orders 144 to 192 parts or 12 to 16 boxes (at 12 parts each) every day. The assembly schedule is still very close to the original demand pattern, but internal component schedules (those for components made in house) start deviating wildly. What ends up at the second-tier supplier bears no resemblance to the original demand. The supplier sees demand as spiking with no coherent pattern and tries to cope with order spreads

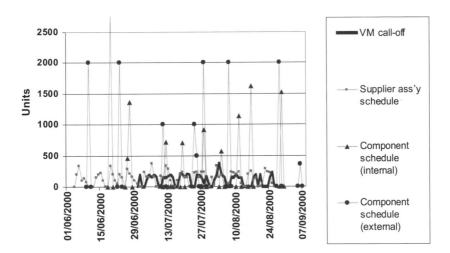

Figure 9.2
Example of how demand amplification artificially induces demand variation in an auto supply chain that provides optional equipment.

of 400–2,000 units, even though actual demand is relatively stable within a narrow range. Regrettably, this situation is the norm rather than the exception—and not just in the auto industry.

Ordering Patterns

The bullwhip gathers momentum as the demand signal deteriorates along the supply chain, taking with it already inflated lead times and expanding to accommodate more hedging. This distortion is fairly obvious. More insidious artificial distortions become visible only after analyzing the order pattern—the way a manufacturer actually receives an order.

Many analysts believe that the industry is compelled to be cyclical because the market demand is cyclical. The peaks and troughs of sales registration are a favorite argument. But in analyzing order patterns from four regions, we found only a weak correlation to sales registration trends. This is not surprising, since the order placement date is typically far from the desired delivery (and hence registration) date.

In a forecast-driven world, where companies hold vehicles as insurance against real or imagined demand peaks, a focus on sales registration might make sense. In a build-to-order world, however, where demand is the starting point, companies must align their processes to an indicator much closer to the customer: the ordering pattern.

Figure 9.3 shows the sales registration pattern for seven regions. Predictably, most countries' sales are lower in the winter and late summer months, when people are vacationing and are less likely to buy a vehicle. This is not particularly disturbing. In fact, manufacturing facilities often time their breaks to coincide with this trough.

Figure 9.3 also shows some odd peaks, however, which seem to indicate that demand is indeed unpredictable. In reality, the spikes have more to do with organizational flukes and national anomalies than with actual demand. In the United Kingdom, for example, most pre-1999 sales increase dramatically around August, not because UK shoppers have the sudden urge to buy a car, but because of registration procedures. At that time, UK registration dictated that in August the license plate letter would change to the next letter, which meant that the registration letter reflected the vehicle's residual value. Obviously, UK drivers would prefer to drive on the "latest plate," so they waited until the letter changed to buy their vehicles. In 1999, the UK government

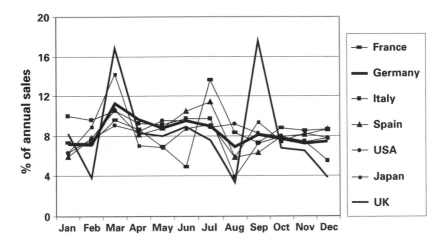

Figure 9.3
Monthly sales registration patterns in major markets (average for 1986–1998). Source: B. Waller, Order and Registration Volatility, 3DayCar Research Report, Solihull, 2002.

realized that such distortions cause unnecessary variability, and introduced biannual letter changes in March and September. Now instead of the one peak in August accounting for 23 percent of annual sales, two peaks account for 16–18 percent of sales each, in March and September. The Japanese have a major buying peak in early spring because it marks the end of the fiscal year and because that is when most companies pay out bonuses.

Aside from these artificial demand distortions, sales cycles are fairly predictable over the year. Figure 9.4 shows the actual daily order intake in the United Kingdom over 6 months for two vehicles. The pattern appears to be somewhere between random and chaotic; however, there is a yearly trend, and there is a weekly cycle. Major peaks occur during the summer, when customers typically place large fleet orders for the coming model year. The weekly cycle stems from the order-entry blackout on weekends. Orders placed over the weekend—often accounting for 25 percent or more of the weekly ordering pattern—are entered on Monday and Tuesday, and that causes artificial order peaks at the beginning of the week.

For the most part, order intake has little bearing on the production system. The customer's delivery expectations have a very strong effect, since some customers will be willing to order their vehicles and wait. Even so, order intake has limited value, because companies do not fully

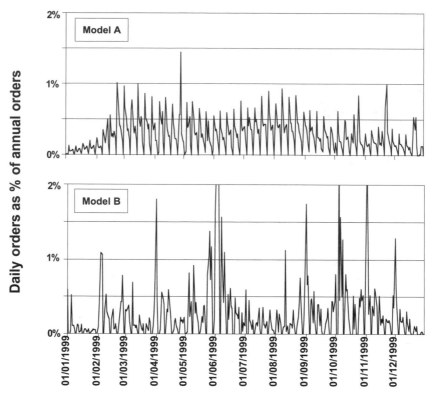

Figure 9.4
Order pattern for two volume models in UK in 1999: a small car (A) and a mid-size car (B). Source: B. Waller, Managing Demand/Selling Time, 3DayCar research report, Solihull, 2001. Large spikes represent sizable fleet orders placed on that day. Fleet customers often order in bulk but expect delivery of their orders over an extended period.

appreciate delivery requirements. A build-to-order system and an attendant focus on actual ordering patterns provides a much clearer picture of customers' true wishes and can greatly reduce if not eliminate demand distortion. As all partners in the value grid focus on what customers have actually asked for, the likelihood of massive overproduction and artificial demand amplification declines greatly.

Process Flexibility and Demand Visibility

First, have a definite, clear practical ideal; a goal, an objective. Second, have the necessary means to achieve your ends; wisdom, money, materials, and methods. Third, adjust all your means to that end.

—Aristotle

The motor vehicle industry, once the trailblazer in process change, is still on the sidelines, shaking its head at the infeasibility of system-wide build-to-order. Meanwhile, other industries are forging ahead. In fact, making demand visible to all key parts of the value grid is no longer a new idea. The grocery sector's Efficient Consumer Response (ECR) initiative has been very successful at linking customer sales to rest of the grid through electronic point-of-sale (EPOS) data—initially to distribution centers and from there to suppliers. The outcome has been faster stock replenishment and faster stock turnover. Other industries have implemented variants of build-to-order with considerable success. Their experiences prove that system-wide build-to-order is viable, and that motor vehicle companies can join others who have responded to customer demand, eliminated artificial demand distortion, restored supplier good will, and abolished profit-eroding incentives.

Lessons from Build-to-Order Success Stories

Some companies in other industries have managed to avoid stockpiling finished products and have been rewarded with superb performance achievements. They have put in place process, product, and volume flexibility, which has allowed them to rapidly provide customized products.

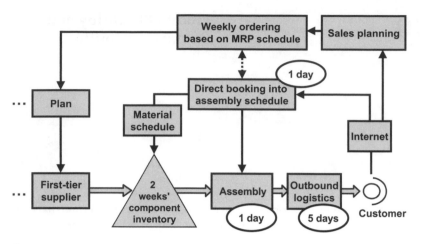

Figure 10.1
Dell Computer's assemble-to-order process.

Dell Computer

Dell Computer has become famous for its ability to transfer a customer's order to the factory within 24 hours of receiving it and to ship the item ordered a few days later. As figure 10.1 shows, Dell's assemble-to-order strategy directly links customer information to production control and from there to assembly operations. The assembly plant receives a new set of orders to be built every few hours and generally builds those orders in less than a day. Crucial to this strategy is a buffer of components that gives Dell the flexibility to assemble any order if components are available. This buffer stock also protects against long supply lead times if, for example, components must come from abroad. While factories are filling orders using components from warehouse inventory, Dell uses forecasting to replenish the warehouse supply.

Dell's assemble-to-order process works well in relatively simple environments with few components offered in many possible combinations. For frequently used components, the reasonably stable demand is visible in the supply chain, even though the component inventory decouples manufacturing from suppliers. The problem comes when volume drops and components stagnate. In the electronics industry, the risk is high that such components will depreciate drastically or, worse, become obsolete.

The advantages of assembling to order are its simplicity and its ability to operate without (in most cases) letting its finished stock go stale. With its much shorter pipeline, Dell has the flexibility to introduce new products about four times faster than some of its competitors.[1] Although Dell's process is not a good match for the motor vehicle industry, it applies to many other industries.[2] Other companies in Dell's industry are unable to mirror its success, in part because they did not start with this process. Compaq, for example, has a huge store-based distribution infrastructure and so is inherently less flexible.[3] Existing infrastructure would not be an obstacle for the motor vehicle industry, however, since dealers would still be needed for servicing, used-car trades, and vehicle demonstrations.

England Inc.

The furniture industry has faced increased competition from low-cost imports, yet England Inc. builds 11,000 chairs and sofas to order each week in its Tennessee factory. Its three-week order-to-delivery time is foundational to its competitive strategy against imported products, which typically have lead times of months. By building to order, England Inc. can also offer variety—85 frame styles and 550 fabric selections for a total product choice of more than 45,000 sofas. One sofa can comprise more than 300 pieces of fabric, wood, and metal, so offering variety on this scale is not as simple as it might sound.

Unlike Dell, England Inc. does not start production as soon as an order comes in, but begins work to coincide with a consolidated outbound delivery truck. Customer orders are small, and the cost of transportation is extremely high, which makes order consolidation critical. The company batches all orders for a particular region and then schedules production so that it can deliver the finished sofas in one delivery load. England Inc. pays its workers extra to ensure their willingness to accommodate demand-driven overtime. It also tightly integrates its suppliers, demanding small and frequent deliveries to ensure its ability to respond to evolving customer taste.[4]

Alcoa

Producers of raw materials are among the least flexible firms in responsiveness to customers' demands. Investments are huge, as are sunk costs in equipment. Processes are rigid, and production batches are large.

For the aluminum producer Alcoa, profits used to go in lock step with the stock price of aluminum. In 1998, however, Alcoa shattered the materials-price profitability link when executives shifted their focus to serving customer demand and becoming more responsive. Alcoa stopped pushing big batches of the same kind of aluminum. According to Alain Belda, chairman and CEO, Alcoa's focus is now to provide customers with what they need, when they need it, making it partners in their customers' cost reduction and efficiency drives.[5] Figure 10.2 shows that Alcoa was indeed successful at breaking away from the cyclical spot price for aluminum. Its quarterly earnings increased despite a relatively flat aluminum spot price.

Many factors will influence Alcoa's long-term success, and the company's strategic priorities may change; however, its short-run ability to decouple its performance from very cyclical aluminum prices is further evidence that a demand-driven system is the next logical step in the evolution of the industry's production model.

Slotting Demand

When a product has multiple variants, the underlying component variety makes build-to-order particularly challenging, which in part is why the auto industry cannot assemble cars in the same manner that Dell builds computers. Storing the 2,000–4,000 components needed for a single car, plus all the variations of each component, is simply too costly.

Another approach, and one that *will* work in the auto sector, is direct order booking. Because it molds order fulfillment and production to

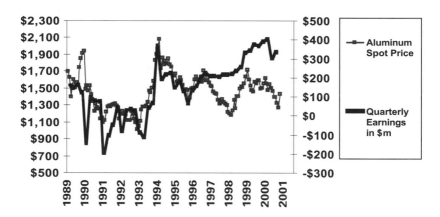

Figure 10.2
Alcoa's earnings vs. spot price of aluminum. (In 1998, Alcoa was able to decouple its share price from fluctuations in the spot price.)

customer demand, direct booking starts build-to-order where it should start, not in some remote area of the value grid, but at the customer—with real data about customer preference.

In this approach, dealers assign incoming orders to slots in the assembly sequence, rather than processing those orders through a network of scheduling systems. Available capacity then becomes the number of free slots, which in conjunction with component availability determines when the order will be built and by which plant. Thus dealers offer slots the way a travel agent or ticketing system offers a list of flights. Once the dealer assigns a customer a build slot, the stability of that order in that slot helps avoid information distortion in supplier schedules.[6]

A direct booking system has two important advantages. First, the dealer can give the customer a *reliable* delivery date at order entry because the assembly date is fixed right after the dealer enters the order. Second, it merges the order bank, scheduling, and sequencing functions into one system, slicing at least 25 days off the order-to-delivery time.[7] (See chapter 2.) Figure 10.3 shows the resulting streamlined flow.

In short, orders are slotted into available production and component capacities, rather than being forecast months in advance. Manufacturers

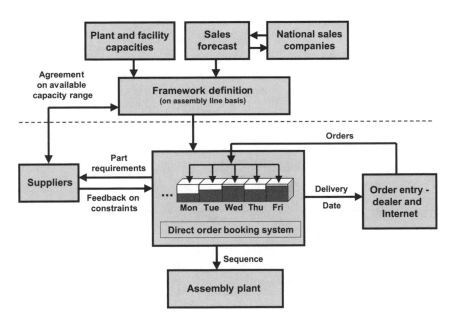

Figure 10.3
Direct order booking, in which the dealer assigns each order a slot on the assembly line.

can determine overall levels of production volumes and component availability, yet still have the flexibility to decide how to match these. Rather than specifying that half of all 2,000 station wagons will get a V6 engine and ABS, they specify only that the plant can build 1,000 V6 engines and 1,000 vehicles with ABS. The exact match occurs only when a customer order specifies it.

Thus, on the *operational level*, direct order booking eliminates much of the demand volatility and amplification, and the assembly sequence becomes the scheduling focal point. True demand is always visible through the assembly sequence, and efforts such as component production and logistics can be synchronized accordingly throughout the value grid.

Because direct order booking locks in the build sequence once it is set, demand stays stable and visible to suppliers and logistics service providers, as figure 10.4 shows. Real-time technology, such as the Internet, communicates demand information, which ensures that the supplier and the manufacturer have the same vision of demand and capacity. Orders go directly to the assembly line, rather than detouring into the body shop. This also adds to the stability of the assembly sequence. Most paint shops rarely attain first-time-OK quality, so this decoupling of paint and body shop from assembly saves time and ensures delivery reliability to the customer. The painted body store becomes a "supermarket" that manufacturers can replenish according to a volume schedule. This decoupling is central to volume flexibility.

Thus, customer demand visibility means that capacity planning and sales forecasting are solidly linked to build scheduling. Capacity and

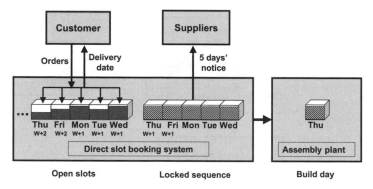

Figure 10.4
How a locked assembly sequence provides demand visibility for suppliers.

constraint management are done in concert with day-to-day scheduling because the orders are slotted according to current component supply and plant-capacity limitations. Instead of fitting demand to resources, companies fit resources to demand, since the available production and component supply resources determine when and where the vehicle will be built.

Managing Demand-Driven Capacity

With direct order booking, the entire value grid becomes more sensitive to demand variability, so under-capacity use is a much more probable threat. Companies must carefully plan capacity use, and the conditions for planning will seem foreign. In the old model, planning and operational levels are tightly coupled: the forecast is issued, and plants respond in the most efficient way to produce the required volume. With direct order booking, there is no forecast-driven order fulfillment, so companies must develop long-term capacity and strategic plans quite apart from operations.

Capacity planning becomes the process of aggregating the national sales forecast and reconciling available vehicle and component production. Suppliers must be part of this process, since component availability is fundamental. The manufacturer and supplier must agree on the degree of capacity flexibility—the extent to which the supplier can alter capacity levels, over what time horizon, and at what cost.

The link between planning and operational levels is a scheduling framework, which defines the vehicle and component production boundaries. Manufacturers and suppliers must adjust this framework at least once a week to be able to cope with changes in demand and provide the right production capacity.

Some companies are already implementing some kind of scheduling framework. Volkswagen's eCap system lets the manufacturer and suppliers communicate online about demand and capacity. In Volkswagen's headquarters in Wolfsburg, the capacity management team sees a screen, which broadcasts green, yellow, and red lights to reflect actual, potential, or no capacity. In 2001, Volkswagen claimed, eCap managed and monitored more than 80 percent of the company's 50 billion annual purchasing volume, and more than 5,500 of its suppliers were at least partially integrated into the system.[8]

Locked assembly slots make it easier for suppliers and logistics service providers because the lock becomes the notice and extent of demand visibility. Suppliers start component production, and logistics companies plan and optimize their loads—both parties work to ensure that the component supply arrives just in time for vehicle assembly, thereby virtually eliminating inventory. With this approach, there is also less need to co-locate suppliers. As stable sequence information allows component production to be planned and executed much further in advance, suppliers much further away can also supply parts in sequence, which in the current system virtually requires co-location in a supplier park.

Currently, most manufacturers lock assembly sequences a week or two before production for all main vehicle characteristics. Variability in first-time-OK quality rates, supplier capabilities, and other factors can cause significant changes to occur much closer to production than that. However, because suppliers *must* have reliable schedule information for their own planning, the vehicle assembly sequence, once set, cannot change. Firms currently exploring build-to-order hence delay firming their production schedules. For Renault, Nissan, and BMW, the lock time is 4–6 days from production.[9] Five days seems a long time, insofar as an order is assigned to an assembly slot in one day; however, taken across the value grid and relative to current OTD times, it is a dramatic improvement. As figure 10.4 shows, locking the assembly sequence for 5 days, with production and distribution taking about 6 days, would result in a total lead time of 11 days, whereas 40+ days is now the norm.

Visibility, Not Variability

We have only to revisit figure 9.2 to understand what a relief direct order booking would be for component suppliers. The visibility of demand and the resulting transparency in the supply chain reduces the many cycles of costly and time-consuming forecasting. Most suppliers now mistrust manufacturer data so much that they end up creating their own forecasts. This second-guessing further distorts the dynamics of the supply chain.

In a value grid where actual demand is visible throughout, component production is strictly coupled to actual demand, and the demand information suppliers see relates to the stocking and decoupling points for their particular parts. Suppliers that must build parts to fit some specified sequence can build the parts that all slotted orders require. Distant suppliers can replenish their parts in accordance with the rate of consumption out of their warehouse. Suppliers beyond the first tier have a reliable understanding of their production requirements: they derive their demand forecast from the production sequence of the manufacturer. For example, if 300 cars with air conditioning are scheduled, the second-tier supplier knows that the vehicle manufacturer will probably need to replenish the supply-chain inventory with that number of air conditioning units.

Keeping demand visibility in real time through online systems keeps variability to a minimum. It also helps manufacturers and suppliers synchronize planning cycles, since suppliers can pull requirements as needed rather than spend energies accommodating pushed requirements in fixed cycles that rarely give them any useful information about actual demand. As a result, IT systems will become simpler, particularly at the manufacturer, where the order bank, scheduling, and sequencing will merge into one system. In the overall value grid, the planning and scheduling systems at suppliers and logistics companies will not only have to plan operations on site, but will also have to communicate and coordinate with other systems in the value grid to synchronize material flow.

The People Factor

As with any change, mindsets can be obstacles. Making demand visible throughout the value grid calls for both organizational and cultural change. Build-to-order is mostly misunderstood, and what people do not understand they tend to regard with suspicion. According to a 1999 survey, most dealers—both volume-brand dealers and specialist-brand dealers—fear that build-to-order and more specifically the Internet will make them obsolete.[10] This only proves our point about misunderstandings. Build-to-order doesn't make the new-vehicle-sales function go away; it merely shifts the dealer's responsibility from managing stock to managing orders. Moreover, new-vehicle sales are only part of a dealer's operations, and the used car retail and service parts remain largely the same.

Granted, the entire sales process will drastically change in a build-to-order world. While dealers may lose on some fronts (e.g., reduced dealer-installed options, and differential benefits depending on current sales practices), many dealers may find this shift to order management easier because they can sidestep investments in vehicle configurations that may not ever find a local customer. In the current model, dealers are motivated to meet customers' needs through inventory, so keeping inventory fresh and moving is their main priority. In a build-to-order system, where virtually no new-vehicle stock exists, dealers are free from an inventory bias and can center on the customer's needs, matching the product to the customer 100 percent of the time. And matching customers' needs also means that dealers will not have to give up their margin to accommodate additional discounts, so the average sales profitability will be more predictable to them. Customers are likely to be more satisfied, which means that follow-on business will increase. Buyers will return for vehicle servicing, new products, and so on, thus opening an entire revenue stream after sales. Build-to-order and the power of the Internet will let dealers farm the customer base and create a stable business model, rather than continuously fishing for customers. Finally, the focus can turn to taking market share from competing vehicle manufacturers, because all dealers have access to the same order bank. In the current model, dealers compete with each other, while customers end up going to other brands. The cost of regaining a customer lost this way is enormous, so channeling dealer energies toward brand competitors and away from infighting over customers represents a significant opportunity to reduce cost and enhance revenue.[11]

Figure 10.5 shows the order-fulfillment process in a build-to-order system. An important organizational change is the de-emphasis on the national sales company. Some have argued that it has no place in a build-to-order system. Vehicle manufacturers will always need a local body to organize the dealer network, arrange legal and contractual agreements, and coordinate national marketing activities. However,

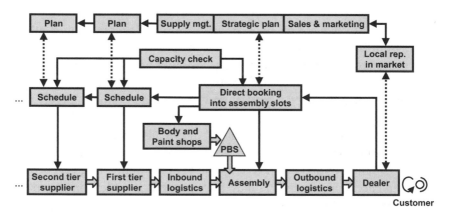

Figure 10.5
Order fulfillment in a build-to-order system.

since a build-to-order system operates virtually without any large stocks, the national sales company is no longer needed to manage and replenish central stock. Another task that might go away is the aggregation of national sales forecasts based on individual dealers' forecasts. While certain market predictions and intelligence will remain essential, those forecasts would no longer be automatically converted into stock orders.

Demand and the Internet

Bill Ford called the Internet the "moving assembly line of the 21st century,"[12] and doubtless the rewards of connecting the consumer to the value grid through a personal computer or a mobile phone are enticing. In the United Kingdom, we found that 18 percent of new vehicle buyers use the Internet in some form in the buying process, with young buyers representing the greatest share.

As table 10.1 shows, however, this percentage is not terribly significant, being larger only than car shows in reflecting where most buyers go for purchasing information. Manufacturers' brochures are the most popular, followed by dealer staff, advice from friends or relatives, and car magazines. Gender made little difference; women tended to consult friends slightly more and rely slightly less on magazines than men.

We also found that customers would rather use the Internet, not as a point of sale, but as a means of gathering product information, searching for products, and getting price quotes. Some dealers transfer up to 11 percent of their orders via third-party dotcoms, such as Autobytel,

Table 10.1
Sources UK buyers used to gather decision-making information.*

Information source	Percentage of customers using
Manufacturer's brochures	61.7
Dealer sales staff	57.4
Car magazine	40.6
Friend or relative	40.3
Newspaper ads	34.8
TV ads	25.3
World Wide Web	18.2
Car shows	5.4

*Source: S. Elias, New Vehicle Buyer Behaviour—Quantifying Key Stages in the Consumer Buying Process, 3DayCar research report, 2002.

Oneswoop, Virgincars, and Carsdirect,[13] but few customers actually end up buying a vehicle through the site. Vauxhall.com in the United Kingdom was one of the first direct-sales-enabled sites, offering a limited product range and £1,000 off list price if the customer would buy online. In the first 6 months, the site logged only a few hundred sales, even though 2,000 customers went through at least part of the buying process.[14] Many other manufacturers also have, or are establishing some form of online sales. Forddirect.com and GMBuyPower.com are examples. These sites, however, typically do not let customers submit orders directly, offering instead to send quotes from local dealers, which in turn often ignore the specification and try to push a stock vehicle that is a "close match."

In the United States, 90 percent of car dealers have an Internet presence, but most have nothing more than this kind of stock-location system.[15]

Being curious academics, we wanted to see how ordering a car via the Internet actually worked. We were particularly eager to see the explanation for dealers' offering different quotes for the same specification. We entered forddirect.com and typed in our request—a base model Ford Escape 2003 XLS with a manufacturer's suggested retail price of $22,550 and an invoice price of $20,947 (as a result of various discounts). The site sent our request to the five nearest dealers, which it had picked according to our ZIP code. Within minutes, we received the canned "we are processing your request" notice from Ford. Hours later, we received personal e-mails from all five dealers. Quotes were from $21,085 to $23,427—at best hundreds of dollars more than the $20,382 and $20,695 Autobytel.com and Carsdirect.com were offering.

Worse, every dealer we spoke to tried to sell us a vehicle that was already in stock and "a better deal" than what we were looking for. Delivery-time quotes for a custom vehicle were between 4 and 10 weeks, and we still had to come into the dealership to complete the order. The entire experience left us wondering if anyone really cares what customers want. And no one explained why we should be getting different quotes for the same specification.

After our experiment, we were considerably less surprised that Internet sales have been sluggish. Obstacles like confusing price structures and arcane state rules that restrict direct sales leave customers no choice but to use the Internet for information gathering and window shopping.

Yet, even with this kind of sabotage, the Internet will eventually become a viable point of sale. It has to, given its rapid household penetration. In 2000 in the United States, 3–7 percent (depending on the brand) of all new-vehicle sales were pure online transactions, and 50 percent of new-vehicle buyers do some shopping on the Internet. This 50 percent has grown from 16 percent in 1997, 24 percent in 1998, and 35 percent in 1999.[16]

Customers told us their biggest reason for shopping online was to secure superior pricing,[17] closely followed by the availability and open disclosure of pricing. "No pressure, no hassle, no haggle" features were also important. Our results are consistent with other surveys that found 15–20 percent of US customers try to avoid dealer contact and thus the bargaining process.[18]

But although we found strong motivation for buying a vehicle online, we also found some serious drawbacks that won't go away no matter how persuasive or convenient the sales mechanism. Relative to airline tickets, books, and CDs, buying a car is far more emotional, which means that a virtual product description won't be enough. Indeed, customers told us that the main disincentive for online purchasing is that they couldn't see or test-drive the vehicle.[19]

In the rest of the supply chain, the Internet has a more defined role as enabler. Manufacturers and suppliers hail it as a tool to cut lead times and connect partners. Both business-to-consumer and business-to-business e-commerce support build-to-order processes. Business-to-consumer e-commerce takes the form of online new-vehicle sales and online trade exchanges, which aid order fulfillment. Business-to-consumer e-commerce establishes online marketplaces that have the potential to lower per-vehicle cost.[20]

One marketplace that benefits tremendously from business-to-business e-commerce is components, where the overall global purchasing volume is an estimated $1.3 trillion.[21] Here, e-commerce can greatly decrease procurement and transaction cost throughout the supply chain. Estimates are that a transaction via traditional EDI costs $8, but could be as little as $1 by adding a first-tier link—that is, by using Internet-based exchanges beyond the manufacturer.[22] This link offers enormous savings. General Motors, for example, manages 30,000 supplier relationships, so a lower transaction cost could decrease per-vehicle cost significantly.

At present, transactions are done through exchanges, COVISINT being the most well known. Individual suppliers and manufacturers also operate several private exchanges, including Bosch's SupplyOn and Volkswagen's vwgroupsupply.com.

COVISINT[23] grew from NewCo—an organization established in March 2000 by executives from Ford's AutoXchange, GM's TradeXchange, and DaimlerChrysler. A month later, Renault-Nissan joined, despite strong opposition from GM suppliers, which considered an alternative trade exchange, but later decided against it. In May 2000 Toyota, Delphi, and Johnson Controls (JCI) also joined. BMW and Volkswagen decided to set up individual exchanges. So far COVISINT partners have invested $170 million in the exchange, with monthly operating costs of $12 million. US partners tend to use COVISINT as an online auction, while Japanese manufacturers use it more as a springboard for collaboration.

Although Ford and General Motors conceived COVISINT with great expectations, much of the initial excitement has vanished. The predicted savings of $1,000 per vehicle have not materialized, and attempts to arrive at that number have brought the exchange close to financial disaster.[24] An important reason is supplier readiness for e-commerce. Only 33 percent of first-tier suppliers have the resources to implement an e-business program, only 44 percent have an e-business strategy, and only 13 percent even *use* exchanges like COVISINT.[25]

Nonetheless, we believe e-commerce applications or something similar will increase. The Internet will connect the customer to the system, as well as provide the tools to synchronize supply and logistics in the supply chain. In 10 years, most of what we can only envision today will be commonplace. For now, it is still early, and vehicle manufacturers are the ones with the technological and financial resources. The smaller and medium-size companies in the second and third tiers still need to catch up.

11 Process Flexibility and Production

Production is not the application of tools to material, but logic to work.

—Peter Drucker

A capable process operating at Internet speed is useful only if the order reaches a capable and flexible factory that can turn it into a product in a reasonable time with acceptable efficiency and quality. Because factory efficiency has been the target of so many improvement efforts, it would seem that very little change is required to provide the needed flexibility. But the value grid is complex, and the secret of flexible factories, as it turns out, rests not in robots and fancy computer systems but in how the factory manages and organizes its work.

The Human Side of Lean Production

As we discussed in our introductory chapter, not all regions understand and implement "lean" the same way. Western manufacturers, for example, have implemented the structural shell of the Toyota Production System, choosing the parts that aided their quest for lower cost. Efforts have focused on reducing the head count in assembly—the main element in labor productivity—and increasing automation in weld and paint. Consequently, Western manufacturers have achieved structural and technological changes, such as less incoming inventory and more flexible automation. The structure of lean production is in place: just-in-time supply feeds into a workload-leveled assembly line for maximum efficiency.

But the hard side of lean production—the structure and technology—is only half the partnership needed to implement flexible production. The soft side of lean production—the workforce—is the other half, and many manufacturers have neglected it.

Possibly they feel it is just too hard to measure. Structural systems have characteristics that are straightforward to quantify, such as takt time vs. stock level and defects per vehicle, but even *defining* workforce quality practices is challenging. Unless companies assess the human side of lean production, however, process flexibility will remain a fuzzy goal at best. There are a series of documented workforce practices that drive efficiency, quality, and flexibility. These are complemented by human resource policies and practices including lean approaches to how workers are compensated, attitudes toward status differences, and workforce training.

Workforce Organization

Many characteristics of work systems drive superior performance. The practices listed in table 11.1 enhance factory performance on three fronts. First, they improve how individual workers do their jobs by offering better-quality tools and the like. Second, they enhance the organization's ability to respond to change (job rotation reduces absenteeism, for example). Third, they enhance information flow and the distribution of knowledge. As the table shows, workforce teams have become a major element in all regions except the United States. The same is true for employee involvement groups and quality circles. The starkest difference shows up in employee suggestions. US workers provide far fewer suggestions than workers in other regions, and US factories fail to implement all but a few of the suggestions offered.

In general, production workers in the United States have the least responsibility for maintenance, equipment set-ups, quality inspection, and statistical process control. Consequently, there is little need to organize or foster teams or to rotate jobs—all of which empower companies to implement and maintain worker-driven quality control and improvement. Teams in Japan and Europe and even in new-entrant countries tend to rotate jobs much more, for example.

In contrast, Japanese producers have continued to use and fine-tune lean work systems. In Europe and new-entrant countries, lean work practices have generally increased also, and more thought is given to their implementation. Suggestion schemes used to be of considerably less value. In one Korean plant we visited in the mid 1990s, for example, management had imposed high quotas of suggestions for each

Table 11.1
Workforce organizational trends for four regions in 1994 and 2000. Because our 1994 and 2000 samples are not identical for these measures, the data represent only trends.*

Work organization measure	US		Japan		Europe		New entrants	
	1994	2000	1994	2000	1994	2000	1994	2000
Plants in regions with teams	35%	46%	100%	100%	95%	100%	64%	87%
Workforce in teams	49.4%	24.6%	56.6%	94.7%	68.2%	82.6%	49.8%	62.9%
Workforce in employee involvement or quality circles	32.8%	25.2%	93.9%	99.0%	62.6%	47.0%	88.4%	47.5%
Suggestions per employee	0.3	0.2	69.1	12.9	1.2	8.3	53.8	7.4
Suggestions implemented	41.8%	31.8%	85.6%	95.7%	38.8%	75.2%	50.6%	30.2%
Extent of job rotation in and across work groups on a scale of 1 (none) to 5 (frequent)	2.0	1.8	3.9	4.0	3.6	3.6	3.3	3.3
Responsibility for quality inspection / SPC on a scale of 0 (specialists only) to 4 (production workers only)	2.4	2.1	1.6	2.7	2.4	3.0	2.2	2.1

*Data for 1994 from J. MacDuffie and F. Pil, "High-involvement work practices and human resource policies," in *Evolving Employment Practices in the World Auto Industry,* ed. T. Kochan et al. (Cornell University Press, 1997), and from Pil and MacDuffie, "Organizational and environmental factors influencing the use of high-involvement work practices," in *Employment Strategies,* ed. P. Cappelli (Oxford University Press, 1999). Fraction of workforce in teams is based only on plants with teams. The extent of job rotation is scored on a 1–5 scale, and the rotation policies are ordered as follows: 1. workers are trained to do one job and do not rotate to other jobs; 2. Workers are capable of doing other work tasks in their work group (or teams if teams are present), but generally do not rotate jobs; 3. Workers rotate jobs frequently within their group, but not outside their group; 4. Workers rotate jobs within their work groups and across work groups in the same department (body, paint, and assembly), but not across departments, and 5. Workers rotate jobs within the work group, across work groups, and across departments. Responsibility for Quality control looks at 4 areas of responsibility: incoming parts, work-in-progress, finished products, and charting SPC data. At one end of the spectrum, quality control staff can undertake these activities. At the other end of the spectrum, production workers can do them (or no one). Other options include skilled trades, first line supervisors, and engineering staff.

employee. Desperate to fill their quotas, and perhaps not fully understanding the spirit of continuous improvement, workers would resort to
ludicrous suggestions like shipping cars with a bucket of paint so that
customers could paint cars the color they wanted.

Compensation

An effective to way to ensure that workers get and stay involved is to
reward involvement at levels and in ways that encourage team- and
department-level participation. Relative to the United States and Japan,
contingent pay schemes are slightly more common in Europe and new-
entrant countries (such as Argentina, Australia, Brazil, India, Korea,
Mexico, South Africa, and Taiwan), but the extreme differences we
observed in 1994 are gone. At that time, Japan was extensively using
contingent pay, the United States was at the other extreme, and Europe
and the new entrants were somewhere in the middle.

Status Differentials

Status levels and hierarchies have also decreased drastically; in most
cases, workers and managers park in the same lot, eat at the same
cafeteria, and so on. In our experience, this is a positive step. The fewer
the status differentials, the more opportunity for informal discussion
and interaction over breaks and the less chance of the "us versus them"
discussions that can destroy team spirit on the shop floor.

Plants can be almost unconscious of what they do to encourage status
differences. During a visit to a French factory, managers told us that
they wore ties when visiting the shop floor so that everyone would
know they were managers and could thus approach them with
management-related issues and suggestions. The managers seemed
pleased that they would take the time to be available for discussion.
Meanwhile, we wondered exactly how often they visited the shop floor
if their ties were the only way shop-floor workers could recognize
them.

Being playful as well as curious, we invented a little test to determine
just how often management actually visited the shop floor. As managers showed us around the plant, we waited until we were in the middle of all the equipment and operations and then asked to use the rest
room. If managers had no clue where it was, they had either bladders of
steel or little familiarity with the operations part of their plant.

Table 11.2
Hours of training manufacturers in four regions provide annually to workers, supervisors, and engineers. Lowest level of on-the-job and off-the-job training across the three groups used to calculate regional average.

Training category	US	Japan	Europe	New entrants
New employees (scale of 0 to 3)[a]	0.5	1.3	1.8	1.6
Experienced employees (scale of 0 to 5)[b]	1.7	3.0	2.0	2.2

a. 0 means less than 40 hours; 3 means more than 160.
b. 0 means less than 20 hours; 5 means more than 80.

Training

When workers are asked to take on broader tasks, and more complex roles, it is important that they have the skills to do so. US plants provide the least training, according to table 11.2; in fact, new workers receive far less training than even workers in new-entrant countries! For experienced workers, the US again shows the lowest levels, although the difference is less pronounced. Japanese training levels are the highest, showing their strong commitment to continuous learning and improvement. Perhaps these numbers explain in part why US productivity has increased dramatically, but quality has not. (See figure 4.5.)

Work Practices and Performance

Understanding work practices means little unless companies can relate them to performance measures, and measuring the performance implications of individual work practices is nearly impossible, given the complex interactions between the practices. Thus, to derive meaningful numbers, we first developed an index normalized for the presence of teams, their tasks and responsibilities, responsibilities for quality, job rotation, and suggestion schemes.[1] The index is based on data from the same 71 plants we used to evaluate factory processes. (See chapter 4.)

Using this index, we linked plant performance directly to the work system being used. We began by splitting data into four work-system groupings, each with the same number of plants.

• The type 1 work system is the direct outgrowth and evolution of the archetypal lean system. The emphasis is on balancing automation use with investment in the workforce. Type 1 work systems heavily use the work practices in table 11.1. Workers are generally well trained, motivated and engaged, receive the appropriate tools, and are part of a well-thought-out communication flow. Plants in Japan, Japanese transplants, and advanced European and new-entrant plants tend to fall into this category.

• Type 2 plants are in transition to lean production with strong elements of Type 1, but vestiges of Type 4. Sometimes the plants do not implement suggestions received to their full potential. In other cases, plants are still working on delegating greater quality responsibility to line workers. Generally, however, these plants are well on their way to having effective and comprehensive lean work systems.

• Type 3 plants are in transition from mass production but still have many more elements of Type 4 than of Type 1. Although they may have teamwork, use is sporadic throughout the plant. Suggestions are rare and when received are often ignored. Some efforts are made to involve workers in quality and rotate jobs, but these are limited in scope.

• Type 4 production systems are engineered to be efficient, usually with heavy reliance on automation and reductions in assembly head count. Plants in this grouping may borrow from lean methods but center their efforts only on the lean structure without the work practices in table 11.1. It is essentially "efficient mass production," coupling an emphasis on high volume with select lean elements. US plants generally fall into this category.

Table 11.3 shows plant performance across these types, and it holds few surprises. Average labor productivity is slightly higher in type 4 work systems, but quality is lower. In fact, the relationship of work system type and quality is linear: The more plants use enablers like quality

Table 11.3
Quality measures of plants using various types of production, by type of work system. Medians exclude South Africa, India, and Turkey.

	Type 1: Lean	Type 2: Transition to lean	Type 3: Mostly mass	Type 4: Mass
Labor hours per vehicle	16.7	15.6	15.9	14.3
Defects per 100 vehicles	33	38	39	49
First-time-OK weld	94.1%	93.6%	90.9%	90.3%
First-time-OK paint	86.8%	88.1%	85.5%	82.3%
First-time-OK assembly	84.6%	82.3%	81.2%	77.5%

circles, teamwork, and job rotation, the higher the quality. Type 1 work systems have nearly a 50 percent higher quality level than type 4 work systems. Thus, although productivity is higher, product and process quality goes down. It is much harder to engineer quality into a system, because quality very much depends on people—their training and motivation and the richness of information exchange.

Within the plant, the quality picture is no different and first-time-OK percentages decline steadily across work system types.

Another interesting difference among work system types is the degree of complexity handled. Table 11.4 shows the average number of platforms, engines, and transmissions used per plant. Lean-production work systems can clearly handle more product variety.

Consistent with the notion of efficient mass production, type 3 and type 4 work systems tend to produce vehicles efficiently for a single platform, with a limited number of engine and transmission derivatives. The leaner work systems cope with much higher levels of product complexity.

Capacity Use

Although not strictly a work practice, another crucial performance dimension is the plant's ability to alter capacity levels at relatively low cost. Figure 11.1 compares the cost across work system types of running a plant at various capacity levels—from 50 percent of full to 10 percent over. Overall, plants split into two groups. In the first are types 1 and 2—lean plants, and those shifting to lean, which despite handling significantly more complexity, incur much less cost when altering capacity. Historically, flexibility of lean plants was facilitated in part by the use of part-time and temporary labor in countries like Japan. Now, the reductions are more likely to come from innovative hour banks, ability to

Table 11.4
Average complexity handled per plant, by type of work system.

	Type 1: Lean	Type 2: Transition to lean	Type 3: Mostly mass	Type 4: Mass
Number of platforms	2.0	1.81	1.45	1.23
Number of engine variations	66	25	6	5
Number of transmission variations	14	13	4	6

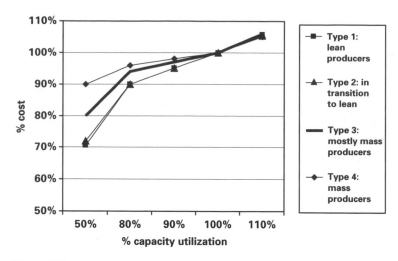

Figure 11.1
Cost of capacity flexibility for various work systems. Capacity cost is percentage of total capacity cost to change to *X* capacity for one week (median, with new-entrant countries excluded except Korea). These averages represent total costs and include direct costs (e.g. labor) as well as indirect costs (e.g. plant and equipment).

re-allocate work, and reduced reliance on massive investments to attain flexibility among others, although the use of temporary workers is once again gaining favor in Japan and some European countries. In the second group are types 3 and 4: efficient mass-production plants, and plants with many characteristics of mass production. Because of their high investments in structural improvements and engineered efficiencies, these plants have actually become more inflexible. In a downturn, this inflexibility is glaring, as evidenced by the cost difference between type 1 (lean-production plants) and type 4 (mass-production plants) when the plant is running significantly below capacity.

Automation

Although much of this chapter's focus has been centered on work systems, it is worth mentioning automation since it has an important bearing on production flexibility (see also chapter 4). As table 11.5 shows, assembly plants have steadily increased their use of automation, with robots being more popular than fixed equipment, which the plant cannot reconfigure. This greater flexibility of equipment is of little value, however, if it is not matched with workforce flexibility, as we discussed earlier.

Table 11.5
Automation (unmatched data; all numbers scale-weighted).*

	1990	1994	2000
Overall[a]	24%	31%	37%
Weld	57%	72%	84%
Paint	32%	42%	52%
Assembly	1.0%	1.3%	2.1%
Robotic index[b]	2.2	3.3	5.4
Number of plants	62	75	71

*Data for 1994 and 1990 are from J. P. MacDuffie and F. K. Pil, "Flexible technologies, flexible workers," in Transforming Auto Assembly, ed. T. Fujimoto and U. Jürgens (Springer-Verlag, 1997). Automation of subareas is weighted as follows in "overall":

31% fraction of spot welds that are automated (includes a conversion for any arc, MIG, and laser welding—these are converted to 150 spot welds per meter weld; other forms of bonding are similarly converted); this is weighted by product volume.

9.5% fraction of sealer application that is automated; this is weighted by product volume.

9.5% fraction of primer, interior, and top coat that are automated, assessed as a fraction of surface area coated automatically; this is weighted by product volume.

50% for assembly of key modules. Assembly assist operations (e.g., via lifter tools or delivery mechanisms) are not counted, nor is automation of materials delivery. Plants are not identical across years.

a. Aggregate of body, paint, and assembly area automation (percentage of production steps automated).
b. Robots per vehicle per hour.

Process Flexibility and Suppliers

Coming together is a beginning, staying together is progress, and working together is success.

—Henry Ford

Suppliers in any industry must be able to respond to changing demand patterns in the market, but in the motor vehicle industry, where typically 60 percent of the product's value[1] derives from internally and externally supplied components, supplier response is critical. A manufacturer must schedule at least 2,000 individual components per final product, with billions of possible combinations. Some of these, such as switching the driver side from left to right and vice versa, require fundamental changes in manufacturing operations.

To date, manufacturers typically rate suppliers according to price first, followed by quality and delivery reliability. In a build-to-order system, location is also important—*where* to source components and subsystems. The industry seems conflicted here, with a widespread move to global sourcing[2] on the one hand and the popularity of supplier parks on the other. Another source of conflict is modular supply. GM's Yellowstone project made headlines in the late 1990s, when the company announced its intent to have suppliers build whole modular systems that production would then install intact on a new type of assembly line in flexible factories that were half the current size. Despite pilot implementations outside the United States, the project failed because of union resistance. In 2000, Donald Hackworth, GM's senior vice-president for manufacturing, said "The word modular is no longer in GM's vocabulary."[3]

But modularity per se is not the culprit. Manufacturers keep trying to solve the supplier-responsiveness dilemma by going for an isolated solution, like implementing a modular supply and using a few major suppliers. Relationships between manufacturers and suppliers, the right level of integration, supplier quality, and operational performance have been discussed to death and even benchmarked—yet we still know very little about what makes suppliers responsive![4]

Measuring "Responsive"

In the current production model, responsiveness is generally viewed in light of inventory levels.[5] If the supplier and manufacturer are correctly aligned, the supplier should be able to use smaller production batches and deliver product more frequently.[6] In a build-to-order system, however, the inventory level is only one of several factors that determine supplier responsiveness. Table 12.1 lists the factors we have benchmarked.[7]

Obviously, in view of the complexity of parts and the number of suppliers, we could not comprehensively cover all part types or even the most valuable parts. Instead, we selected five component categories, which are based on the components' complexity and customization level: *Nonspecific* parts are batteries and spark plugs, and the like. *Standard* components include such things as metal pressings and suspension parts. *Subassemblies* are units like headlights or seats. *Option* parts include air conditioning and navigation systems. *Color-coded* parts included painted wing mirrors and bumpers.

Table 12.1
Framework for benchmarking supplier responsiveness.

	Factors considered
Second-tier supply	Order lead time
	Material availability
	Product variety
First-tier supply	Inventories
	Lead times
	Capacity
	Batch sizes
	Product variety
Inbound logistics	Distance
	Mode of transport
	Frequency of delivery
Vehicle manufacturer	Demand information: forecasts, schedules, call-offs, late amendments
	Demand consistency (forecast vs. call-off)

We then split our survey results into these categories wherever appropriate.

Interpreting the Demand Signal

Responsiveness starts with the demand signal from the manufacturer. The more variable and unpredictable the signal, the harder it is for a supplier to respond. The first-tier suppliers we surveyed generally receive a number of forecasts and schedules as well as call-offs on daily requirements (specific orders on what they must deliver that day). Typically they receive forecasts that come at intervals of a month or two, covering the next 6 months, monthly schedules covering 2 months, and twice-weekly call-offs covering 1 week.

Suppliers saw information quality about customer demand as a major problem. They expressed little confidence in the manufacturer's delivery schedule, blaming poor communication and delays in the system. Predictably, they perceived the information as more useful the closer it came to actual production and the more frequently the manufacturer updated it. Forecasts scored worse than schedules, which scored worse than call-offs. Overall the deviation of forecasts and schedules is relatively low, with an average forecast and schedule error of less than 15 percent and 7.5 percent, respectively. This small deviation is understandable, insofar as manufacturers issue call-offs after they establish the vehicle build sequence.

But although the deviation between forecast and schedule was small, information was still unreliable because manufacturers would often phone in changes on or very close to the delivery date. Typically, a production controller in the assembly plant would ring his counterpart in the supplier, changing the delivery quantity on the same day the supplier was to deliver it. Fully 94 percent of suppliers we surveyed permit these changes, and they occur an average 3.4 times a week, which translates to nearly every other working day. (Quite a few suppliers operate 7 days a week.) Clearly, late amendments distort the demand and cause uncertainty, although we cannot measure exactly how because few suppliers record these calls.

Production Batching

In studying batching, we noted a curious phenomenon. Most suppliers generally linked component assembly to manufacturer call-offs, and they made parts daily, but they completely disconnected the subcomponent production from final assembly. We found production batch sizes of 3 to 20 days in the component production and machining departments, but saw batches of less than 1 day in assembly. This decoupling can have serious consequences in the supplier's ability to respond to a parts-requirement change.

As table 12.2 shows, the average total inventory for the suppliers we surveyed was just short of 22 days, with a concentration in raw materials and bought-in components. The highest levels were in the nonspecific category and the raw material level in the color-coded category. Processes underlying these component types include injection molding or wire drawing, which are generally batch-driven, and the manufacturers that supply the raw materials for these processes tend to deliver them in large quantities.

The lowest stock levels were in standard part and subassembly suppliers, where the low levels of finished or semi-finished products indicate a close coupling to actual requirements. Overall though, the high levels of finished products indicate that suppliers are using inventory as a buffer against what they perceive is uncertain demand.

The Uncoupling of Demand and Supply: A Case History

To understand how suppliers manage (or rather mismanage) the link between orders and production, we researched a headlight supplier for the European market. The supplier makes 300 pairs of headlights (600 total) daily in five basic variations, as well as after-market parts. It supplies these daily to the client manufacturer's warehouse 45 miles away. The manufacturer's demand gives 3 weeks advance notice of orders, split into daily requirements.

The material requirements planning (MRP) computer system,[8] which is connected to the manufacturer's Electronic Data Interchange (EDI) system, issues weekly work schedules for subcomponent production and orders to suppliers of raw material and bought-in components. For a particular part, the supplier makes the main components in-house. It buys 30 bought-in components from 85 second-tier suppliers and 10 raw material types from 15 raw material suppliers. The main manufacturing steps are to injection-mold the frame, housing, lens, and reflector and to lacquer and plate the inner frame and reflector. Lens molding and lacquering are in a separate clean room to protect the process from dust and dirt. Even so, the daily scrap rate is an astounding 10 percent.

Table 12.2
Inventory levels for first-tier suppliers (days). (Because not all suppliers buy subcomponents or have all assembly stages, total levels are not the sums of the subcategory averages, but represent what we measured across all respondents.)

Component group	Raw material	Bought-in components	Components built in house	Pre-assembly work in progress	Assembly work in progress	Finished goods	Total
Nonspecific	23.0	60.0	30.0	15.8	NA[a]	13.8	57.5
Standard	2.5	4.0	1.5	2.6	1.6	1.2	7.6
Subassembly	15.8	9.7	7.3	2.5	0.8	1.1	14.8
Color-coded	25.0	12.5	Not applicable	12.5	1.5	7.7	33.7
Option	10.7	13.5	2.0	2.2	3.3	4.0	19.4
Average over sample	13.1	11.6	5.7	6.2	1.9	4.5	21.9

a. Not available.

As is true of many first-tier suppliers we visited, the headlight supplier's order-fulfillment process operates on two levels. The assembly
cells, where the supplier integrates the final product, constitute one
level. These are very flexible, having a changeover time of less than 10
minutes, and can thus produce to exact daily requirements. On the
other level are all remaining operations, which operate on the weekly
schedule the MRP system issues. Between the two levels sit several
days' inventory.

Table 12.3 shows the average inventory held on site, and the planning
and ordering times. On the customer side of the flexible assembly cells
were 2 days of finished goods inventory, which the supplier likely kept
as a buffer against demand variation. We saw this layout in other suppliers, particularly when subcomponent production fed into an assembly or
paint and assembly step. A metal-pressing supplier averaged 1 to 2
weeks of finished goods inventory, with batch sizes of up to 4 weeks, for
example.

Before assembly, subcomponent production is the typical MRP-driven
batch production that we found at many suppliers. Oddly (although
unfortunately we found the same thing at many suppliers), the supplier's MRP system runs every Thursday, even though the new schedule
from the customer is not available until Friday morning. Information
then waits 5 production days to be used! Moreover, after the MRP system
issues weekly schedules to all subcomponent production steps, supervisors smooth them by manually altering them to suit their needs. Both

Table 12.3
Inventory levels and planning and ordering lead times for a European headlight
manufacturer.

Process stage	Inventory level	Planning or ordering time
Finished products	2 days	Daily shipping schedule
Assembly work in progress	Hours	Daily shipping schedule
Bought-in components	A parts: 5 days B parts: 15 days C parts: 30 days	Weekly order
Components built in house	1–2 days, 5–10 days for small parts	Weekly MRP schedule, manually altered
Component production work in progress	3–5 days	Weekly MRP schedule, manually altered
Raw materials	40 days (mainly granulate, held in silos)	5 weeks fixed orders, weekly delivery

these events contribute greatly to unsynchronized production, which in turn creates the need for the supplier's substantial inventories.

This case, which unfortunately is typical shows to what extent demand can become decoupled from component and subcomponent production—even when the manufacturer provides 3 weeks of stable demand. Between component production and vehicle assembly are three stocking locations: Supplier post-production (finished goods) inventory, manufacturer warehouse buffering, and manufacturing line-side inventory. Thus, disconnects occur on two levels: first, within the supplier (assembly-component production) and second between the supplier and manufacturer. If there is a 2-day stock at the supplier, what is the point of an interim warehouse? Yet, according to the supplier's plant manager, the manufacturer never mentioned the need for tighter coupling to the build sequence or more frequent deliveries.

In addition, although we could not evaluate to what extent quality issues actually disturb the process, the high scrap rate suggests that suppliers also create inventory buffers to offset sub-standard process quality.

Production Capacity

On the surface, it seems obvious that supplier responsiveness depends on the available production capacity. However, for the supply chain to fit well in a build-to-order system, both the manufacturer and supplier must understand to what degree capacity directly affects responsiveness and why. Table 12.4 shows two measures of capacity use for the suppliers we surveyed: the *current capacity*, or actual labor and machine production

Table 12.4
Current and manned capacity and average production hours in suppliers surveyed.

Component category	Average current capacity use (% of actual use)	Manned capacity use (% of theoretical use)	Production as % of 24-7 work week	Effective 24-7 capacity use
Nonspecific	81.3	83.3	90.5	75.4%
Standard	75.9	80.3	62.5	50.2%
Subassembly	82.5	82.5	72.3	59.6%
Color-coded	86.3	88.3	70.8	62.5%
Option	84.6	95.0	56.0	53.2%
Average over sample	82.4	84.3	69.3	58.4%

time, and the *manned capacity*, the time machine and labor are theoretically available for production. It also shows what percentage of a 24-hour, 7-day work week production takes up. Production hours determine the manned capacity, since the more production hours worked, theoretically, the more machine time and labor are available for production. Suppliers use their production processes and machines only 82.4 percent of the time (average current capacity use). Manned capacity is slightly higher at 84.3 percent.

In these terms, a supplier can increase capacity two ways. It can reduce downtime and thus increase current capacity, or it can provide more labor to increase production hours and thus increase manned capacity. The effective 24-7 capacity use is, then, a combination of the current and manned capacity use, given the actual production hours per week.[9] As the table shows, the suppliers had an average 58.4 percent effective 24-7 capacity use. In other words, an average 41.6 percent capacity[10] is available if any increase is called for and the supplier is able to extend production hours to a 24-7 week.

The table shows the potential for overall increase, but we also used the data to investigate the degree of volume flexibility and discovered an interesting response pattern. Given a month's notice, the suppliers claim, they can increase their overall capacity by 40.4 percent; within a week by 22.3 percent and within a day by 6.7 percent. Obviously the shorter the notice, the more difficult it is to put on extra shifts, get the necessary workforce in place, and provide the raw materials needed. Nevertheless, overall, suppliers appear to be extremely flexible to high demands. On the other hand, the data is concerned with *total* capacity, so capacity for a particular part number might not be as high. Moreover, certain resources could cause a throughput bottleneck, or other parts made by a different supplier could affect them. Hence, additional supply-chain flexibility is determined, not by the average flexibility among suppliers, but by the *least flexible* supplier.

Our interviews suggest that, although overall capacity increases are generally feasible, suppliers tend to rely on overtime and extra shifts. What affects flexibility here is the lack of qualified labor and the inability to reduce or increase available labor on short notice. Hence, suppliers cannot sustain these extra capacity levels for more than, say, several weeks in a row. Suppliers also suggested that volume changes were often far less problematic than the changes in the product mix that vehicle manufacturers often demand.

Second-Tier Relationships

This confusion about capacity led us to ask the same suppliers another set of questions about what constrained their companies from being responsive. No factors clearly emerged as consistent causes. Indeed, the data strongly suggests that individual suppliers face very specific problems related to their unique circumstances. No one mentioned the quality of the demand signal from the vehicle manufacturer, but instead cited factors like labor flexibility and availability, changeover and batch sizes, and material availability and quality. From these we identified a major influence on first-tier suppliers' flexibility: their relationship with second-tier companies.

The typical first-tier supplier we surveyed used about 150 bought-in parts, relied on only a handful of raw materials, and had an average of 45.7 second-tier suppliers per first-tier plant. This strongly suggests that first-tier purchasing and inbound logistics functions are extremely complex.

Table 12.5 shows the average order lead times from second-tier companies, delivery frequencies, and delivery performance (how often deliveries were on time). This data gives a quantitative picture of the link between first- and second-tier suppliers.

The order lead times average 42 and 20 days for raw materials and components, respectively, indicating that second-tier suppliers offer little flexibility. Some raw material suppliers show a particularly high degree of inflexibility, which contributes greatly to supply-chain inefficiencies. And although the average delivery is made nearly daily and no less

Table 12.5
Order lead time and delivery performance of second-tier suppliers.

Component category	Order lead time		Deliveries per day, raw material and components	On-time delivery, raw material and components
	Raw materials	Components		
Nonspecific	7.0	30.0	1.5	96.7%
Standard	46.0	12.8	0.6	98.4%
Subassembly	46.8	13.7	0.6	87.1%
Color-coded	66.8	26.8	0.5	99.1%
Option	35.2	27.5	0.2	96.8%
Average over sample	42.5	20.3	0.7	95.6%

frequently than once a week, on-time delivery performance is inconsistent. Indeed, suppliers cited it as one of the strongest inhibitors to responsive operations.

Thus, flexibility is affected both within and outside the first-tier supplier. The internal factors are process reliability and large batches. External factors are last-minute changes, second-tier order lead times, and to some extent the distance to the second-tier supplier. The uncertainty from both sets of factors causes first-tier suppliers to create buffer inventories.

Does Co-Location Matter?

In recent years, the auto industry has made a lot of noise about co-located suppliers, wondering if such a strategy is the answer to supply-chain responsiveness. Yet despite the rhetoric, most regions have done little to reduce the distance between suppliers and the assembly plant. As figure 12.1 shows, Japan has the closest supply base. This has been a significant source of competitive advantage for Japanese products.[11] North America and Europe show similar profiles, except that Europe uses supplier parks, so it shows at least some co-location (thin gray bar at the bottom). Co-location is most prevalent for new-entrant countries, since manufacturers could not depend on the country's existing infrastructure and so persuaded suppliers to go with them. When General Motors built its plant in Gravatai, Brazil, in 2000, for example, it received large government subsidies to locate there and build its $600 million plant

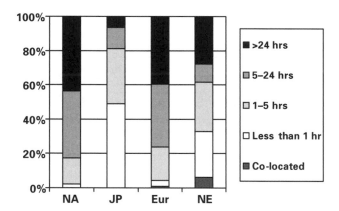

Figure 12.1
Distance (in hours) of suppliers.

with a capacity of 120,000 vehicles per year. It persuaded 16 large suppliers to follow along. Interestingly, these suppliers did not receive any government subsidies, so their overall risk of going to Brazil was comparatively much higher than GM's.[12]

Another reason to co-locate suppliers when moving abroad is the possible break in import duties. Brazilian laws, for example, set import duties at 35 percent for vehicle manufacturers with local production and at 60 percent for those without it. When Chrysler moved to Brazil, it took Dana with it to supply a rolling chassis in sequence to Chrysler's Dodge Dakota pickup truck assembly plant. The rolling chassis represents one-third of the vehicle cost, and contains parts from 70 other suppliers. Chrysler was able to launch the Dakota with 52 percent local content because sourcing the rolling chassis from Dana counted as local, even if many bought-in parts in the chassis were imported.

Our data strongly suggest two patterns that affect quality: The farther away the supplier, the more difficult it is to fix a problem, *and* the more stock held in the pipeline, the longer it takes to fix a problem. For example, if someone finds a defect in a component and the pipeline is holding 5 days' worth of that component, the waste is tremendous. And quality is not great—on average suppliers quoted their own quality as just under 99 percent, or 10,100 defective parts per million.[13] If we exclude all the nuts and bolts and assume this quality for, let's say, the 200 main components of a vehicle, the chance of building one without defects drops to 13.1 percent.

These patterns have serious implications for supplier responsiveness in a build-to-order system. When suppliers are located days away from the final assembly facility, how can they alter component supply to match a short-term evolution in customers' needs? For example, if a Western European supplier relies on a wire harness supplier days away in Asia, that supplier must depend on forecast schedules to manage production. If there is an order change close to the build date, the custom harness will have to be scrapped once it finally makes its way to the automobile assembly factory, and the changed order will be delayed while the replacement is shipped.

Stock levels correlate with the assumption that long distance means longer to fix. In Japan, where proximity is high, median stock level in warehouses is 6 hours. In contrast, stock levels are 15 hours in North America and 48 hours in Europe. Although new-entrant countries use co-location the most, the stock levels are the highest (multiple days) because some plants receive large quantities of components from their home countries.

Revisiting an Old Idea

The motor vehicle industry began as a completely integrated plant. Ford's original River Rouge complex was very integrated, encompassing most basic building blocks needed for automobile production. "The Rouge" was the largest manufacturing complex in the United States, with peak employment of about 120,000 during World War II. Here Henry Ford achieved self-sufficiency and vertical integration in automobile production—a continuous workflow from iron ore and other raw materials to finished automobiles. The complex included dock facilities, blast furnaces, open-hearth steel mills, foundries, a rolling mill, metal-stamping facilities, an engine plant, a glass manufacturing building, a tire plant, and its own power house supplying steam and electricity.

As decades passed, however, variety and specialization increased, and suppliers became increasingly independent. They were now producing parts for a range of factories, and eventually began supplying even their manufacturers' customers. In the late 1990s, this statement of independence perhaps reached its full definition when the parts businesses of General Motors and Ford spun off and became Delphi and Visteon. Now, GM and Ford are drawing the same independent suppliers back into the nest, as they form supplier parks across Europe and new-entrant countries. Has the industry gone full circle?

Yes and no. Supplier parks do not work well for every region. Although Europe has close to 20 parks and operations in new-entrant countries such as Brazil place tremendous reliance on them, developed countries like the United States have practically none. Gary Cowger of General Motors gives one major reason: "When you're building a new plant in the middle of an old plant and you have a lot of supplier base around, why make your suppliers build new plants?" However, GM's Opel does have several supplier parks in Europe, such as at its Rüsselsheim plant in Germany,[14] and Ford will operate its first North American supplier park at its Chicago assembly plant.

The proliferation of supplier parks also has much to do with government subsidies. Ford would probably have been far less likely to build a supplier park in Chicago without the attractive benefits package of $110 million offered by Chicago and the state of Illinois.[15] Many manufacturers established their current supplier parks in Europe, not to have greater flexibility, but to reduce their initial investment.[16]

Are Supplier Parks Mandatory?

Supplier parks, the co-location of key module and system suppliers adjacent to assembly factories, are the best known form of co-location, although their essence dates to the industry's beginning. They fit well with a build-to-order system for several reasons. It is far easier to supply complex modules in sequence and synchronize component production to meet short response times. Admittedly, not all suppliers are affected by assembly-sequence reliability to the degree that module and systems suppliers are, but the whole issue would become moot if manufacturers could simply provide stable information about the final production sequence. Currently, the reason for co-locating these suppliers of modules and systems is often that the vehicle manufacturer cannot determine which vehicle goes onto the assembly track more than a few hours in advance. The supplier is forced to meet this tiny window, and solutions can get quite original. One plant we visited had inserted an additional buffer, a tunnel, between the painted body store and assembly just so that the call-off lead time for suppliers would be longer. This inventory served *no* other purpose!

Besides providing greater assembly-sequence reliability, supplier parks make it easier to transport fragile integrated assemblies and to resolve quality problems. It is far quicker and easier for a quality engineer to pop over to his counterpart at the supplier in the supplier park than to drive somewhere and take an entire day for the same discussion.

Of course, supplier parks have their downside. Suppliers find it harder to balance volume fluctuations for multiple customers, to locate and retain low-wage workers, next door to well-paying vehicle manufacturers and to keep overhead costs reasonable. A commitment to co-locate with multiple manufacturers is difficult and costly. Not only must the supplier build one satellite near each customer at a significant investment, the volume of those co-located facilities is now completely dependent on the volume produced in that manufacturer's plant. If the supplier can locate more optimally between several plants, it can balance reductions in volume demand from one manufacturer with increases from another, or even volume changes for one product with volume changes in a different product built at a different plant of the same vehicle manufacturer. Overhead costs have a tendency to shoot up in multiple co-locations because certain labor functions cannot be divided. For example, no matter how small the facility, you still need an entire manager, engineering, and so on.

Perhaps the biggest problem is the massive investment required. If a supplier has three to five main manufacturing customers—and many do—is it going to build one satellite plant at each client location? Some suppliers like TI Automotive have taken that route. Their brake systems are problematic to ship over long distances, so they have small operations next to their customers. The main operations that make the tubes serve these satellite plants, and the satellite plants bend and assemble the systems and ship them in sequence to the automobile factory.

Six years ago, PPG, which makes glass and industrial coatings, built several satellite plants close to its customers' vehicle-manufacturing factories. Before that, PPG was shipping glass products in large quantities to those factories, where employees of the vehicle manufacturer would unpack the material, sequence it for installation on the vehicles, and attach components such as the buttons needed for connecting rearview mirrors and lift plates for door glass. The company now ships the glass in bulk directly to the satellite plants, which then deliver glass to the auto factories in the order and quantity needed for that hour's production, with all the necessary attachments already installed.

Some manufacturers are using logistics suppliers as an alternative to supplier parks. TNT picks up components for BMW's Spartanburg plant, processes them off-site, sequences components, and delivers components line-side for installation. At the GM plant in Lansing Michigan, TNT assembles door panels.[17]

Implications for Build-to-Order

Regardless of its form, some co-location is necessary for a successful build-to-order system. Suppliers of complex, customized parts *must* be located close to the assembly plant, for example, because otherwise the delay to wait for these parts will have a direct effect on the order-to-delivery time for the entire vehicle. A manufacturer cannot build the car in days if it takes the suppliers a week to make and ship the customized interior, dashboard and front-end modules.

For parts that do not have to be built in sequence, supplier location is not as critical, but it directly affects the amount of inventory the supplier holds. The farther away the supplier, the greater the inventory. Suppose a Michigan-based manufacturer decides to source a part in Northern Mexico rather than in Southern Canada or locally. Is the cheaper labor worth the cost of maintaining inventory, transporting stock, and addressing quality problems? The answer cannot be conclusive, since demand conditions are never stable—even the slightest demand variation can cause tremendous havoc in the supply chain. Yet manufacturers routinely assume that conditions are stable when they decide to source parts. And despite the lower labor cost (usually a nominal decrease), they end up spending a small fortune on emergency air freight and on rectifying inventory and quality problems.

Again, build-to-order works only if the *entire* supply chain is responsive. It makes no sense to reduce labor cost only to create rigid structures that add cost elsewhere. Second-tier suppliers, for example, must also be flexible. If first-tier suppliers face long order lead times and great distances to their raw material suppliers, they end up getting squeezed between increasing demands for small-batch delivery from their manufacturer customers and demands to source large batches of components from their inflexible second-tier suppliers. Locating first-tier suppliers close by might not be enough if the rest of the supply chain is far away.

Build-to-order forces manufacturers to think about flexibility, not solely cost reduction. If they fail to evaluate *all* opportunities for greater flexibility, most strategies, co-location included, will not give the expected return.

13 Process Flexibility and Logistics

It is good to have an end to journey towards, but it is the journey that matters in the end.

—Ursula K. LeGuin

When manufacturers look for responsiveness in the supply chain, logistics—transporting vehicles from the assembly plant to the dealership or even directly to the final customer—tends to be overlooked. The process seems straightforward. You ship the vehicle from point A to point B. What has to be flexible?

But in a build-to-order system, everything links, and logistics is about linking the whole production chain to the dealers and ultimately the customer. To not do so can have a considerable effect on the cohesiveness and responsiveness of the supply chain. Renault is a case in point. In 1998, Renault started its build-to-order project, "Projet Nouvelle Distribution," with the goal of a 15-day order-to-delivery time. Apart from initial problems, mainly what to do with the stock of new vehicles still in the market, the project was going very well. The stock in Europe decreased quickly and sharply, and executive vice-president Pierre-Alain de Smedt announced a reduced expenditure of €513 million in the first 6 months of 2001 at the Frankfurt Motor Show. "We're economizing in logistics, reducing stocks, shortening delivery times, and simplifying the entire delivery chain,"[1] he happily reported.

Yet in late 2001 Renault had to revise its order-to-delivery target to 21 days. "We haven't managed the 15-day lead time," said Francois Hinfray, Renault's senior vice-president for sales and marketing. In 2001, only 21 percent of customers received their car within the goal of 15 days. In the end, the delivery time was closer to 21 days for most.

Not that the project didn't have other benefits. In fact, the build-to-order system as a whole succeeded on several fronts: Finished goods inventories went down 21 percent, profit margins improved as buyers had less room to haggle over the price of a car built to their specifications, and factories became more customer focused.[2]

What went wrong? Order-to-delivery time didn't increase 6 days because demand was too variable or factories couldn't cope. Renault had to add those days solely because of logistics and transportation. Moving a product in Europe typically requires 10 to 15 days,[3] but railways are notoriously unreliable, particularly in France, where strikes are frequent. And road transportation has issues, too, such as sporadic strikes, and a perennial truck shortage during times of peak demand.

Transportation vs. Everything Else

The United Kingdom is a good backdrop to explain obstacles and opportunities in the logistics part of build-to-order.[4] UK manufacturers tend to use road, overwhelmingly, rather than rail when they are not using the Eurotunnel. The information flow generally originates from a central system within the manufacturer, passes to the logistics company's headquarters, and is then sent to the actual site or local operation, where workers consolidate loads and allocate trucks. Once the route planning is done, the logistics company sends a request to the finished car lot in the plant to prepare the load and then sends the truck to pick it up.

The trucks deliver to regional storage compounds or distribution centers, where the dealer staff signs delivery notes acknowledging receipt. The logistics company continuously updates the vehicle tracking system, which provides load and individual vehicle status, including estimated time of arrival and, when available, estimated time of collection (ETC).

The average delivery time was 3.8 days in the United Kingdom for the manufacturers we surveyed. This is a significant delay in the whole order-fulfillment process, especially when the physical part of the transportation accounts for no more than 12 hours. Lack of information accounts for the rest: Logistics companies simply do not have enough details to do any meaningful forward planning or to arrange backloading. Forward planning is the process of arranging loads to the dealerships or customers. Backloading—a financially crucial logistics element—is the process of gathering vehicles to fill a transporter after it delivers its initial load so that it does not return empty. Backloading helps the logistics company maintain the cost efficiencies that vehicle manufacturers demand. In fact, manufacturers often build backloading into the pricing at levels up to 60 percent capacity use. Since the logistics company doesn't get paid by distance, but by the volume of vehicles moved, it is under tremendous pressure to achieve the specified capacity use without prolonging delivery time. Unfortunately, this balancing act is difficult and, delivery time is often compromised, as logistics firms aim to enhance backload efficiencies.

To add to the mess, even though backloading is crucial to profitability, vehicle manufacturers do not explicitly consider it in their arrangements. Instead, they have informal understandings with the logistics providers that backloading is a necessary factor in their cost equation. In fact, a logistics company cannot even arrange backloading until it gets enough information to fix the outgoing dispersion load.

Both our interviews and questionnaire responses identified the lack and quality of information from the vehicle manufacturer as the main inhibitor to efficiency and responsiveness.[5] Daily information is severely lacking. One planning manager told us that his company often didn't know which cars to ship "until they are driven into our compound." Only then could the company start planning.

If the industry continues to embrace these practices, shorter delivery time would raise the cost of transportation, as figure 13.1 illustrates. Outbound is the cost from the factory to the distribution center.

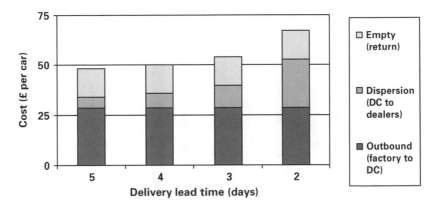

Figure 13.1
How reduced delivery time would affect transportation cost for one brand, assuming 250 dealers, and 100,000 units in UK. Source: J. Gregory, "Vehicle logistics and the Three-Day Car Programme," 3DayCar Annual Conference, Stratford upon Avon, 1999.

Dispersion is the cost from the distribution center to the dealers, and Empty is the cost for running empty on the way back. With shorter delivery times and thus fewer vehicles per load, the dispersion run to deliver the loads would be less efficient and without adequate lead time there would be little backloading to offset it, so transportation cost would increase significantly.

Bigger Isn't Always Better

Logistics, like the other parts of the value grid, suffers from the influence of mass production, where the motto is low cost, high load efficiency, and equal treatment of all orders. Distribution is not timed, and delivery time is compromised in the same way—whether the car has been sold and has a waiting customer or has not been sold and will sit in dealer inventory for 2 months anyway.

As figure 13.2 shows, the transporter fleet profile is best summed up as "lumbering." Most of the 1,537 fleets have transporters that can hold 10 to 12 cars each, thanks to past cost-efficiency pressures that looked more at transportation cost than delivery times. The more cars per transporter, cost-efficiency experts reasoned, the more economic the overall movement per vehicle. All this grand scheme did was introduce inflexibility into the scheduling, since now the overarching objective is for trucks to be full. The larger the transporter, the longer everyone waits to fill it with vehicles.

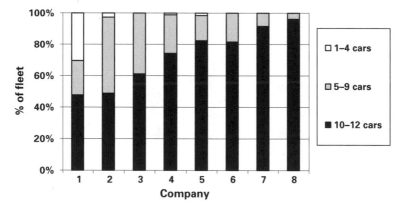

Figure 13.2
Transporter fleet capacities for 1,537 fleets in UK. Source: Holweg and Miemczyk, "Logistics in the three-day car age."

Fortunately, the industry is coming around to the idea of "less big." Shorter, more flexible delivery, as well as the potential to deliver to individual customers has many companies looking at increasing the number of smaller transporters.

To date, only a few companies deliver directly to the customer (usually a large fleet buyer or some special operation, or in some countries an independent Internet-based sales company). For large fleets, the logistics companies can generally use larger transporters because of the volume involved. Internet-based companies, however, deliver mainly to individual private customers on residential streets, so smaller transporters are required to handle the handfuls of customers in a given area. For these deliveries, companies typically use either single-car trucks with optional trailers or two-deck transporters that hold up to three cars.

Most logistics companies see the investment in small transporters as essential, but also as an additional operational expense, since drivers need more training to interface with the customer. Training can be anything from vehicle checking to managing potential conflicts with the end customer. Companies tended to disagree about how much additional cost would be involved, and manufacturers are not likely to explore the effects of increasing direct deliveries because of the political and legal consequences for their dealer networks.

The Cost of "Oops"

Damage is another factor that causes additional delays and uncertainty, and freshly painted cars seem to invite scratching and denting. Our survey revealed damage levels from 0.4 percent to 2.0 percent, with an average 1.5 percent. While overall, this seems low, *any* damage level will invariably mean a late delivery to the customer. Transit damage, for example, represents the possibility that 1.5 percent of the vehicles built will arrive late to the customer. At about £180 per car damaged (averages are from £110 to £250), repair cost is only £2.63 per vehicle transported. The cost in customer goodwill, however, is considerably more.

The main source of damage appears to be unloading and loading (66 percent), and damage during transport, such as scratches from low-hanging trees. Miscellaneous causes such as storage-related damage occur rarely. During transit, most damage occurs to the car body and paint, with occasional instances of dirty internal trim.

Solutions to prevent damage tend to be costly. Manufacturers have considered protective panels, but the reverse flow was a problem. Once these panels are dirty from the inside, they cannot be put into contact with paintwork again. Some luxury-car makers, including Porsche and Aston-Martin, even deliver cars in containers or closed transporters, at considerable cost.

The whole vehicle inspection process in its current form is a major nuisance, giving rise to inconvenient policies such as no night deliveries to dealers because someone must be there to inspect the incoming vehicle. When vehicles *are* inspected, it is often in inclement weather, and the potentially responsible parties (the manufacturer, logistics company and its contractors, and dealer) disagree about what constitutes "undamaged."

When someone notes damage, vehicle manufacturers, dealers, and logistics companies often debate about which party pays for the repair. If each party has its own insurance, the blame game starts in an attempt to avoid higher premiums. Some UK companies we surveyed use a scheme in which all partners pay equal amounts into a shared fund that pays for repair work. On average this fund amounts to £2 to £3 per vehicle. Any scratch, dent or blemish, however small, is considered transit damage unless someone can prove that the vehicle left the factory in that condition.

New Metrics and an Attitude Adjustment

To overcome logistics' operational problems and shorten distribution times, manufacturers must be more forthcoming with timely information. Monthly volume is not enough, especially since the forecast tends to be inaccurate most of the time. A capacity guideline cannot take the place of a detailed plan.

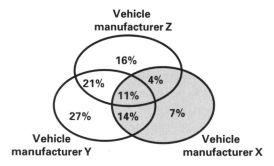

Figure 13.3
Potential overlap of supplier collection.

Manufacturers must also rethink current performance measures. Concepts such as "one delivery time fits all," be it stock or individual customer, usher in dysfunctional dynamics. Likewise, focusing on cost per vehicle, rather than on lead time in conjunction with cost, shifts the strategic focus to economies of scale.

Transporting products for multiple franchises and industries is one strategy logistics companies—both inbound and outbound—can use to improve capacity use and maintain short lead times. Figure 13.3 quantifies the overlap of parts-collection schemes operated by one inbound logistics company for three manufacturers. Of the 200 to 300 suppliers for each scheme, 11 percent supply all three vehicle manufacturers, and 50 percent supply at least two at a time. Despite this considerable overlap, the logistics company makes most collections individually.

14 Product Flexibility

They can have any color, as long as it is black.
—Henry Ford on the Model T in 1926[1]

Product variety was Henry Ford's Waterloo and what finally eroded Ford's market share. Yes, the T's standard chassis was versatile; customers could have a two- or five-seat open touring car, landaulet, coupe, van, or truck. With a special body, the Model T could become a small bus, a taxi, a racing car, or a tractor. The design was clean and production efficient. Bolt the body on the rolling chassis and paint it black, the color that dries the fastest.

Customers were okay with this as long as cars were a novelty, but when the new-vehicle market saturated around 1927, they began to grumble. Meanwhile, Chevrolet, Ford's main competitor, had introduced the 490 in 1917 in a range of five very stylish body styles. The 490 was a modern, fresh-looking car with a selective transmission as opposed to Ford's foot-pedal-operated one. More important, Chevrolet had become a division of General Motors in 1918, and it was already benefiting from Alfred P. Sloan's strategy of promoting multiple brand and multiple models. When Sloan took the helm, in 1923, he was prepared to have GM offer everything from an entry-level Chevrolet 490 to a Cadillac. In the 1924 annual report to shareholders, he stated that GM would be offering "a car for every purse and purpose."

In retrospect, the results were predictable. At the start of the 1920s, Ford sales were five times those of General Motors. By 1940, GM held 40 percent of the market, while Ford had less than 20 percent. Sloan had not only modified Ford's mass-production system to generate and manage product variations, but he had also established brand portfolios that gave customers the ability to select the status level associated with their chosen brand. The industry soon recognized that variety was the key to blanketing market space and locking in a range of customers with diverse but related requirements. Like companies in other industries, automobile manufacturers now attempt to top and re-top the range of their offerings. Market pressures force manufacturers to anticipate and preempt competitor offerings and to form strategies to differentiate their products from all the others out there. These differentiation strategies have outdone each other in an attempt to provide distinguishing variety to the point that one product can have thousands of possible feature combinations.

In their scramble to be noticed, manufacturers have forgotten why they began to be different in the first place: customers. For any of these strategies to matter, the customers must have a real chance of securing the product they desire. Meanwhile, variety at this level introduces complexity into the value grid, which translates into long order-to-delivery times. There is a tension between those who market this much variety and those who must produce the envisioned products. Keeping the right balance between these parties is challenging.

Any tinkering with the variety level can upset the balance. Too little variety and customers go to the other showroom, where they have more choices. Too much variety and production and supply become problematic.

So the strategy is to offer enough variety to entice without impeding efficient and effective production. Product variety marks the critical interface between marketing and operations, customers, and factories. The tradeoff between potentially lower revenue from lack of variety and escalating design and production costs is the theme of endless and delightful debates between marketing and manufacturing. Even so, no one has written much about variety's effect on the value grid. About all we know is that marketing pushes for choice, design departments convert variety into infinite design complexity, and the factory, which has little input at either stage, ends up having to produce the vehicle.

It would seem, then, that the first step to managing variety successfully is to understand it and how it affects the value grid.

The terms used to describe the different forms of variety are given in table 14.1. Other terms are helpful in putting these definitions into perspective: *Model* means a vehicle that might share a platform with others but has significant differences in sheet metal (the rule of thumb is 75 per-

Table 14.1
Terms for forms of variety.

Internal	The variation in processes and parts to create products. Consists of three subtypes that may or may not translate to external variety:
	Fundamental Product structures and platforms that form the basis around which everything else is made. For automotive platforms, these include a unique underbody and wheelbase.
	Intermediate Number of wire harnesses, powertrains, and vehicle colors.
	Peripheral Overall number of components and variety of these components for product variations.
External[a]	Range of choice offered a customer at a point in time (body styles, colors, options, and so on).
Dynamic[b]	Amount of external variety offered over time. Driven by two key factors: model range (range of products offered for a given model) and product life cycle (how often the product is replaced).

a. Sources: H. Mather, "Optimize your product variety," *Production and Inventory Management Journal* 33 (1992), no. 2: 38–44; J. MacDuffie, K. Sethuraman, and M. Fisher, "Product variety and manufacturing performance: Evidence from the International Automotive Assembly Plant Study," *Management Science* 42 (1996), no. 3: 350–369.
b. Source: M. Fisher, K. Ramdas,, and K. Ulrich, "Component sharing in the management of product variety: A study of automotive braking systems," *Management Science* 45 (1999), no. 3: 297–315.

cent of the surface area). *Body styles* are variations within models (two-door, four-door, and so on).

Variety as Choice

Variety as customer choice, or *external variety*, is the marketing side of the balancing act we described above, and attempts to increase it seem limitless. Gimmicks have contributed significantly to the variety explosion. Another source is model proliferation, which is reaching ridiculous proportions. In the 1970s all you could get were small, medium, and executive vehicles, trucks, and —possibly a sports car. Now we have the SUV, the MPV, the UAV,[2] and their subsets.[3] Most customers do not know what the acronyms mean, let alone the differences among the classes.

Model proliferation can happen subtly. Japanese manufacturers, for example, have been driving proliferation since the early 1970s by offering vehicles outside defined segments. Examples are the super-minis below the compact class, small sports cars like the Toyota MR2, and pseudo off-road vehicles like the Suzuki Samurai. As figure 14.1 shows, Japanese manufacturers now offer an average 3.5 more models than their Western

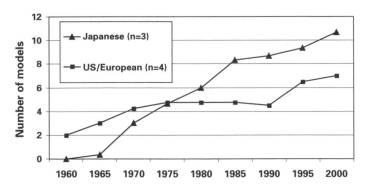

Figure 14.1
Average model ranges offered in UK, 1960–2000.

competitors (Japanese vs. US/European), most of which they import from Japan.[4] In addition, model offerings have doubled in 30 years for all manufacturers.

Within individual models, variety has also increased, but here the customer *perception* of variety—more specifically, of variety's value—becomes important. For most mainstream vehicles, manufacturers offer a choice of body style, engine type, color, trim, and options. External variety grows exponentially with these combinations, especially with options because a manufacturer seldom offers them separately. Thus, two options translate to four possible combinations, four to 16 and so on. Moreover, a manufacturer might offer a different set of options for each model derivative. An optional roof rail may be offered only on station wagons, whereas the sunroof is not available on the convertible versions, and so forth. This starts to get complicated, which is seldom a good thing for the customer.

Table 14.2 gives an overview of important European, American, and Japanese high-volume vehicles as their manufacturers offered them in the United Kingdom in 1999. Every model has multiple body styles, power trains (engine/transmission), and interior trim and exterior paint combinations. Except for Mercedes, the products have a relatively consistent range of paint or trim combinations, but numbers differ radically when comparing total product variations. For some models, the numbers are in the realm of the absurd. For example, Mercedes offers far more variations in its S-class and E-class models than the company could ever sell in its entire existence, let alone during the lifetimes of those products.

Table 14.2
External product variety and sales in the UK automotive sector. The total number of variations takes combination restrictions into account (e.g., no automatic transmission offered with 1.4-liter engine). Product variety, the number of vehicle permutations offered for a particular model, depends on the market. Air conditioning that is standard in the UK might be an option in Germany, for example.

		No. of body styles	No. of power trains	No. of paint-trim combinations	No. of options	No. of possible variations	UK sales (units/year)
Nissan	Micra	2	4	36	5	1,656	47,775
	Primera	3	5	60	2	820	21,714
Honda	Accord	2	4	30	2	529	19,024
	Civic 5-dr	1	6	27	8	1,348	31,596
Vauxhall	Astra IV	4	13	44	41	55,425,024	81,494
	Vectra	3	13	46	22	5,843,600	77,479
Ford	Mondeo	3	8	92	16	171,584	77,183
	Fiesta	2	6	63	12	22,368	99,830
	Focus	4	6	64	18	1,070,592	103,228
VW	Golf IV	2	9	211	22	154,964	63,715
	Lupo	1	5	85	10	176,576	4,642
Renault	Clio	2	6	91	6	1,514	63,991
	Megane	2	7	104	0	448	65,127
	Laguna	2	9	65	1	1,196	30,475
Peugeot	206	2	4	43	14	7,520	58,788
	306	2	8	59	9	6,928	53,447
	406	2	7	64	8	20,796	42,442
Mercedes	E-Class	2	9	121	41	3,933,000,000,000	12,930
	S-Class	2	6	480	22	3,205,000,000	2,653

Does anyone really need this much variety? Our research on customer focus groups and interviews with manufacturer's sales and distribution managers found that customers cannot judge the difference between the less than 1,000 variants of the Honda Accord and the trillions of variants on the Mercedes E-class. Body style, engine, exterior color, and radio type are the most considered features. Other features and options are less critical. In other words, 17,424 variations matter on the E-class, but the rest of the value grid must still deal with the remaining 99.9999996 percent that the customer doesn't even recognize.

Table 14.2 also gives sales volume because volume per product derivative (the possible combination of features per model), not variety per se, affects the value grid. The manufacturer is likely to make more of the product derivatives with high volumes, for example.

Our analysis of sales data for major European volume cars in 1999 and 2000 revealed not the 80-20 relationship we expected (80 percent of the volume accounted for by 20 percent of the specifications), but for many vehicles, 0.1 percent of the specifications already accounted for 50 percent of sales.[5]

Product variety proliferation shows no signs of slowing, and its patterns are difficult to predict. We analyzed the historic development of four major high-volume cars (and their successors) offered in the UK market from 1964 to 1999. As before, we measured variety as the number of body styles, power trains, paint/trim combinations, and options, and we also measured sales volume.[6]

As table 14.3 shows, we found no clear trends across the four models. Ford, for example, has been reducing its product variety since the mid 1980s. The 1999 Mondeo is available in 0.01 percent as many variants as its 1983 predecessor, the Sierra. Vauxhall, the British GM subsidiary, has a confusing profile. It tried to reduce its product variety by bundling options in the early 1990s for the Astra III but then offered many options with the Astra IV, which has taken it back to the variety level of the Astra II. Rover's variety was consistently below 25,000 until BMW's takeover and the implementation of a revised options policy, which rocketed it to 2 million. Volkswagen has steadily increased variety, offering a wide range of paint-trim combinations and options.

Thus, variety has increased, sometimes dramatically, and again, variances are largely due to options, not body styles, colors, or power trains. Variety is driven by company policy for each individual model and does not exhibit a systematic trend.

Electric Doors and Other Sales Gimmicks

Understanding variety from the customers' viewpoint is tricky because it has to do with their perceptions of the choice offered. People are fickle creatures, and what they perceive changes quickly. Entire disciplines are built up around understanding the elements of perception, so it is a challenge to know what the customer "values" until it is out there being either ignored or sought after. And if it is sought after, who can know for how long? Despite this uncertainty, manufacturers seem willing to base sales on short-term preferences rather than on long-term solutions. Of course, few industries are exempt from at least some fad fallout, but the motor vehicle industry has become shameless in its pursuit of what is "in." Some customers, particularly younger ones, do buy cars and trucks in the same way they would shop for clothes, but many more do not. A large customer segment cares about buying a car at a reasonable price with reasonable features. For some reason, these shoppers tend to be ignored. Instead, manufacturers cater to the impulse buyer and have become willing entrants in the "I can guess what's in" race or the "you thought of it, but I can do it better" contest.

The sliding door on multipurpose vehicles is the perfect example. In 1996, Chrysler took the industry by surprise and introduced a second sliding door on the driver's side of its mini-vans. Not to be outdone, other companies enhanced access to the rear of the mini-van via the driver's door, followed by their own dual sliding doors. These soon became electrically powered with remote control and now include novel features like obstacle detection and motors integrated inside the door. Various types of innovative folding and disappearing seat arrangements became another prominent source of differentiation. The gun has fired and the race is on. As we write this paragraph, the latest gimmick is an electric rear hatch.

Some manufacturers are seeing the folly of such pursuits. Robert Lutz, vice-chairman of General Motors, recently commented "Much of today's content is useless in triggering purchase decisions." He was referring to the plastic cladding on the Chevrolet Avalanche that wasn't selling and was costing an additional $750 per vehicle. GM had finally decided to remove it.[7]

Suppliers have helped combat the lure of gimmicks as they become more consolidated and attempt to offer full service—designing and delivering portions of vehicles. Over time, their input will help control

Table 14.3
Historic product variety in four high-volume models.

		No. of body styles	No. of power trains	No. of paint-trim combinations	No. of options	Total no. of variations[a]	UK sales (units/year)
Vauxhall							
Viva I-HA	1965	1	2	17	1	59	NA[b]
Viva II-HB	1967	2	4	20	4	728	100,220
Viva III-HC	1970	3	5	23	8	15,848	76,338
Astra I	1983	4	10	28	10	1,495,104	62,570
Astra II	1984	4	11	22	26	53,575,680	56,511
Astra III	1993	4	11	30	15	76,972	108,204
Astra IV	1998	4	13	44	41	55,425,024	81,494
Rover/Austin[c]							
1100 MkI	1964	1	1	10	3	240	NA
1100 MkII	1967	3	4	12	3	864	131,282
Allegro I	1973	2	4	NA	3	448	28,713
Allegro III	1979	3	6	11	6	1,056	59,885
Maestro	1983	1	5	NA	11	NA	65,328
Maestro	1987	1	4	105	7	1,132	43,815
(Rover)							
200	1991	2	8	44	17	21,792	68,122
200	1998	2	9	60	10	14,960	64,928
25	1999	2	8	106	18	2,742,656	1,170
Ford							
Cortina I[d]	1964	3	3	14	5	2,688	NA

Cortina II	1968	3	5	NA	NA	2,880	137,873
Cortina III	1972	3	7	28	12	702,464	187,159
Cortina IV/V	1982	3	6	275	28	219,576,000	135,745
Sierra	1983	3	9	110	35	1,278,852,000	159,804
Mondeo	1993	3	7	51	19	315,072	88,660
Mondeo	1999	3	8	92	16	171,584	77,183
Volkswagen[e]							
Golf I	1980	2	6	26	7	7,216	NA
Golf II	1985	2	6	29	8	2,192	31,145
Golf III	1995	2	11	93	8	16,968	44,111
Golf IV	1999	2	9	211	22	154,964	63,715

a. Number may differ slightly from actual offer because of model year changes and other influences.
b. Not available.
c. Austin brand only. Morris, MG, Riley, Vanden Plas, Wolseley versions not considered.
d. Excluding Cortina GT and Lotus Cortina.
e. Excluding station wagons, sedans (Jetta, Vento, Bora), and convertibles. We analyzed the Golf only from 1980 on.

faddish influences, since every manufacturer will be buying the same "innovations" from the same suppliers.

From Customer Choice to Production

External variety is what the customer sees—the choices of body style, paint, and options that make up the desired car. Manufacturers see variety very differently: Their focus is on how to translate external variety into requirements for the manufacturing process and value grid. These requirements dictate a product's *internal* variety—how complex it is to make. Again, the number of body styles, engines, colors, paint-trim combinations, and options figure in, but with far more nuances and subtle interactions that affect the value grid. Japanese automobile manufacturers in Europe, for example, have few offerings per model (low external variety), but find it almost impossible to build to a customer order.[8] Volvo and Mercedes, in contrast, build a very large proportion of their production to order, despite extremely high levels of product variety.

The starting point for most vehicles is the *body-in-white*, a welded steel monocoque (shell). The body-in-white (BIW) reflects the number of apertures and model styles of the particular vehicle, and may be customized to handle specific options that the vehicle would ultimately have. BIWs might vary according to engine type or the presence of air conditioning, sunroof, and other options. The more options offered, the more BIW variants. The BIW complexity, in turn, determines the variety in the process before painting and, ultimately, the number of painted body variants the plant has to manage.

Of the 20 models we analyzed to determine external variety, we obtained detailed data on nine for an assessment of internal variety. Table 14.4 presents the results of analyzing nine models from this sample (disguised for confidentiality). Pre-assembly complexity does not relate to size; small cars can have as much complexity as large ones, sometimes more. Rather, the number of BIWs seems to dictate complexity, since the number of paints sprayed is fairly constant at 12 to 15. The A-segment car is an exception, because it uses independent body panels, but even here pre-assembly complexity is low.

BIW complexity—having a different BIW for various engines and options—varies greatly and does not seem to mirror external variety. That is, a different BIW is not required for each new feature. In many cases, manufacturers can use the same BIW for different engines, left- or right-hand drive, and air conditioning.

Table 14.4
Internal vehicle complexity for nine models in Europe in 2000. (A: supermini. B: subcompact. C: compact. D: mid-size. BIW: body in white. RHD/LHD: right- or left-hand drive. A/C: air conditioning.)

Model segment	No. of body styles	No. of BIWs	No. of paints sprayed	Total no. of permutations (pre-assembly)	Different BIW for			
					RHD/LHD?	Engines?	Sunroof?	A/C?
A	2	2	2	4	Not applicable	No	No	No
B	3	9	14	144	No	No	Yes	No
B	2	9	14	126	Yes	No	Yes	No
B	2	158	10	1,580	Yes	Yes	Yes	Yes
C	4	32	14	448	Yes	No	Yes	Yes
C	5	36	14	504	No	No	Yes	No
C-D	3	243	10	2,430	Yes	Yes	Yes	Yes
D	2	20	12	240	Yes	Yes	Yes	Yes
MPV	1	4	13	52	Yes	No	Yes	No

According to our interviews with manufacturers, plants use more BIW variants (rather than having one BIW fit several designs) to reduce the number of brackets and welds needed to adapt the BIW to a particular design. Others desire a change but have no input into the variety inserted at the design stage. "We know," said a production controller at a European subsidiary of a Japanese manufacturer, "that the complex design makes our manufacturing inflexible. . . . But both design and tooling come from Japan, and we have no real influence on the [fundamental] variety before it gets here."

How Types of Variety Relate

To investigate the link between internal and external variety, we did a simple correlation analysis between the elements that define each one. We found that body styles, power trains, and options positively correlate with overall external variety, but that BIW variety bore no relation to the number of body styles offered in the market and little relation to external variety overall. A more detailed analysis of the assembly plant survey data highlights additional and more nuanced disconnects between internal variety and external variety. For example, engine compartment variations bear no relation to the number of engines or transmission variations offered to customers. Likewise, the number of body-side variations bears no statistically significant relation to the number of door variations offered. Clearly, it is possible to build vehicles with high external variety using body structures that vary little. Translation: Building a car that offers a lot of choice to the customer doesn't have to be any more complex in production.

So how does customer choice affect production cost? We found that the main production costs stem from features or options that customers either rarely choose or choose nearly always. These items affect production on the margin. But narrow-focus option parts, such as side airbags in low-end vehicles, often have take rates of less than 5 percent. At the other extreme are air conditioning or automatic transmission, which for some vehicles have take rates well above 98 percent. In both these cases—features rarely taken and those taken nearly always—cost implications are dramatic. In research for a major vehicle manufacturer, we found that if more than 60 percent of the customers requested ABS, it was cheaper to offer the ABS system to all customers than to have an ABS and a non-ABS model. The ABS parts were more expensive but economies of scale, reduced error rates in assembly, reduced complexity

in materials handling, and higher purchasing volumes provided opportunities to offset the extra parts cost.

A larger problem is that not everyone sees the need to make these
kinds of translations. A cost analysis takes resources, and the marketing
unit, the declared champion of customer responsiveness, is likely to ask
"Why are we doing this?" Marketing personnel usually take the tack
that if someone wants it, the company should offer it, no matter how few
people express that preference. Manufacturing and purchasing costs are
not relevant.

This attitude is not always due to conflict of interest, however.
Sometimes manufacturers do not see compelling evidence (translation:
cost savings in hard numbers), and "increased flexibility" is just a little
too vague for their tastes. A case in point is a European manufacturer that
offered only two body styles, but had a highly complex BIW. One feature
that introduced complexity was the through-hole for skis, which
required an additional cut into the rear wall of the sedan's passenger
compartment. The cut entailed a direct-labor cost of $40 per car. It was
impossible to convince management that standardizing the sedan's BIW
by cutting the through-hole into *all* vehicles, regardless of whether or
not the ski bag was fitted, would be far cheaper. The savings were due to
increased plant flexibility, however, and no one could attach a monetary
value to that. In the end, the $40, being the only thing well understood,
swayed the decision to keep cutting that hole as needed.

Variety and the Vehicle Life Cycle

In addition to coping with external and internal variety, manufacturers
must manage *dynamic* variety—how often the manufacturer replaces the
product. The more product generations offered, the more dynamic variety available to the customer. Thus, a company whose replacement cycle
is roughly half that of its competitors offers twice the choice to its customers over time.

The common perception is that vehicle life cycles have decreased
drastically over the past few years. Although the "decreased" part is certainly true, we found the trend to be more gradual than drastic. Figure
14.2 shows the average model life cycle for the UK market over 30 years,
which we derived from analyzing the life cycles of 19 significant volume vehicles in the United Kingdom, from their introduction to replacement or major facelift. As the figure shows, life-cycle reduction has been
fairly constant from 7.5 years in 1970 to just over 5 years in 2000.

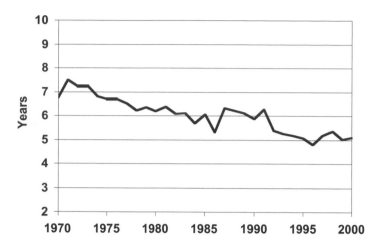

Figure 14.2
Average model life cycle in UK market over 30 years, derived from analyzing life cycles of 19 major volume vehicles from introduction to replacement or major facelift. Data shown as 5-year moving average.

The long life cycles in the 1970s were an aberration from earlier years. For example, in the 1960s, low product complexity meant that successor models generally shared many components with their predecessors. This meant manufacturers could develop them quickly. The Ford Cortina II, for example, had the same engine, running gear, and floor-pan structure as the Cortina I. The models introduced in the early to mid 1970s, however, were more likely to be stand-alone developments, but manufacturers still had vastly different approaches. Some US companies, for example, accelerated changeovers by simply altering the appearance of external body panels and interiors. Ford GB, Ford of Germany, Vauxhall, and Opel thus had models with far shorter life cycles than their European counterparts. Volkswagen, Fiat, and Renault preferred to keep a model in production longer and then replace it with a completely new model with very different components. The best example of this approach was Citroen, with long-lived models such as the 2CV, DS, GS/GSA, and CX.

In the late 1970s, as technical advances began to make cars more complex and the US economy took a downturn, model cycles in the United States lengthened, but since the early 1990s cycles in all regions have been shortening. As figure 14.3 shows, the US producers are only now catching up with their Japanese competitors, which very steadily have pursued a strategy of 4–5-year model cycles.

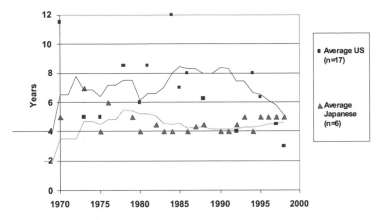

Figure 14.3
Average model life cycle for US market over 30 years, derived by analyzing life cycles of
23 volume vehicles (17 domestic and 6 Japanese). Upper line: 5-year moving average for
US manufacturers. Lower line: Japanese manufacturers.

High dynamic variety—bigger model range and shorter model life
cycles—means better choice for the customer, but it comes with sobering
ramifications for manufacturers. More models with shorter lives means
fewer sales per model, and in an industry where product development
cost for a new model is easily $1 billion, sales volume cannot tolerate
even a nudge in the negative direction. Manufacturers offer more choice,
but they have less chance of recovering production cost and staying
profitable over the long term.

Thus, on a global scale, market volume is steadily growing, but where
it comes from makes a huge difference. Incentives are offered, cars sell,
and everyone is relieved. On the surface the volume from incentives
seems to be smoothing everything over, but as we have shown, behind
the "sales are up" sign, vicious cycles are grinding away residual values,
brand identification, and eventually profit.

Managing Variety

The previous sections should have provided some flavor of how variety
can affect the value grid. And they should have also clarified why managing that variety in one part of the grid doesn't necessarily reap benefits
in other parts. A manufacturer can offer customers many choices and
still have manageable production complexity, but the reverse could also
be true—few choices, unmanageable production.

In addition to generating conflict in the value grid, variety is a source of intra-organizational conflict for manufacturers. Within each manufacturer are multiple stakeholders, each with a separate, often conflicting, agenda. The marketing unit views external variety as critical to attracting customers. Product design groups view increased internal variety as a source of cost savings. Manufacturing wants to lower internal variety to reduce complexity. All that variety must be stored somewhere, and someone has to manage the logistics associated with storing and handling so many parts. More parts handling for direct workers means they have more time that is not value-added. More variability in assembly time means that balancing the workload becomes more difficult, and so on and so on.

The key to managing variety to achieve product flexibility is to generate it at minimal cost without compromising the responsiveness of the wider manufacturing system. Researchers and consultants have advocated a range of strategies, which promise greater variety with superior responsiveness at minimal cost.

In view of the ease with which companies can inadvertently choose the wrong path, we developed the framework shown here in table 14.5, which assesses the effectiveness of these variety-management strategies in the context of both build-to-forecast and build-to-order systems. In this case, "management" means effectively mitigating variety's adverse effects, and we deliberately restricted the framework to a simple distinc-

Table 14.5
Strategies for managing (mitigating) product variety. Higher number of + signs indicates level of applicability of the strategy in each scenario.

Value grid system	Mutable support structures	Modularity	Late configuration	Option bundling
Build-to forecast (BTF), emphasis on post-customization	+ Economy-of-scale advantages only	+ Labor-cost advantage through outsourcing	+++ Increases choice without increasing fundamental variety	+++ Reduces forecast error and inventory risk
Build-to-order-(BTO), emphasis on pre-customization	+++ Increases flexibility in manufacturing	++ Enables postponement and order-driven production	+ Can reduce internal variety	No true advantage

tion between the two systems. We also recognize that these strategies can run in parallel at various tiers in the value grid.

In a build-to-forecast system, as the framework implies, the aim is to keep external product variety low because the more variety offered, the more stock ends up being held to try to pair the existing product with a customer. And the more variations, the less likely the pairing will be successful. Peugeot and Nissan in Europe are among the manufacturers that have opted for central stocking locations to try to increase the odds of matching a customer to a product. Their strategy is to use both option packaging to reduce customer choice and late configuration of some items (radio type, spoilers, and other options that the central stocking location or dealership can add on).

How external variety translates into internal variety in a build-to-forecast system is irrelevant because a flexible manufacturing process and minimal internal variety do little to facilitate a customer-to-product match.

In a build-to-order system, external variety matters only to the extent that it alters the level of internal variety. Matching products to a customer through inventory is not relevant at all, since the customer is linked to the product from the outset and stays linked until the sale is complete. The complexity *before* customization is critical and calls for strategies that lower fundamental and intermediate variety. These include platform sharing and the use of mutable body shells, which minimize the required number of body variants and let the plant decouple body and paint from assembly. At all times, the focus must be on customer-driven production. BMW and Volvo, for example, have introduced smart painted body stores that let the plant resequence vehicles along with decoupled assembly processes, and mutable support structures. Tony Koblinski, GM's executive director of global order-to-delivery, put it this way: "OTD is much more than a logistical challenge. It is an initiative that includes virtually every aspect of designing, engineering, building, and selling vehicles."[9]

Option bundling and late configuration are most effective after customization, as the framework shows, since they reduce overall external variety, but are of limited use in a build-to-order value grid. In contrast, modularity and mutable support structures offer little advantage for a build-to-forecast grid, but are highly effective before customization. Both will increase a manufacturer's ability to build products to order by reducing the challenges associated with internal variety.

The Leveraging of Platforms

Some manufacturers are experimenting with strategies to combat the cost of dynamic variety. One that has seen widespread use recently is to engineer platforms that suit multiple products. Volkswagen's Jetta and Beetle and Audi's TT and A3 share the VW Golf IV platform, for example.

As figure 14.4 shows, many manufacturers are adding vehicles and body types to a platform. Developing platforms is expensive, so the more bodies per platform, the more development costs can be recovered. Also, platforms share many parts for suspension, exhaust, braking, and in many cases even power trains, so the manufacturer also gets economies of scale in purchasing.

Platform leveraging is thus a way to compensate for falling volumes per model. As long as the industry continues to proliferate crossover vehicles (UAVs, SUVs, and so on) in the name of customer choice, finding ways to absorb the cost of lower per-model sales is important, and platform strategies are quite significant to this. As can be seen in figure 14.4, the number of vehicles/body types per platform has been steadily increasing, and this has resulted in an increase in the average production volume per platform, thus offsetting reductions in volumes per body type and model. From 1990 to 2002, the number of body types per platform for eight vehicle manufacturers operating in Europe increased from 1.5 to 3.9, while volumes per body style dropped from 129,000 to

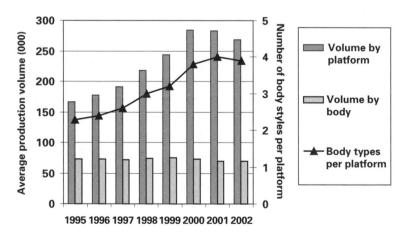

Figure 14.4
Model proliferation and platform use in Europe, 1995–2002 (eight manufacturers).

69,000. However, because of the increase in body styles per platform, average platform volume increased by more than 40 percent over the same time period. These trends are expected to continue. For example, Volkswagen's new PQ35 platform, host of the Audi A3 and the Golf V, is forecast to exceed annual production volumes of 2 million vehicles by 2007. Other companies are taking similar measures. General Motors is cutting its passenger car platforms from 13 in 2000 to 7 in 2005, and Nissan and Renault are moving to 10 shared platforms.[10] Nissan alone had 24 platforms in 1999.[11]

Although platform leveraging takes some of the pressure off suppliers to achieve economies of scale, manufacturers must be careful not to overuse it. As recent criticism in the motor vehicle press shows, manufacturers are concerned that brand differentiation will be harder if platforms are shared across brands. Volkswagen's A04 platform, for example, is shared across not only the models mentioned earlier, but also the Seat Toledo, Leon, and Skoda Octavia models.

Toward Mutability

Although the framework shows this as one strategy, it is really the beginning of a fortunate chain reaction. Mutability means that the support structure can, unaltered, accommodate the variety of options specific to a vehicle. Mutable support structures, for example, offer extreme flexibility because although they have standardized and generic interfaces, they do not require standardized parts. Production is happy because the plant can rapidly swap one support structure for another, which makes the assembly sequence more predictable and stable. Customers are happy because they get what they want. Suppliers are happy because they can deliver components according to stable assembly sequence.

Leveraging mutability involves reducing BIW variants or adapting other support structures (e.g., wiring harnesses). It also decouples assembly. With fewer BIW variants, the plant can separate body and paint from assembly and use an interim painted-body store to house bodies that are ready to be customized. A decoupled system lets the manufacturer assign orders much later in the process.

Companies that are adopting build-to-order will find that this combination is a powerful tool for reducing internal variety, while maintaining an acceptable level of external variety. Mutable support structures are of little benefit to a build-to-forecast system. The entire point of mutability and decreased internal variety is to implement customer responsiveness across the value grid. The expense of building mutable support structures is hardly worth it without that perspective. Let us look in more detail at efforts to enhance mutability.

Mutable Support Structures

Many manufacturers are opting to make major components mutable. The wiring harness is only one example. Other manufacturers have chosen to reduce the number of BIW variants or to use a different body shell, such as a space frame. All these structures help reduce internal variety.

Example: Wiring Harness

The wiring harness connects all the car's electric items. It consists of several incredible lengths of cable, often unique to that vehicle, which workers must assemble manually in a long, tedious process. Because of the task's labor-intensive nature, assembly plants tend to outsource the making of wiring harnesses to low-wage countries. This decision is short sighted because the penalty for doing so is a very long lead time: The build program must be decided as long as 6 weeks in advance to make sure that the vehicle has the right harness when it is built.

Almost all assembly plants manage at least 19 types of wire harnesses and most have many more. They can generally be tweaked to accept specific combinations of options, but do not tolerate order swapping unless the same combination is involved, which is highly unlikely. Thus, in a build-to-order system, if the harness has problems, the customer waits. This is less of an issue for a build-to-forecast system, where finished products wait for customers.

Manufacturers are addressing the wiring-harness problem in various ways. For some of its products, Volvo is working on reducing the number of harnesses so that they can handle any combination of electrical components. For some products, Volvo's European customers can alter electrical options via their dealer up to 4 hours before the vehicle enters the assembly line. Volvo's success proves that the wiring harness need not limit the level of variety that can be offered, nor be a bottleneck in customization.

Some companies have solved the problem by doing away with the harness. Peugeot relies on multiplexing in its luxury 607, replacing the entire cable structure with a networked bus system, just like a computer bus. Electrical elements are connected to a vehicle-wide common bus system, rather than through individual connections or cables.

Again, we see the success of looking at product complexity in a holistic way. A mutable wiring harness or multiplexed bus is certainly more complex from a design standpoint, and the harness is even more expensive to produce because the cable has excess wires and connectors for options that might not be installed. Still, the reduced internal variety lets manufacturers accept order changes late in the order-to-delivery cycle and easily swap options.

Simplifying BIWs

In this strategy, rather than assign specific BIWs to orders, the manufacturer adapts a set of standard BIWs to fit each model's design. A production engineer of a European manufacturer told us that having simpler BIWs worked well for his company. With fewer painted body variants, the plant could assign painted bodies to the most urgent customer orders and increase delivery within the acceptable time window.

BMW recently announced that it would reduce the number of BIW variations from 40,000 (3-series) to 16 (new 3-series E46) to reduce its internal variety.[12]

Although some manufacturers believe that assigning specific BIWs to orders (staying with the traditional system) puts more pressure on the plant for continuous improvement, we disagree. As we described earlier, we found the body shops' average first-time-OK rate (percentage of BIWs not needing repair) was 94–97 percent, and the paint shops' average was a disappointing 83–87 percent. (See chapter 3.) In simpler terms, 20 percent of vehicles don't make it through the body and paint shop without corrective repair. If customer orders are tied to specific BIWs that cannot be substituted, those orders are delayed.

Of course, each BIW design must be well thought out, since one BIW might have to accommodate a range of engine variations, options, and so on. However, the benefit of far simpler logistics and manufacturing processes for the build-to-order system as a whole makes a more complex design seem trivial. One manager at a US vehicle manufacturer was particularly enthusiastic,

"We had serious trouble achieving a stable assembly sequence, which affected the delivery reliability to the customer. With the reduction in BIW derivatives, we can use the painted body store to restore the correct order, even if an order gets delayed in the body or paint shop. That way, we can achieve almost 100 percent reliability of the originally planned sequence."

Space Frames

Much of the motor vehicle industry thinks the space frame is a new invention and that models such as the recent Fiat Multipla, Renault Espace, and aluminum-built Audi A2 and A8 are some of the first to use it for volume applications. Actually, Saturn introduced the space frame in the 1980s. While valuable in principle, the space frame concept was not compatible with the rest of GM's vehicle design approach and thus fell from favor when the company began building new products that leveraged GM designs.

A space frame and a monocoque differ structurally. A monocoque's outer skin is structural and must provide a certain strength for impact integrity and passenger protection. As a result, it is generally steel. (In some high-end products, it is aluminum.) In contrast, a space frame's skin is nonstructural. A structural frame supports outer panels, which can be of almost any material—steel, aluminum, even plastic.

The space frame is a promising alternative to the monocoque. First, it lets plants bring customization closer to the customer because the plant can clip on the colored body panels even after most of the product is complete. As a result, the customer can choose the vehicle color very late in the process. The actual frame is the same across a range of vehicles, which gives a lot of flexibility in assigning orders to vehicles. Saturn paints the load-bearing frame black and installs the colored plastic panels only at the end of the assembly line. This has the added benefit of reduced paint scratching in assembly.

Second, by using a space frame the manufacturer can add flexibility within the product's life cycle. The MCC Smart, for example, has two basic colors for its partially visible frame, and customers can choose from a range of colored panels. Because the dealership can replace these panels within 90 minutes, customers can change the color of their vehicle very easily. Being able to alter the vehicle's exterior look with no change to its core is an attractive way to provide greater dynamic variety.

Finally, because they can use different materials, space frames offer the opportunity to selectively reduce vehicle weight and improve fuel consumption. The Volkswagen Phaeton, which uses a steel monocoque, and the Audi A8, which uses an aluminum space frame, are roughly the same size (differing by only 4 millimeters) and share a significant number of parts—same all-wheel drive system and almost identical suspension. Yet the aluminum A8 weighs 1,780 kilograms and the steel Phaeton 2,319 kg—an astonishing 539-kg difference. On average, every 100 kg of curb weight increases fuel consumption by 0.1 liter per 100 kilometers.

Decoupled Assembly

In a decoupled system, as figure 14.5 shows, the painted-body store separates body and paint processes from assembly. The result is increased throughput reliability because if one BIW doesn't make it through the paint process, the plant can quickly substitute another one.

A decoupled system works roughly like this: The manufacturer does not send customers' orders into the body shop, as in the traditional system; instead orders are sent to a special painted body store governed by an automatic storage and retrieval system. The painted body store can hold as many as several hundred car bodies. Even with a few BIW variants and 10 to 15 colors, the plant can quickly make virtually any shell that might be needed. Thus, when an order for a blue three-door car comes in, the plant pulls a blue three-door body from the painted body

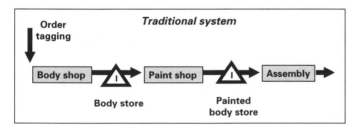

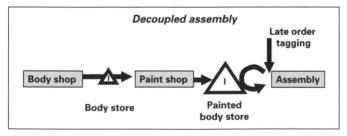

Figure 14.5
Order tagging in traditional system and in a system that decouples body-shop and paint-shop processes from assembly and implements late order tagging.

store, which signals other parts of the value grid to replenish the store. The replenishment follows the *kanban* supermarket principle[13]: Removing one item off the shelf triggers a "pull" signal into the grid to obtain replenishment. As the figure shows, order tagging is delayed until the vehicle enters the assembly track, which means that customer orders drive the assembly sequence.

Apart from flexibility, a decoupled system solves another major problem in current vehicle assembly operations: how to deal with an unpredictable assembly sequence. Unpredictability occurs for two reasons: efficiency strategies such as batching and line balancing dictate changes, and rework levels, especially in the paint shop, throw off the original sequence.

In a build-to-order system, the manufacturer must be able to tell customers when their cars are actually ready. A decoupled system stabilizes the assembly sequence, and a stable sequence is paramount to making a build-to-order system work. Several manufacturers have recognized this relationship and are working hard to make the needed changes. BMW's reduction in BIW variants was part of a larger strategy to create mutable body shells that would let the plant resequence body and paint activities and delay the customization for a customer order to where it enters the final assembly process—essentially implementing the decoupled system in figure 14.4.

A variant of the completely decoupled system is *volume-based* decoupling. The basic flow is the same except that final order tagging occurs at the exit of the painted body storage, at the entrance to assembly. Yet the paint shop and the body shop are driven by a separate schedule that aggregates the volumes of bodies that make up the assembly sequence. Thus, in volume-based decoupling, individual orders do not determine the schedules for paint and body (such as "make a red three-door with sunroof"); schedules are based on volume ("make X number of three-doors with a sunroof and Y without"). The idea is to build in a certain flexibility for swapping orders if a quality issue causes a delay. The overall flexibility is far less than that in a complete decoupling scenario, however.

Modularity and Outsourcing

The use of modular components and the outsourcing of production are neither new ideas nor exclusive to the motor vehicle industry. Computer hardware manufacturers, for example, combine diverse components with few compatibility issues thanks to standardized protocols and interfaces.

Modularity arose in part because more vehicle manufacturers began outsourcing production in an attempt to convert their fixed costs to variable, to lower labor cost, and to leverage economies of scale at suppliers. The larger economies of scale across fewer first-tier suppliers have resulted in simpler assembly and logistics operations, since the manufacturer's assembly plant ends up dealing with less complexity.

Thus, modularity not only reduces design complexity, but also helps simplify the manufacturing process by shifting complexity off the main assembly line into subassembly lines where variability is less critical. Subassembly lines are in essence separate from the main lines, so anything that happens there tends not to affect the broader production process as severely. The plant can also test subassemblies before inserting them into the main production process. Thus, for example, the whole dashboard assembly can be tested while its subcomponents are still accessible—something that is much more challenging when the dashboard is embedded in the vehicle.

Many have hailed modularity (often coupled with outsourcing) as a solution for all ills: A select group of trusted suppliers provide a dozen or so modules per vehicle. These suppliers often reside in a supplier park adjacent to the assembly plant or (when union rules permit) in the plant. It is, then, easy for suppliers to produce and transport the modules as the assembly sequence requires. It is a great vision, and sensible, too, so why are initial enthusiasts, like Ford, hastily backpedaling on their strategies to "completely modularize the next-generation vehicles"?

The short answer is that it is too much work with too little measurable return.[14] Modularity requires both standard interfaces and mutable support structures, and the module design doesn't always deliver dramatic reductions in manufacturing complexity. As figure 14.6 shows, most of the plants participating in the 2000 study of global assembly plants bought the left front headlight, parking light, and turn signal as one integrated piece—neat, clean, and predictable. On the other hand, the number of fastening points for the headlight varied dramatically, from three to more than ten, so why have an integrated module? Manufacturing complexity doesn't go down because production must still deal with the fastening points.

This example is one of many that suggest companies are failing to look at design from a manufacturing standpoint, but have simply relied on outsourcing to work out the kinks. When manufacturers make

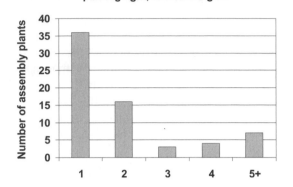

Number of components
in front left headlight (high/low),
parking light, and turn signal

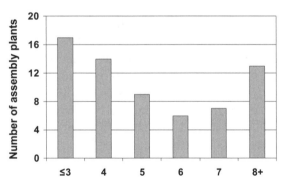

Fastening points
for front left headlight (high/low),
parking light, and turn signal

Figure 14.6
Number of components in a left headlight purchased by plants and number of fastening points in assembly, including components assembled either on a main line or in a subassembly area. Data from Global Assembly Plant Study.

outsourcing decisions without considering the full system, unhealthy dynamics ensue.

Modularity and outsourcing can set up some unpleasant and precarious situations. Suppliers end up with a much larger design role and consequently more long-term bargaining power. Manufacturers end up wondering if they'll be locked into the same supplier. Intier, for example, will supply complete interior modules for the 6-series and the new

Figure 14.7
How outsourcing affects employment at manufacturers and suppliers, and the labor-cost differential that drives it.

Cabriolet. Intier already supplies the entire Mini interior, apart from the seats.[15] Being in such a position is very different from being "just another seat supplier."[16]

The main reason manufacturers give for outsourcing of their activities is difference in labor cost between manufacturer and supplier.[17] As figure 14.7 shows, while outsourcing has certainly boosted the number of supplier employees, wages have not increased proportionally. This does not mean that suppliers do not face some labor cost challenges. For example, as we saw earlier, when suppliers are pressured into co-locating with vehicle manufacturers, indivisibilities in management and engineering staff can significantly increase cost. A manager or engineer can service a certain level of production, but below that it is difficult to justify paying a full person.

Although many manufacturers see outsourcing as a way to convert costs from fixed to variable, many suppliers end up with higher capital costs. A module supplier might end up producing the entire dashboard, when it started out producing only the instrument panel. Now that it is supplying modules, it must buy in parts from other suppliers, receiving only a small handling fee. Overall, then, the supplier has taken on more responsibility, but its financial statements are worse than before!

In an unusual move, Toyota decided against outsourcing modules and thus transferring design capabilities to suppliers. Instead it is promoting joint ventures among suppliers and takes equity share in the resulting entity. For example, it created a joint venture between Toyoda Gosei and Horie Metal Co. to set up the FTS Company with the goal of building resin fuel tanks. Toyoda Gosei made resin products, and Horie Metal Co specialized in metal fuel tanks. Toyoda Gosei owns 50 percent of FTS, Horie Metal owns 30 percent, and Toyota owns 20 percent.[18] In this way, Toyota is reducing its in-house design efforts by leveraging supplier know-how, but it still retains significant control over both the innovation process and output.

Focusing on the short term and on what is easy to measure (e.g., labor cost) is a shaky basis for going outsourcing with modularity. On the other hand, modularity's true contributions—simplified production, enhanced quality via testable functions, management of different component life cycles and technologies, etc., have remain unsung.

Late Configuration

As the framework shows, the last two variety-management strategies are considerably less important in a build-to-order system. Late configuration is simply correcting the inability of not being able to make what the customer wanted in the first place. Its sole purpose is to increase external variety, which is not a concern in building to order, since every customer already receives precisely the desired combination. The idea is to add options at a distribution center or dealership rather than at the car factory, thereby giving more choice without incurring more fundamental variety. This strategy works best for easily added features such as radios, alarms, alloy wheels, fog lamps, and body kits.

In Europe, Honda routinely configures body kits, alarms, and trim accessories in its distribution centers. According to its sales and distribution manager, the company sees distribution centers, not just as stock buffers, but as "value-added operations" to configure and prepare vehicles to customer specifications. The company believes the strategy takes complexity out of assembly operations while providing more flexibility in meeting customer requirements. The result is fewer finished product variants in inventory. Other manufacturers were not as optimistic, expressing concern that late configuration might not be of the quality that could be attained in the assembly plant.

For customers, late configuration is largely invisible, although it can sometimes compromise quality. For example, retrofitting sunroofs is problematic because the sealing is often substandard, causing the roofs to leak.

Bundling Options

"If you want fog lights, they come in a package with heated mirrors, and a windshield defogger," says the salesperson to the customer. "Sorry, those aren't available separately." This conversation, or something like it, is common in dealerships around the world. Although manufacturers theoretically offer variety, the customers still aren't getting what they really want. Option bundling, as the framework shows, has no advantage in a build-to-order system.

In a build-to-forecast system, manufacturers use option bundling to reduce forecast error and thus the risk that stock will become obsolete.[19] Again, the focus is on one part of the value grid. Customers dislike option bundling. They do not want all the options and they end up paying for something they do not want. In the long run, how can irritating the customer be profitable?

A Final Word about Variety

In the current forecast-driven model, external variety's leftovers translate to excess stock and discounting, part of the two vicious cycles that erode customer satisfaction and thus profitability. The more variety a manufacturer offers, the more the desired vehicle becomes the proverbial needle in the haystack. And even with the lowest number of variants, the haystack is too big to fit into a distribution center, which means that customers have slim to no chance of finding the needle—the precise combination of features they desire.[20]

In a build-to-order system, variety is managed holistically across the value grid. The customer specifies his or her desired vehicle and the manufacturer implements strategies that preserve customer choice without burdening production unnecessarily.

I've got my head in the freezer and my feet in the oven, but on average the temperature is quite pleasant here.

—folk saying

Delivering the most vehicles at the lowest cost has been the operating principle of vehicle assembly plants since their conception. Decades later, plants still strive to attain and leverage scale. It is what they do—not because it is a well-thought-out strategy but because they have been carefully programmed to repeat an ingrained pattern. Volume, as we described earlier, has always been the shining prize, awarded to those who can squeeze the last bit of capacity from their facilities. Manufacturers raise the bar, and plants oblige by accepting the *minimum* efficient scale of 200,000 vehicles per annum.

The problem is that companies rarely attain the right volume. The minimum scale soars, demand shifts, inventories grow, incentives are offered, customers grudgingly drive the cars off the lot, and everyone goes home happy that sales are up.

Not that volume per se is a bad thing—in theory, economies of scale can do wonders for a bottom line—but the emphasis on capacity use has blinded manufacturers to volume's darker side. There is volume that responds to natural customer demand, and then there is volume pumped up by sales incentives. Thus, when analysts come to the earth-shaking insight that high capacity use is a main determinant of profitability,[1] we have to say "That depends on what you're using the capacity for." In 2002, sales were decent and capacity use was good in most factories, but on average the industry paid $1,873 in incentives per vehicle in the United States, and the average of each of the Big Three exceeded $2,300.[2] So the savings from higher capacity use and economies of scale went to subsidizing product sales. Would the same analysts agree that robbing Peter to pay Paul is a sustainable business model?

Fortunately, the industry is waking up, and critics of the mass-production logic are becoming more numerous. Many realize that such a static and inflexible model clashes horribly with the dynamic characteristics of the present-day market. The world is on Internet time, and the motor vehicle industry is back in the 1920s. Monolithic factories that push out finished vehicles restrict opportunities for innovation, customer responsiveness, and employee development. They simply cannot respond quickly enough to market change, and their rigid cost structure makes it difficult to modify volumes as demand changes. The only good thing about them is they force companies to think about managing scale more intelligently.

The Cost of Change

Part of the impetus for rethinking scale is that capacity alterations come with a serious cost penalty. As table 15.1 shows, running an automobile assembly plant at 50 percent capacity for one year costs on average 76 percent of full-capacity operating costs. The average cost of running at 50 percent capacity for one week is even higher, almost 80 percent of full-capacity operating costs. This explains the strong incentive not to reduce capacity use when demand drops, but rather to push volumes out and gamble that—despite costly incentives—the resulting sales will help cover the fixed cost. And demand variations *are* frequent. Not only do vehicle sales follow a seasonal pattern; demand for a particular vehicle shifts considerably over the vehicle's life cycle.

Table 15.1
Costs of capacity-use change over one year and one week (means representing total costs, including direct costs such as labor and indirect costs such as plant and equipment).

Capacity level	Change	
	Over year	Over week
50%	75.5%	78.7%
80%	90.0%	92.2%
100%	100%	100%
110%	105.1%	106.1%

How does an inflexible factory cope with fluctuating demand? As the quote at the beginning of this chapter implies, some plants run over capacity, others run under, but the averages look good, so no one complains.

This strategy is prevalent in North American factories, not because managers cannot plan capacity properly, but because a factory running close to capacity tempts the company to build a new one. The reasoning goes something like this: The company sees that the plant is working at 80 percent capacity, assumes that demand will increase and render its current production capacity insufficient, so it decides to build another plant before that happens. With this capacity management strategy, small wonder that no one gets the full-capacity-use prize and that demand rarely catches up.

Figure 15.1 shows capacity use across 19 assembly plants over time for one vehicle manufacturer. It was pointless to include any others: not only would the graph be unreadable, the results would be no different. For all assembly plants, use varies dramatically over time, even within the same company, and the dramatic variations come with equally dramatic costs, including overtime expense, underused equipment, unstable stock flows, and layoffs.

In short, volume flexibility is a product of many factors, not just labor cost per vehicle, and until companies understand those factors, they cannot effectively balance capacity use across facilities.

In a build-to-order system, volume flexibility is critical. A forecast-driven system can stabilize volumes using forecast orders, but a

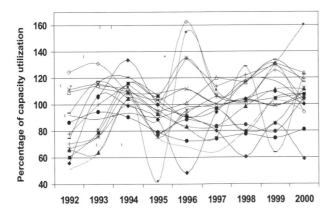

Figure 15.1
Capacity use in 19 plants for one manufacturer, 1992–2000. Data Source: *Automotive News Data Book*, various years.

demand-driven system must follow demand's rises and falls, which makes it extremely vulnerable to drops in capacity use. Manufacturers told us that this vulnerability poses the greatest financial risk and the greatest operational challenge in adopting a build-to-order system. The response to that is that any production system is vulnerable if demand drops, whether it stockpiles products or builds to order.

Being able to manage short-term variability in demand is crucial, and manufacturers who aspire to volume flexibility often have similar goals: to maintain efficient production and to be elastic enough to change production volume on short notice. These goals translate into two interrelated strategies: to increase responsiveness at the factory level and to manage demand flow. The first strategy addresses workforce flexibility and suppliers, which have the same volume rigidities as the assembly plants. The second strategy addresses seasonal swings in demand, which can be significant for some companies. The Italian motorcycle maker Ducati experiences sales swings of 5:1 throughout the year, for example.

Working with Reality

Perhaps the most important goal in volume flexibility is to stop and think about scale as it affects the value grid within the constraints of the infrastructure already in place. Despite our earlier description of large factories as being out of step with modern markets, we are not advocating that they disappear overnight. Not all large-scale operations are dinosaurs, and smaller operations are not the comprehensive solution in the hyperlinked digital age. The truth is more complex than such polarization; it requires not that manufacturers rush from one end of the spectrum to the other, but that they pause and consider what scale means to the entire value grid.

In other words, manage production scale intelligently. Do not subscribe to narrow-focus thinking about volume. The industry is rife with "good ideas," and some have elements worth considering, but no single idea should be taken as a complete solution. Some suggest that car dealers could become micro-factories, locally assembling vehicles to customer order, for example.[3] With the sunk costs of existing facilities, liability issues, and supply-chain efficiencies, micro-factories are neither practical nor feasible. However, the spirit of the idea—bringing customization closer to the customer—is worth pursuing. Likewise, manufacturers must understand where scale is needed in the value grid and where they can attain responsiveness by sacrificing scale economies.

Manufacturers cannot be lazy about looking for ways to manage scale. They must look relentlessly both inside and outside—at small competitors, supply-chain partners, customers, and so on—to identify opportunities to create volume flexibility. Suppliers, for example, have the same volume rigidities as the factories. To address this, some manufacturers have begun to insert volume- flexibility windows in their contracts. These windows give them room to change the amount purchased without cost penalty, but the percentage they can change varies with time. For example, the manufacturer can change an amount by only 5 percent if the supplier has only a week's notice, 10 percent with 2 weeks' notice, and 20 percent with a month's notice. Without some imposed flexibility requirement on the supply base, measures to implement volume flexibility at the assembly plant will not be very effective. Toyota is a case in point. Its build-to-order efforts are constrained by its rigid scheduling in Japan. Its contracts with suppliers specify maximum weekly schedule fluctuations of 10 percent, which enables stable *kanban* links to the supplier yet does not allow the flexibility needed to build the majority of vehicles to customer order on short notice.

Building knowledge, getting closer to customers, developing managerial talent and monitoring technological change are all important reasons to consider smaller operations, but they add value only if they become part of a company's overall strategy to manage scale.

The Power of Small Scale[4]

One way to manage demand and to increase responsiveness at the factory level is to integrate large and small operations. The concept of minimum efficient scale has biased industries to think that bigger is better and biggest is best. Every year, integrated steel mills should produce more than 5 million tons of steel, beer breweries should churn out 8 to 15 million barrels, and automotive factories should build 200,000 vehicles. The message is that facilities and operations smaller than the current yearly magic number are not cost effective and hence not commercially viable.

But small-scale operations have advantages that larger facilities cannot provide to the same degree. One is that smaller operations give companies the *flexibility to be creative* when responding to the needs of both industrial clients and end customers. PPG's satellite plants (see chapter 12) aimed to create stronger relationships in the highly competitive market for automotive glass. Its small-scale facilities, with fewer than 100 employees each, provide just-in-time sequencing to automotive assembly factories. These small-scale plants are now critical to ensuring capacity use at the much larger float glass and fabrication plants that produce windshields and other automotive glass products. This capacity use is critical to the larger plants, which are both scale-intensive and capital-intensive.

PPG's proximity to the businesses it supplies has been a boon for everyone involved. PPG has benefited from having a better understanding of its customers' needs, thus increasing the likelihood that relationships will last over the long term. The vehicle manufacturers benefit because they can move labor-intensive assembly tasks to a lower-cost supplier and reduce the logistical and managerial complexity of handling the integration activities in house.

For end customers, small operations are equally effective. German auto manufacturers had long faced the problem of how to decrease shipping time to Japanese customers. Their solution was to leverage small-scale facilities in South Africa originally built to bypass South African import duties and begin producing right-hand-drive vehicles. DaimlerChrysler's East London plant in South Africa produces all right-hand-drive vehicles for the Mercedes-Benz C-Class models, and BMW's Rosslyn Plant produces 3-series cars for export to Japan, Taiwan, Singapore, New Zealand, Hong Kong, and Australia. Producing in low volumes in South Africa shaves a week off shipping time to Japan and the rest of Asia.

Small-scale facilities are also uniquely suited to *react to market demand* and to *manage lower-demand product variants that do not justify the use of large-scale facilities*. Japanese manufacturers commonly use parts makers to assemble vehicles, thereby using supplier capacity to meet customer demand. We found more than 20 such assemblers producing a variety of cars, trucks, and RVs under the umbrella of large manufacturers. Relationships with these small-scale producers are tight, and the supplier often benefits from the exchange. In 1992, for example, Mazda asked Kurata to produce the AZ1 two-seater at its Yano plant, with a target volume of only 1,000 vehicles per month. When demand collapsed in June 1993, Mazda canceled AZ1 production, but Kurata continued to be a Mazda supplier. Although Kurata had been building Mazda vehicles only a short time, the production opportunity at this low scale greatly strengthened its engineering and manufacturing capabilities, which in turn increased its value as a traditional supplier for Mazda.

Japanese manufacturers have taken great pains to ensure that only companies within their *keiretsu* (enterprise group) undertake small-scale production. The risk of not doing so is that other companies will gain too much knowledge about the manufacturer's products. For example, the small-scale operator Karmann produces fewer than 60,000 cars per year but is responsible for a variety of high-end niche products for several manufacturers.[5] Consequently, Karmann has built up specific expertise in small-scale manufacturing approaches, such as the use of plastic rather than metal tools and dies for small stamping runs. And it is taking on more and more engineering tasks.

A less threatening side of growing expertise is that it is *easier to find and develop talent*. Individual small-scale operations are less critical to overall corporate performance, so the manufacturer risks little in letting managers prove themselves, and the manager is highly visible. It is easier to screen a younger managerial cohort than to sift through teams of managerial candidates that have evolved along the longer career paths typical of a larger facility. For example, many senior managers have proved their skills at the small operations in South Africa. Keith Butler-Wheelhouse became president of Saab after a stint in South Africa and is now CEO of Smiths Industries. Jürgen Schrempp went on to be CEO of DaimlerChrysler, Carl-Peter Forster became CEO of Opel AG, and Bernd Pischetsrieder progressed to CEO of Volkswagen AG—impressive results for managers of operations that together produced only as much as an average-size auto factory in the United States or Europe.

A third advantage of small-scale operations is that they can *tap into labor markets without disrupting them*. A large automotive assembly factory employs more than 5,000 employees. Hiring enough workers within commuting distance strains local labor markets, resulting in increased wages. Smaller scale not only lets firms "cherry pick" labor from competing markets; it also provides more variety in choosing an operations site. Smaller-scale operations effectively diffuse union power, although we do not advocate that companies use them for that purpose alone. Mini-mills such as Nucor, Chaparral Steel, and Florida Steel are an example—their lower labor needs, coupled with the conscious locating of facilities in right-to-work states, have prevented unionization. The result is more flexible work rules and efficient labor use through extensive performance-based pay.

Finally, by examining small-scale activities that others are experimenting with and establishing small facilities in "hot spots," companies can *uncover radically new technologies and managerial approaches*. Forming alliances and buying small-scale innovators outright are ways to evaluate this new knowledge. The manufacturer can also look at other parts of its established value grid. Is it leveraging all the capabilities of its smaller operations?

Although these advantages seem obvious, many companies won't implement small-scale operations unless they can plainly see financial benefit. The intent of the facilities in South Africa, for example, was to serve the South African region and bypass import duties, not to groom stellar talent. Companies cite many reasons for their reluctance: "We cannot divide our labor talent and equipment." "Our flow processes will be destroyed." "More competitors will enter the market." (The last reason alludes to the belief that scale economies bar new entrants: if the minimum efficient scale already meets the demand, new production capacity will drive product prices below the new entrant's unit cost.) These reasons flow from a misunderstanding that operations must be all large or all small. This is not managing scale intelligently. And some of the reasons are no longer valid: technology is breaking down the labor indivisibility obstacle, for example, and companies can reduce labor costs by sharing engineering talent across multiple facilities.

Many companies have built their success on rethinking scale, and they keep on doing so. Nucor is now experimenting with even smaller facilities that directly cast molten steel into its final shape and thickness, bypassing the need for any rolling at all. That process would further reduce energy costs and the need for capital equipment. The company believes that it will be able to run mills that are one-eighth the size of the current mini-mills, and that in the long run it will be able to co-locate these smaller facilities with large customers.

Workforce Planning

Another way to manage scale intelligently is to remove the financial pressure to keep the factory going at the same rate all year. The workforce is an important part of why a factory succeeds (labor costs are the lion's share of operating expense), yet in addressing capacity use many manufacturers focus only on process inefficiencies. Thinking of ways to reduce labor costs, other than simply laying off workers, seems to be a distant priority.

Some factories, mostly in Europe, use hours banks, in which workers agree to put in so many hours per year and within agreed-on limits can work those hours according to demand. Thus, they might work more hours during high-demand periods and, rather than receive overtime pay, work fewer hours at other times. The hours bank reduces the impact of demand swings on labor costs and eliminates the need for costly overtime or for untrained temporary workers (who might compromise quality). Unfortunately, because of differences in national laws, only 30 percent of global assembly plants can have an hours bank.

A related strategy to reduce labor costs is to shift labor across the company to meet volume variability. BMW, for example, can shift a group of trained agency workers across multiple plants in Germany to meet shifts in demand for products from each facility.

Outside the automotive sector are other interesting approaches to flexing labor resources. A classic example is Mettler-Toledo, a Swiss-American joint venture that makes industrial scales. Mettler-Toledo is the market leader for weighing instruments for laboratories, industrial use, and food retailers. It provides a textbook case of how an integrated workforce can provide volume flexibility and enable adoption of a build-to-order strategy.

In the mid 1980s, Mettler was managed like most manufacturing organizations, with rigid production programming and lots of finished stock in the warehouse. Profitability was lacking, and development times exceeded 2 years. In 1986, facing bankruptcy, the company introduced an ambitious manufacturing strategy to produce scales solely to order. It simplified production and outsourced bits that were not critical to former employees who had formed specialized supplier companies. Because scales were not coming from component stock, integration with the new suppliers had to be tight.

The human side of this strategy was even more innovative. Mettler realized that its workforce had to be motivated and flexible to achieve the desired turnaround. The company empowered employees to come and go at their leisure. They had to be present only during 4 common hours each workday and no more than 10 hours. Apart from monthly constraints, it was up to each employee to decide when he or she needed to work.[6] The results are amazing: During high demand, the product-development team pulls together to help meet volume needs, so the plant can shift its capacity use from 50 percent to 160 percent with minimal notice. Performance-based pay helps ensure that every employee has an incentive to keep the system working. Absenteeism is 3 percent in Mettler's German plant (unheard of in other German manufacturing businesses), and the firm is consistently profitable.

Wearing Many Hats

The twin of managing scale is managing demand, and one way to manage demand is to diversify production plants. The idea is to have large, efficient, but less flexible plants supplying the base-line demand while potentially higher cost flexible plants cater to demand fluctuations on the margin. The flexible plants can also manufacture products whose volumes do not justify dedicated facilities.

The extremely inflexible steel industry offers an interesting example of successful plant diversification. Steel making is a sequence of three processes: sintering iron ore, coke, and limestone; producing iron in a blast furnace; and turning the iron into steel by reducing its oxygen content. The steel is then cast and rolled into sheets, beams, or wire. The rigidities of these processes severely restrict the industry's ability to respond to demand swings. To address this problem, large steel firms have begun relying on mini-mills. These provide additional volume and cast specialist grades of steel, while the large mills produce major volumes and large orders. Mini-mills melt down scrap steel, but lack the sintering plant and blast furnace needed to make the iron at large mills. The mini-mills cannot meet all the demand for steel or make all varieties, but they give large mills a way to cope with demand swings and variety.[7]

Another approach is to use "swing plants," which manage deviations on the margin from forecast demand. In the textile industry, swing plants are purposely close to the customer base, generally in higher-wage locales. In the auto industry, swing plants that produce the variable component of demand are located in countries that have generous policies toward subsidizing worker salaries when plants are not operational.

Other companies specifically design plants to manage large quantities of low-volume products. The Nissan Revival Plan reduces variety and increases volumes at most factories while maintaining one plant that manages most low-volume variety. Nissan's Shatai plant will be managing eight platforms, while the other Nissan plants in Japan will manage between one and three platforms each.

Time-Based Pricing

Managing demand also means intelligently gauging what the customer will pay. Differentiated pricing is common in service sectors and is usually related to the urgency a customer expresses. Getting photographs developed in an hour should cost more than getting them in 3 days, which cost more than 10-day mail service, for example. In other words, customers select a price-responsiveness tradeoff they find acceptable.

Air travel is another example. If you want to fly to New York tomorrow, you will most likely pay the full ticket price. If you book a month in advance, you get a better price. If you go stand-by on the day of departure, you might get an even better deal.

To explore the price variation for a single flight relative to booking time, we tracked four economy return flights on a route in Europe and one in the United States. We looked at British Airways from London to Hamburg and one of its discount airline competitors, Ryanair, on a similar routing. Likewise, we looked at American Airlines from New York to Oakland, and collected similar information for its discount airline competitor JetBlue.

As figure 15.2 shows, this comparison was not as straightforward as we expected.[8] First, no airline uses a standard linear pricing model, whereby the flight simply becomes more expensive the closer the booking is to the flight date. Instead the companies continuously adjust airfares according to demand and available flight capacity. Consequently,

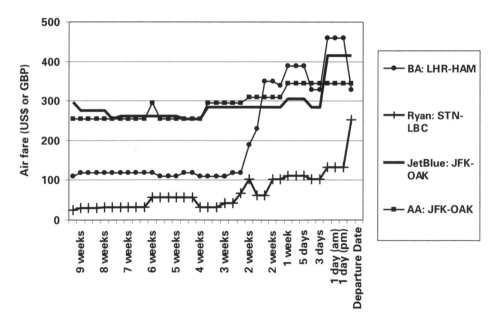

Figure 15.2
Air-fare pricing relative to booking time for four flights. Source: each airline's online reservation site.

overall revenue generated from available capacity was the critical factor, not capacity use itself. The lesson here is that full capacity does not equal maximum revenue; sometimes, maximum revenue comes from selling less for more.

Indeed, British Airways expects to gain an extra 3–7 percent in revenue by continually altering its product offering and pricing; some of its competitors believe they can achieve up to 10 percent.[9] And their expectations *are* realistic. A typical European short-haul flight has nine major pricing categories, which can yield more than 100 ticket prices for the same flight. Thus, any two people on the same flight are likely to pay different prices for the same service.

Dell Computer simultaneously manages both demand and supply. It works closely with its corporate customers to manage demand, and tries to anticipate and cater to large orders. Dell also gets direct feedback from its suppliers about available capacities and potential problems. If one supplier indicates a capacity problem with a 60-GB hard drive, for example, Dell can alter the prices and make the 80-GB hard drive more attractive. That way, customers are much more likely to choose the 80-GB drive, thereby alleviating the volume constraint.

In the motor vehicle industry, sales are price sensitive only to the extent that some promotion forces them to be. Customers who do not succumb to the promotion or incentive are punished twice—first by paying full list price and second by having to wait several months for the vehicle. The mindset that drives these promotions and incentives is "We must maintain recommended retail pricing." The company believes it cannot lower retail prices when demand is low because, once it lowers the retail price, it can never raise the price again without negative publicity. The only strategy left is to lower retail price through incentives. The customer pays the nominal price, and "cash backs" and other direct and indirect payments make up the discount.

A build-to-order system offers far more opportunities to use a time-based pricing structure because there is no need to reactively manage the disposal of excess inventory. Moreover, such a structure lets the manufacturer keep the factory's capacity use at acceptable levels. This does *not* mean that prices must always be so low that the factory runs at 100 percent capacity all the time. At the heart of volume flexibility is finding the volume that gives you the most revenue, not the one that gives you the cheapest factory. Selling cars below cost, as is common today, is not a long-term sustainable solution.[10] Strategies centered on discounting to attain volume eventually backfire, and there is no way a production system can succeed without sustained demand for the product.

Time-based price structuring can take several forms. Order slotting, which we discussed in chapter 10, is a possibility. The price then depends on when the slot is scheduled. Products ordered well in advance will be cheaper, since they create long-term demand visibility, which in turn helps manufacturers manage and smooth capacity use in assembly and the supply chain. Passing these savings on to the customer encourages the most beneficial flow of demand: a production slot for delivery in a week could be at 100 percent of the list price, a slot a month out could be at 97.5 percent, and a slot even further out might be as low as 95 percent.

Of course these strategies assume that the industry will finally migrate from reactively managing stock to actively managing demand and in the process rid itself of the notion that unit cost is a critical internal measure of profit. The current accounting sleight of hand is an amazing feat. In this trick, a vehicle becomes revenue the moment it leaves the assembly line, yet months after counting the revenue from the "sold" vehicle the manufacturer is paying to get rid of the same vehicle through incentives, discounts, and marketing gimmicks.

Smoothing Orders

Demand management assumes that the company knows its customers and what they expect. Everyone likes to chat about this topic, and most discussion is based on two assumptions: that all orders are the same and that all customers need the same level of service.

Both assumptions are false. In reality, customers fall into many distinct groups, as table 15.2 shows. These different groups present a significant opportunity to achieve volume stability through the judicious management of different customer types. The manufacturer can buffer high-margin orders from private customers who want their vehicles "yesterday" with predictable and stable orders, which are not so time critical yet which potentially offer more demand visibility. Similarly, export orders from distant destinations are another base load for the order portfolio. Export orders can be used to smooth the regional order flow, as both Toyota in Japan and Volvo in Europe have discovered. Toyota builds 60 percent of its vehicles to order, and Volvo approaches 80 percent on certain models.[11]

Table 15.2
Segmentation of new vehicle orders for UK volume car segment.*

Type of customer	Typical volume	Current discounts	Can be postponed?
Private retail	40%	0–10%	With discounts
Retail fleet	20%	10–20%	Negotiable
Direct fleet	25%	30–40%	Negotiable
Employees	10%	15–20%	Yes
Demo and showroom	5%	—	Yes (short term)

*The data were assembled from various interviews at vehicle manufacturers and further secondary sources (*Automotive News Europe, Automotive World*). This table is an illustrative example—the segmentation will differ considerably by vehicles and segments. Compact and mid-size segments generally show a far higher fleet content than smaller vehicles, for example.

Fleet orders also provide opportunities for order smoothing. A large volume goes to fleet orders for rental companies, large corporations with a mobile sales force, government purchases, and the like. In Germany in 2002, for example, 26 percent of all new cars were sold to companies (as opposed to private households), and a further 8 percent of sales went to car rental companies.[12]

Here, the actual lead time is not always critical. We found that 75 percent of fleet managers would accept a 2-week window of delivery for each batch of new cars as long as they had a few days' notice of the actual delivery time. Only 16 percent found this unacceptable. (The rest responded "don't know.") Of those accepting the manufacturer-specified delivery date, almost 40 percent said that the delivery should then happen on that date with no further delays. The burden is then on manufacturers to improve processes so that they can meet specific delivery dates.

Orders from employees provide similar opportunities for smoothing. We were surprised to learn that a huge percentage of vehicle sales go to the manufacturer's employees and employees of their suppliers. For Ford this percentage is estimated at 15–20; for Mercedes and BMW it is estimated at more than 20. Substantial sales discounts are granted to employees—often as high as 15–20 percent of the sales price. So employees buy or lease the new cars at the discount rate, and manufacturers push volume without straining the vehicle's brand image through discounting to private buyers or pre-registering[13] or auctioning them off.

Because employee sales account for such large volumes,[14] why not continue to sell cars to employees at discounted rates but, in return, ask employees for some delivery flexibility? Why not ask that they be willing to pull forward or postpone exact delivery times to make way for urgent private customer orders that herald full profits or ensure capacity use when demand is low? When we proposed this approach to several manufacturers, we met fierce resistance. A common reaction was "Our employees are not second-class customers." These are people whose wage level and job security depends on the manufacturer's profitability. We are not sure how asking them to be more flexible constitutes making them second-class customers. It merely invites them to participate further in making their company's bottom line more attractive.

The last customer group we identified consisted of those who buy demo and showroom vehicles and pool cars. Together, these cars account for around 5 percent of the overall production volume. Buying a car is an emotional process. Customers like to see, drive, and "feel" cars, so having demonstrators and showroom vehicles at dealers is important. Yet again, within limits, these orders do not have a critical lead time. Dealerships may want models on display and ready for test drives, but if the dealer sells a showroom or demo car, handing it over to the customer could easily be aligned with the arrival date of its replacement.

Figure 15.3 shows how the picture of capacity use changes when manufacturers exploit these opportunities for order smoothing and buffering. Of the vehicles listed in table 15.2, 40 percent are destined for large fleets, employees, and dealer showrooms. For these orders, lead time is not critical, so they can form an order buffer—a short-term pool of orders that provide some flexibility as to when the manufacturer can build them. Their flexibility is certainly not infinite, so the order-fulfillment period would be negotiated.

Creating a flexible order-driven process can lead to significant competitive advantage, as Dell has shown quite dramatically. On the other hand, it also carries high risks, as Dell has also seen in its huge demand swings. Between 1998 and 2002, Dell's order bookings across product lines ranged from 35,000 to 110,000 units per week. Consequently, Dell has started managing capacity use by collaboratively planning large orders with corporate clients. The automotive assembly process is orders of magnitude more complex, and the cost of altering an existing plant's capacity is tremendous, as we described earlier. Therefore, proactive demand management to minimize the financial risks of idle capacity is critical to the long-term success of a build-to-order system.

Figure 15.4 shows how segmenting and prioritizing orders using assembly slots helps a manufacturer to stabilize its use of production capacity.

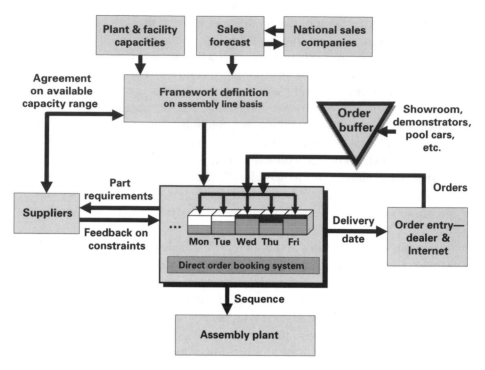

Figure 15.3
Creating an order buffer of long-lead-time vehicles to stabalize capacity use.

What You Measure Is What You Get

As we implied earlier, the measures the auto industry uses to determine profitability are severely flawed. This extends to the way companies reward managers. Most assembly plants, for example, are evaluated for their daily production volumes and their minimization of labor use. Product and volume flexibility or customer responsiveness is largely ignored. In fact, just over one-third of the plants we surveyed did not track individual orders. Among those that did, on average, 10 percent of vehicles were not produced within 3 days of the target production date. Several plants did track customer orders and were pretty good at producing them in a reasonable time, but many more did not. Those that failed to do so missed an opportunity for improvement. Without measuring this aspect of the production process, they cannot hope to improve this dimension of responsiveness.

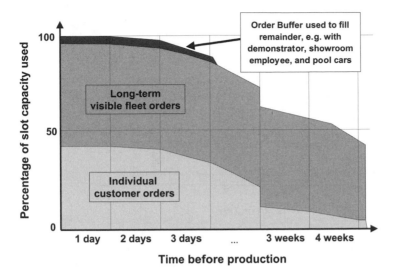

Figure 15.4
Using order segmentation and assembly slots to optimize capacity use.

Again, much of this attitude is ingrained. Current performance measures logically devolve from forecast-based logic, following the theme of cost minimization: assembly plants are measured on achieving the predicted volumes, not on making the right cars on time. National sales companies are measured on how well they dispose of the vehicles. Dealer incentive structures are based on sales volume, not on how many vehicles actually match the specifications the customers wanted.

The incentive structure is particularly insidious. Dealer incentives are based on monthly sales, which distorts the sales pattern over the month. Dealers are less inclined to give incentives at the start of the month and prefer to wait until closer to the end of the month to see how far they are from their sales target. Then they pour on the discounts and incentives to attain the desired volume for the month.

Figure 15.5 shows the distribution of actual sales over 3 months for UK dealerships of various brands. Other industries have also observed this effect, which is dubbed the month-end "hockey stick" because of the large uptick in sales toward the end of the month or quarter after a period of relatively stable and flat sales.

The "hockey stick" is a natural response to the task of getting rid of product and achieve the monthly sales target, which is what the forecast-based system requires of its distribution system—the national sales

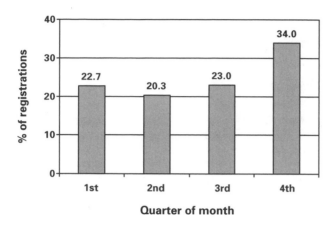

Figure 15.5
The "hockey stick" syndrome, reflecting incentives used to reach target sales at end of month. Source: B. Waller, Sales Channel for Build-to-Order, 3DayCar research report, Solihull, 2002.

companies and dealerships. The more product pushed into the market, the greater the reward. "More is better" permeates the organizational culture. Market share, production volume, productivity, and unit cost become the live-or-die measures.

In a build-to-order system, volume-based dealer incentives are unnecessary. Instead, producing vehicles to customer order in a short time with stable capacity use is the performance yardstick. Assembly factories are measured on how well production matches the schedule. Dealers are measured on how successfully they brokered vehicle delivery in view of the order flow. Component suppliers are measured on price per unit *and* flexibility. Finally, logistics must also be driven by something other than price—particularly on the distribution side, where the lead time is most visible to the customer. Cost of delivery is still important, but time frame and reliability are important too.

Clearly, then, for a build-to-order system to succeed, manufacturers must abandon many established notions about volume and must incorporate flexibility, responsiveness, and proactive order management throughout the value grid.

Breaking the Cycle

I cannot understand why people are frightened of new ideas—I'm afraid of the old ones.

—John Cage, composer[1]

Over the last century, the automobile has ingrained itself in society and in daily life. The industry that Peter Drucker called the "industry of industries" 50 years ago[2] is even more prominent today in terms of employment and economic impact.[3] However, the industry is also notoriously slow to embrace change. In 1950, some predicted that at the start of the new millennium cars would leave the road and take to the air. As far back as 1970, General Motors had designed a fuel-cell vehicle. But today cars still travel on roads, and in many ways little has changed between Carl Benz's prototype of 1886 and today's offerings. The vast majority of cars are still propelled by internal-combustion engines, and structurally a car is still a metal box on wheels, much like what the Fisher-Budd Company produced for the Dodge brothers in 1914.[4] In the same tradition, manufacturing and distribution strategies have changed little from their ancestors that governed manufacturing a century ago.

By no means do we wish to discredit the very real productivity and quality improvements at the many factories around the world that have made the transition to lean production. But even factory-level improvement must be brought in line with the overarching goal of a systemically efficient and responsive value grid. Otherwise, any change can backfire. The auto industry has been the reference model for lean production, but it is now also the classic example of how creating islands of excellence can inhibit responsiveness. What use is a factory that saves minutes in assembly when the finished product sits in stock for months? Rigid line balancing and long-term production smoothing may increase labor productivity. However, if the benefits come at the expense of the overall system's efficiency and responsiveness, customers gain little value. The auto industry, like many others, must reconsider to what extent the quest for efficiency inhibits the flexibility of the overall system.

The sustained demand that drove the development of today's production strategies has long been absent in the Western world. The current production model drowns the market in inventory but provides little insight into customers' real desires. Long lead times in information flow and an emphasis on local optimization create dramatic cycles of boom and bust. One year the industry sees prosperity and financial gains; the next year it may see the opposite. Industry experts and practitioners simply accept this, attributing it to the economy. Larry Yost, CEO of ArvinMeritor, sums up the prevailing attitude: "We're slow growth, low returns, and extremely cyclical."[5] Cyclical businesses, however, need not suffer dramatic profit-and-loss cycles, as the auto industry now does. We blame the current versions of mass production and shop-floor-centered lean thinking, and their sibling, the forecast-based production system. The specific problems the auto industry has to deal with today are the results of decisions made months ago. Making to forecast is probably as effective as attempting to drive a car by looking in the rear-view mirror—by the time you see the turn, you're past it, and the opportunity for redirection has been lost. And the slower the feedback from the market, the starker the response has to be. As a result, the insidious cycles have drastic adverse implications for production volumes, for suppliers, and for the workforce.

The Case for Responsiveness

As John Devine (CFO of General Motors) recently observed, "business is highly cyclical [but a number of businesses] do very well operating in a cyclical area."[6] Companies that manage to separate profitability from the business cycle do so by creating responsive systems driven by customers' orders rather than by long-term forecasts. Among the many success stories are those of Dell Computer and the raw-material producer Alcoa.

The problem is that feedback from the market is often too slow. The resulting profit-and-loss cycles drive stockholders to press for short-term management action rather than long-term systemic improvements and endanger the availability of capital needed for expansion and investment. Equally disturbing, the cycles are coupled with unacceptable employment swings.

Responsiveness cannot break the economic cycles entirely, but it can reduce the troughs. Build-to-order systems are more stable, since a company can counteract small dips immediately. The more closely the reaction matches the behavior of customers, the more responsive the organization will be to shifts in the market and the less "counter steering" will be required.

Process: Reconnect the Customer

In this book we have explored process flexibility, product flexibility, and volume flexibility, which are prerequisites to implementing any build-to-order system. Let us now summarize these three kinds of flexibility.

The point of process flexibility is to reconnect the customer to the value grid. Without this fundamental step, the focus of everyone from production workers to logistics companies will remain on local rather than system-wide improvements. Any value grid is doomed if there is no demand for the company's service and products at the customer end. In the short run, demand may be sustained via incentives or price reductions, but the industry is eating the planting seed. As the airline industry recently discovered, anyone can cut costs by cutting peanuts, but sustaining long-term profitability requires superior matching of production and services to customers' needs and wishes.

At the most rudimentary level, reconnecting the customer to the value grid means making the customer's needs the standard that drives all tradeoffs between local optimization and grid-wide responsiveness. Production schedules, supplier management, and logistics planning must be driven by actual orders, not by sales predictions or by power struggles among regional distribution units. When underlying demand is directly visible, there is no need to correct for unpredicted market evolution. Demand visibility plus active demand management is an effective formula for dissolving much of the artificial cycle we now see, as is strategic decision making centered on the customer as the source of long-term profitability.

Moving away from a single-minded pursuit of local efficiency and cost minimization requires examining what each segment of the value grid contributes to responsiveness. Rather than squeeze suppliers and shift activities to low-wage locales, for example, companies should explore how they can structure relationships with others in the value grid to enhance customer responsiveness. Modularity, outsourcing, and logistics restructuring can be ruts of rigidity or founts of flexibility. Companies can explicitly evaluate or model responsiveness opportunities and bottlenecks to gain insight into how to make the transition to this new mode. With a host of electronic communication tools and information technologies, they can make this transition happen. "The dream of a three-day car built to order is far closer than any of us thought possible just 3 years ago," Gary Cowger, group vice-president for manufacturing and labor relations at General Motors, recently said.[7] The challenge lies in reorienting the value grid away from cost minimization and efficiency and toward responsiveness and long-term revenue enhancement.

Product: Harness Variety

The common perception that customer choice translates to unmanageable production complexity is misguided and shows that neither variety nor its effect on the value grid is well understood. Variety challenges all parts of the grid, but much depends on the business model chosen. In the current model, external variety is the bane of many executives as they try to foster matches between existing stock and potential customers. Using discounts to deal with the discrepancy between aging inventory and discerning customers is nothing but a barrier to sustainable profitability.

In a build-to-order system, external variety is of little importance, since the customer defines the product's specifications from the start. No product matching is necessary. Thus, all the energy that used to go to managing the customer-product match must be redirected. Now internal variety becomes a formidable hurdle: How does a company attain enough manufacturing and system flexibility to produce vehicles quickly enough? Products that offer choice to the customer need *not* be more complex to make. Our findings support this unequivocally. Delaying the impact of variety as late in the value grid as is possible and late order tagging help keep the process flexible without limiting choice. Mutable support structures can be designed into the product from the start to ensure that the company can respond on short notice to any demand variation.

Volume: Manage Demand and Scale Intelligently

Capacity, demand, and customers' expectations interact in complex ways that generate multiple tradeoffs, which must be balanced. In the current model, manufacturers ignore the balancing problem and simply disconnect the value grid from the market by maintaining large inventories. Imagine the same logic applied to a service industry. A night in a hotel or a seat on a Boeing 747 flight cannot be put into inventory; if it isn't sold when it becomes available, its residual value is zero.

Efforts in other industries have demonstrated that a company can exploit flexibility and still meet demand. For example, customer segments can be tied to certain order lead times, since some customers express a much greater willingness to wait than others. In this way, active management of demand and time-based pricing harness the flexibility inherent in customers' expectations and differences. The customers who are willing to wait should be rewarded with discounts. In the perverse reality of the current model, they are penalized; they pay more and wait longer for the car they want. Customers who express their true preferences for a car provide invaluable information on market expectations and desires, which in turn empowers companies to smooth out their order flow and demand.

In managing scale, companies now believe that anything less than 100 percent capacity use represents forgone profit opportunities. However, as the service sector has shown, revenue management means achieving the greatest profit by managing demand and price accordingly. And maximum profit doesn't necessarily require maximum volume. Instead, profit is achieved by building fewer products at a higher return per unit.

The cost of altering capacity is not a reason to avoid responsiveness. Using flexibility in customers' expectations, leveraging the needs and expectations of different customer segments, and actively managing demand reduce the need for wide swings in capacity use and free firms to focus on real profitability. Responsiveness is an idea whose time has come. The long-term profit margins of most major players are less than 5 percent. What do firms have left to lose?

The Road Ahead

The auto industry has historically been a strategy trailblazer. Lean production has not only transformed the building of cars; it has also led to improvements in banks, in hospitals, and in software development. Becoming more responsive to customers' needs and building products to order is the next logical step.[8] The opportunities presented by responsiveness are arguably even greater in sectors outside of manufacturing. If a vehicle manufacturer builds a car no one wants, it can be stored on a lot. If no one enters and uses the services of a fully staffed bank branch, the employees' potential effort cannot be stockpiled.

There are no shortcuts to responsiveness. The best we can do is offer guidelines. Lean production, which offered the initial guidance to attaining efficiency and better quality, also facilitates product flexibility and volume flexibility, but responsiveness requires a more systemic approach. We have outlined the major changes that must take place if the auto industry is to move toward the neo-lean model of build-to-order: redirect the focus from local optimization, explore the link between internal complexity and external variety, and manage demand and scale intelligently. These changes are profound, not just because the adjustments to organizational structures and strategies seem daunting, but also because they force everyone to set aside long-held values and beliefs about what drives sustainable long-term performance.

Our research has focused on the motor vehicle industry, but the challenges and opportunities that come with these changes apply to many other industries too. Firms in all industries have worked hard to create islands of excellence in the value grid. It is now time to connect these islands to the one element that can drive long-term success: the customer.

Notes

Introduction

1. See J. Womack, D. Jones, and D. Roos, *The Machine That Changed the World* (Rawson Associates, 1990); David Hounshell, *From the American System to Mass Production, 1800–1932* (Johns Hopkins University Press, 1985).

Chapter 1

1. P. Eisenstein, "Just what the customer ordered," *Professional Engineering* 13 (2000), no. 14: 36–38; L. Chappell, "Makers face challenge of '5-day car,'" *Automotive News*, January 22, 2000; J. Cantwell, "Forrester: Build-to-order will save makers money," *Automotive News*, October 15, 2001: 40; W. Weernink, "Supply connect: Build-to-order drives BMW's future growth," *Automotive News Europe*, December 2, 2002: 28.

2. Nissan also is working toward build-to-order in Japan. Sparked by the takeover by Renault in 1999, Nissan started a 14-day-car program called SCOPE in Europe in 2000.

3. Toyota traditionally had five domestic sales channels into which vehicles were grouped, all of which had separate dealerships: Toyota (luxury cars), Corolla (compact cars, largest channel), Toyopet (medium-size cars), Netz (for young buyers), and Vista (family cars). In 2003, Toyota announced a new strategy that would merge the existing Netz and Vista channels and introduce Lexus as a new luxury channel in Japan.

4. Counter to common perception, Nissan's build-to-order program started long before the merger with Renault. Nissan has similar approaches underway in Europe, where the RESPONSE system was updated to D-6 scheduling under the SCOPE system, and in the USA, where the MAPS system was updated with the ICON system, introducing weekly ordering. These projects are much less advanced than the ANSWER II system in Japan. The distribution system in the US is posing the greatest obstacles so far. In comparison, Nissan's build-to-order ratio is around 15–20% in Europe and 2–3% in the US.

5. We found three differences between Toyota and Nissan that explain Nissan's ability to operate with less stock in the marketplace. First, Toyota's production is based on forecast, whereas Nissan's is based on orders. Toyota dealers have a binding contractual agreement with Toyota on the volume front, and primarily amend the forecasted volumes they have agreed to take. Nissan dealers do not have any volume commitment. Second, interviews with Nissan managers suggested that the pressures for change resulting from

Nissan's near bankruptcy and the Nissan Revival Plan (devised by Charles Ghosn in 1999) also fostered an environment in which change was enabled. The NRP clearly states a reduction of finished car inventory as one of its main goals. Third, the ownership structure of their domestic distribution systems differs drastically. Nissan owns 60% of its local dealers. This facilitated encouraging dealers to adopt build-to-order as a strategy. In contrast, Toyota dealerships are independent, and thus cannot be forced into adopting new policies. Technically, Nissan dealers are still allowed to order for stock, but the dealer then bears the risk for that stock. On the other hand, Nissan dealer contracts do not have volume targets, whereas Toyota contracts explicitly specify binding volume targets for each dealer.

6. Research in the UK shows that supermarket items are available at 98%, although the first several hundred top-selling items have much higher availability. Nevertheless, when selecting a specific basket of ten different items, on average only 80% of all items will be available.

7. G. Williams, Progress towards Customer Pull Distribution, research paper 4/2000, International Car Distribution Programme, Solihull, UK, 2000; "European new vehicle supply—the long road to customer pull systems," *ICDP Journal* 1 (1999), no. 1: 13–21.

8. M. Anderson, "Autos in the networked economy—the next wave," ICDP Sponsors Meeting, Solihull, March 2000.

9. G. Williams, "Progress towards lean distribution," ICDP Supply and Stocking Meeting, Solihull, January 27, 2000.

10. E. Elridge, "Expiring leases lift used car supply," *USA Today*, July 13, 2000.

11. S. Finlay, "Ford Credit refocuses to recover from losses," *Ward's Dealer Business*, August 1, 2002.

12. We used the value-stream-mapping methodology, which was originally developed by Toyota. See M. Rother and J. Shook, *Learning to See* (Lean Enterprise Institute, 1998); D. Jones and J. Womack, *Seeing the Whole* (Lean Enterprise Institute, 2002). A similar logic of mapping the order-fulfillment process has been proposed by B. Shapiro, V. Rangan, and J. Sviokla ("Staple yourself to an order," *Harvard Business Review* 70, 1992, no. 4: 113–123).

13. This theoretical measure is directly derived from the system structure, which drives a system's dynamic behavior, and thus provides the crucial understanding of the dynamics and processes that drive the actual lead times. See J. Sterman, *Business Dynamics* (McGraw-Hill, 2000).

14. Focusing on the capability of a system rather than on the actual lead times achieved was also suggested by G. Stalk ("Time—the next source of competitive advantage," *Harvard Business Review* 66, 1988, no. 4: 41–51).

15. We created the generic process map by first comparing the different tasks undertaken within each of the six processes (for example the development of a weekly production schedule by assigning orders to a production week of a particular plant). We then compared task functionality and sequence, which revealed little difference among the manufacturers analyzed. We assembled a generic task sequence by choosing a resolution level high enough to exclude any firm-level idiosyncrasies. Finally, we evaluated each task's structural (not average) delay, which enabled us to benchmark the capability of the system.

Chapter 2

1. G. Williams, Progress towards Customer Pull Distribution, research paper 4/2000, International Car Distribution Programme, Solihull, 2000.

2. For more on the scheduling systems at Nissan Sunderland, see D. Sennechael and I. MacLean, "Car-sequencing challenge at a Nissan plant calls for complex scheduling," *APICS—The Performance Advantage*, March 2001: 39–40.

3. On average, European dealers add 9 days to the delivery date given by the manufacturer, according to Geoff Williams of the International Car Distribution Programme. Our research with Nissan in Japan suggests that Japanese dealers add a similar number of days.

4. We analyzed the inbound-logistics schemes of three major assembly plants in the UK. The cases, selected to be representative of volume factories, cover one scheme each for the two main Western makers, plus one Japanese scheme for the analysis. In total, these schemes link in excess of 670 supplier manufacturing sites to three assembly plants.

5. The cost data are based on Goldman Sachs internal estimates. Similar data have also been reported by P. Wells and P. Nieuwenhuis (*The Automotive Industry*, British Telecommunications, 2001).

6. Cross docks are facilities operated by logistics companies enabling them to consolidate loads originating from multiple destinations into single outbound trucks. This independently optimizes the collection of loads from disparate origins, as well as the delivery of those loads that are going to a common destination.

Chapter 3

1. While many plants still focus on batching body shells to increase the number of vehicles of one color going through the paint shop at any one time, the advantages of such batching have decreased significantly in recent years. Purge times and the amount of lost raw material and increased pollution associated with *not* batching are so minimal that batching is no longer critical. However, some firms, including Honda, have designed their whole processes around product batching in paint shops as well as in weld and assembly processes.

2. Kosuke Ikebuchi, "More than just a production method," *World Automotive Manufacturing*, October 13, 1999.

3. The research into the logistics of vehicle distribution was carried out in several phases. After initial focus group research, the first phase was primarily qualitative in nature, creating a high-level process map to gain a complete understanding of the basis subprocesses. In the second phase, a quantitative data collection was conducted with the major vehicle logistics players in the UK. A sample size of eight service providers was used, covering c. 3.1 million annual vehicle movements and a pool of 1,537 car transporters. The companies involved cover 10% of the total European vehicle transportation volume and a majority of the UK market. As the assessment of build-to-order's consequences is based on a theoretical future situation, it was decided by the research focus group to model the main characteristics of the vehicle delivery process on the basis of times, distances, load capacities, and utilization, using a logistics provider's proprietary

software program. In the third phase, the data gathered from the process mapping and questionnaire survey was used to model the effects of more responsive delivery. In particular, the modeling exercise was used to test focus group scenarios for reducing the cost and environment effects in order to indicate whether these yielded the expected gains. The input data was based on dealership locations in the UK (by post-code), factory locations, transport capacities and frequency and timing of supply to these locations. All three research stages were complemented with semi-structured interviews. Eight managers were interviewed at operations and strategic planning (or business development in some cases) level in order to capture several perspectives across three vehicle logistics organizations. In all, eleven interviews were carried out, with some individuals interviewed more than once. For related material, see M. Holweg and J. Miemczyk, "Logistics in the three-day car age," *International Journal of Physical Distribution and Logistics Management* 32 (2002), no. 10: 829–850.

4. Distribution centers are sometimes called vehicle storage centers (VSCs) or regional distribution centers (RDCs) when multiple national centers are operating. A market compound differs from a distribution center (DC) in that a compound is an intermediate stocking location where new loads are assembled for the dispersion routes and where unsold stock is held. This stock is used to replenish dealers as they sell their own stock. A distribution center fulfills the same function as the compound but is further used to encourage dealers to deliberately source new vehicles sales from the distribution center, permitting them to select from all unsold stock in the center for their customers.

5. J. Gregory, "Vehicle logistics and the Three-day Car Programme," 3DayCar Programme Annual Conference, Stratford upon Avon, UK, December 1999.

6. In figure 3.3, all order-to-delivery times represent calendar days, excluding delays due to weekends and shift patterns. We normalized this time basis to address two variations. The first is the working hours of the scheduling operations. Most schedules exclude the weekend, although some manufacturers create extra schedules on Friday for Saturday and Sunday if the plant is operational. The second is the differences in working hours in the plants. Some assembly plants work on a 7-day 3-shift pattern, but most operate on a 5-day, 2-shift pattern. Therefore, we assumed that all order processing and manufacturing functions are executed 7 days per week and that shift patterns do not cause additional delays. The lead times or delays within the information flow are directly related to the system run and update frequencies. For example, an overnight batch process induces a delay of up to 1 day, and systems running once a week induce an average delay of 3.5 days—plus potential further delays for overnight processing depending on particular system run times and length of processing. The material flow delays are calculated as the system fill divided by the hourly output (Little's Law states that the minimum throughput time is determined by system inventory and output over time—see John Bicheno, *The Lean Toolbox*, PICSIE Books, 2000). In the case of loading delays, average performance figures are used. Distribution times refer to the manufacturer's data for average delivery times from the plant to a dealership in the plant's home market.

7. This tool was originated by M. Norman and B. Stoker in their 1991 book *Data Envelopment Analysis* (Wiley).

8. The European Commission is considering a project proposed by the European Auto Supplies' Association (CLEPA) under the Framework Six Initiative.

9. R. Hall and L. Tonkin, *The Manufacturing 21st Century Report: The Future of Japanese Manufacturing* (Association of Manufacturing Excellence, 1989).

Chapter 4

1. Volkswagen added a superscript 2 to the abbreviation KVP.

2. The data for 1989 were collected by John Paul MacDuffie and John Krafcik and formed the basis for *The Machine That Changed the World*. For the original discussion of productivity and quality for this time period, see Krafcik, Learning from NUMMI, working paper, IMVP, MIT, 1986; Krafcik, Comparative Analysis of Performance Indicators at World Auto Assembly Plants, Master's thesis, MIT Sloan School of Management, 1988; Krafcik, "Triumph of the lean production system," *Sloan Management Review* 30 (1988), no. 1: 41–52; Krafcik and MacDuffie, Explaining High Performance Manufacturing, working paper, IMVP, MIT, 1989; MacDuffie and Krafcik, "Integrating technology and human resources for high performance manufacturing," in *Transforming Organizations*, ed. T. Kochan and M. Useem (Oxford University Press, 1992). Data for 1994 were collected by John Paul MacDuffie and Frits Pil. For a discussion of the approach used for that time period, see MacDuffie and Pil, "The international assembly plant study," in *Lean Work, Empowerment and Exploitation in the Global Auto Industry*, ed. S. Babson (Wayne State University Press, 1995). For discussions of performance in the mid 1990s and its determinants, see Pil and MacDuffie, "The adoption of high-involvement work practices," *Industrial Relations* 35 (1996), no. 3: 423–455; MacDuffie and Pil, "High-involvement work practices and human resource policies," in *Evolving Employment Practices in the World Auto Industry*, ed. T. Kochan et al. (Cornell University Press, 1997); MacDuffie and Pil, "Flexible technologies, flexible workers," in *Transforming Auto Assembly*, ed. T. Fujimoto and U. Jürgens (Springer-Verlag 1997); Pil and MacDuffie, "Transferring competitive advantage across borders," in *Remade in America*, ed. J. Liker et al. (Oxford University Press, 1999).

3. The foundation for the productivity methodology was initially developed by John Krafcik. See his Master's thesis: Comparative Analysis of Performance Indicators at World Auto Assembly Plants (MIT Sloan School of Management, 1988). Refinements are discussed in J. MacDuffie and F. Pil, "The International Assembly Plant Study: Philosophical and Methodological Issues," in *Lean Work, Empowerment and Exploitation in the Global Auto Industry*, ed. S. Babson (Wayne State University Press, 1995). Productivity figures are adjusted for product characteristics, vertical integration, and working time differences. With respect to vehicle characteristics, in the body shop, the most important vehicle characteristic considered is weld content. This is assessed as a total of all spot welds (which including total manual and automatically applied spot welds, and spot-weld equivalent conversions for MIG, arc, and laser welding (150 spot welds per meter), as well as conversions for non-traditional techniques such as screws). In the paint shop, two product characteristics are controlled for: sealer content in relation to average world sealer content, and vehicle size in relation to average world vehicle size. In the assembly area, vehicle adjustments are based on option content (added labor time based on average world installation time for components), and vehicle size. All vehicle adjustments are weighted by production volume of different products produced in the plant. Vertical integration adjustments are based on a set of core activities that are done in house at most plants. Lastly, differences in working time, breaks, and absenteeism are removed. A number of factors, including automation and product design-related issues are not controlled for. These will be discussed separately in this book.

4. Since the data were collected, there has been a dramatic increase in the use of temporary labor in Japan.

5. *100 Events That Made the Industry* (Crain Communications for *Automotive News*, 1996), p. 162.

6. We are grateful to J.D. Power and Associates for sharing raw data so generously with the International Motor Vehicle Program. Data reported are adjusted to solely reflect assembly plant-related defects. For a discussion of the initial quality methodology, see J. MacDuffie and J. Krafcik, "Integrating technology and human resources for high performance manufacturing," in *Transforming Organizations*, ed. T. Kochan and M. Useem (Oxford University Press, 1992). We are grateful to John Paul MacDuffie for his invaluable help in understanding these data. The methodology was modified to adjust for survey enhancements undertaken by J.D. Power and Associates. It only reflects quality items that could be compared across all time periods and that still reflected defects originating in the factory.

7. For more on this, see J. Bicheno, M. Holweg, and J. Niessmann, "Constraint batch sizing in a lean environment," *International Journal of Production Economics* 73 (2001): 41–49; M. Holweg, "Dynamic distortions in supply chains—a cause and effect analysis," in *Manufacturing Operations and Supply Chain Management*, ed. D. Taylor and D. Brunt (Thompson International, 2001).

8. See R. Schonberger, *Japanese Manufacturing Techniques* (Free Press, 1982); Y. Monden, *The Toyota Production System* (Productivity Press, 1983); R. Hall, *Zero Inventories* (McGraw-Hill, 1983). These were the first standard books on just-in-time, yet not until the publication of *The Machine That Changed the World* did the public outside academia take more interest.

9. The Smart project was initially founded in 1994 between Daimler Benz and SMH (Swatch). After disputes about vehicle pricing, a too-conventional product layout, and the vehicle's environmental performance, Swatch left soon after the joint venture. In 1995, the design was frozen, and after 18 months of construction "Smartville" was opened in 1997 in Hambach—after fierce negotiations with various governments as to where the factory would be located. The assembly line is shaped like a plus, with a central repair area in the middle—which much to our amusement, can be overseen from the cafeteria. Co-located around the factory are the system partners, each providing a key element of the vehicle or the process: the body-in-white (Magna, paint supplied by Eisenmann), the plastic panels (Dynamit Nobel, Cubic for plastic surface enhancement), the cockpit (Mannesmann-VDO), the back-end module (Krupp-Hoesch Automotive), the front module (Bosch), the doors (Uniport), and the trim (Dynamit Nobel). Together, the seven co-located suppliers on site provide 50% of the value of the vehicle. The engine is manufactured in Daimler's Berlin engine plant, and shipped into Krupp's back-end module assembly on site. MCC Smart has only 15 direct vehicle suppliers. Faurecia, for example, is located 100 kilometers from the plant, yet delivers the seats in sequence. (Data based on research visit in mid 2000.)

10. C. Osburn, "Ford to share savings from warranty gains," *Automotive News*, March 11, 2002: 24.

11. D. Kurylko and R. Sherefkin, "DCX spells out vendor liability," *Automotive News*, June 10, 2002: 1.

12. These large system suppliers are often referred to as "0.5-tier suppliers," since they essentially provide an interface between the VM and its previous first-tier suppliers.

13. C. Whitbread, "Valeo trims some suppliers, coddles others," *Automotive News*, July 29, 2002.

14. Quoted on p. 144 of *100 Events That Made the Industry*.

15. Womack et al., *The Machine That Changed the World*.

16. M. Ihlwan with C. Dawson, "Renault Samsung," *Business Week*, October 7, 2002.

17. *Financial Times*, July 11, 2002, p. 33.

18. K. Clark and T. Fujimoto, *Product Development Performance* (Harvard Business School Press, 1991).

Chapter 5

1. David Cole, cited in speech by Dana vice-president Steve Hanley, Management Briefing Seminars, Traverse City, Michigan, August 2001.

2. *Financial Times*, May 22, 2002, p. 16.

3. J. Brewis, "M&A in the Fast Lane," *Corporate Finance* (London), April 2000.

4. Luca Ciferri, "Fiat Auto cuts losses in third quarter," *Automotive News*, November 4, 2002; Dave Guilford, "Fiat feels pain, too, as GM stock slumps," *Automotive News*, October 21, 2002.

5. Y. Yamaguchi, "Cami: The bone in Osamu Suzuki's throat," *Automotive News*, September 2, 2002: 6.

6. The estimates are from a 2000 study by CLEPA, the European Suppliers' Association. Of the $932 billion, $210 billion is based in Europe. Of the total market, 74% is the result of sales to vehicle manufacturers, and the remainder from aftermarket sales.

7. R. Sherefkin, "Debt is the key factor in TRW deal," *Automotive News*, September 2, 2002.

Chapter 6

1. Central Policy Review Staff, *The Future of the British Car Industry* (HMSO, 1974).

2. Source: G. Williams.

3. T. Koblinski, speech at Management Briefing Seminars, Traverse City, Michigan, August 2000.

4. The 3DayCar New Vehicle Buyer Survey, conducted by Simon Elias at Cardiff Business School, surveyed 1,033 customers in the UK in 2000 and 2001. See also S. Elias, New Vehicle Buyer Behaviour—Quantifying Key Stages in the Consumer Buying Process, 3DayCar research report, 2002.

5. Initial research in car retailing has been reported (see e.g. R. Delbridge and N. Oliver, "Just-in-time or just-the-same?" *International Journal of Retail and Distribution Management* 19, 1991, no. 2: 20–26), yet it took until 1992 for the first comprehensive benchmarking study to be commissioned by the Royal Motor Industry Federation. The research carried out then evolved into the International Car Distribution Programme (ICDP). Since then, the benchmarking rounds in 1994, 1997, and 1999 of European vehicle supply systems have created a strong longitudinal database of performance data, which largely will be used in the following to describe the vehicle supply system's performance in the UK.

6. Figure 6.2 is based on manufacturer interviews about lead times for both custom-built orders and orders that have been matched with stock orders in the pipeline. The average lead time is thus shorter than it would be—all vehicles were custom-built, which makes it unsuitable as a basis for comparing system capability.

7. Survey conducted by Gartner, published on www.eyeforauto.com February 9, 2001.

8. T. Koblinski, Management Briefing Seminars, Traverse City, August 2000.

9. J. Bolte, speech at Management Briefing Seminars, Traverse City, August 2001.

10. A. Robinson, "Toyota to test quick turn on Solara," *Automotive News*, August 9, 1999.

11. According to consumer research commissioned by Nissan.

12. "GM delays Saturn build-to-order," *Ward's Dealer Business*, January 1, 2002.

Chapter 7

1. The average gross profit on new vehicles is 5.9%, versus 11.1% on used vehicles (NADA average dealership profits, quoted in *Automotive News* Market Data Book; Crain Communications Inc., 2003, p. 52).

2. Ibid.

3. G. Lapidus, "eAutomotive: Gentlemen, start your search engines," Goldman Sachs, New York, 2000.

4. Dealer stock is typically financed by the vehicle manufacturer or the national sales company for 30 days. The dealer bears the cost of holding the stock beyond this. If however, vehicles are not sold within 6 months, the vehicle manufacturer or national sales company commonly helps finance special discounts to clear the stock.

5. In particular, brakes, tires, batteries, and exhaust systems suffer from damage due to prolonged storage, as well as the exterior paint due to exposure to weather and sunlight. These defects, often invisible at the point of sale, are likely result in early warranty claims by the customer.

6. L. Ciferri, quoting Nick Scheele, "Building to order could save €99 a car," *Automotive News Europe*, June 3, 2002: 4.

7. Ibid. Estimated average wholesale price of €7,824; finance rate 11%; cost of 8 weeks in inventory €132; cost of 2 weeks in inventory €33; total saving €99.

8. Ibid.

9. Specialist vehicle manufacturers considered in ICDP surveys: BMW, Jaguar, Mercedes, Saab, Volvo.

10. G. Williams, "Progress towards customer pull distribution."

11. Stock objectives describe a vehicle manufacturer's planned new vehicle inventory in the marketplace, i.e., the combined dealer and compound/distribution center stock. Stock objectives have been used by ICDP as benchmark for tracking the actual versus planned improvements.

12. The manufacturers spent $7.9 billion on advertising in 2002 in the US, the biggest spenders being Chevrolet ($795 million), Toyota ($626 million), Nissan ($543 million), and Ford ($542 million). Source: K. Jackson, "Automakers to spend $8 billion in ads," *Automotive News*, March 31, 2003: 39.

13. NADA average dealership profits, quoted in *Automotive News Market Data Book* (Crain Communications, 2003), p. 52.

14. It could be argued that the 22% who admitted to changing their specification is an underestimate of the tendency, as some consumers may have made a change but not interpreted it as a compromise. That specialist buyers were slightly less likely to take an alternative reflects the more discerning buying stance they take for a high-value product, where they are more used to detailing specification. In the cheaper market segments, customers may be more used to getting what is in stock.

15. D. Guilford, "Incentives still needed, Wagoner says," *Automotive News*, September 9, 2002: 10.

16. J. Cantwell, "Porsche tells US: No more rebates," *Automotive News*, August 26, 2002: 8.

17. "Buy now, pay later," in *100 Events That Made the Industry* (Crain Communications for *Automotive News*, 1996), p. 72.

18. Chrysler offered $2,824 on average per vehicle, Ford $3,230. Source: D. Guilford, "GM vows to keep incentives," *Automotive News*, October 28, 2002.

19. "Coming soon: Built-to-order cars delivered in 10–15 days," *Atlanta Journal-Constitution*, March 26, 2001.

20. Data from various interviews with British Vehicle Manufacturers.

21. J. Kohn, "Studies rebates are strong poison," *Automotive News*, September 2, 2002: 6.

22. *Financial Times* (US edition), May 20, 2002: 18.

23. The "Monroney sticker," named after Senator Mike Monroney, has been in effect since the 1959 model year. The law imposed fines of up to $1,000 for dealers for tampering with the sticker price. "By establishing a uniform price," it is noted on p. 118 of *100 Events That Made the Industry*, "Monroney provided a basis for bargaining."

24. A. Sawyers, "Wholesale auction prices dive," *Automotive News*, October 21, 2002: 18.

25. Source: conversation with Christophe Chabert, assistant to Renault's PND Project Director, at ICDP Conference, St. Paul de Vence, October 2000.

Chapter 8

1. Source of financial data of Fortune 500 companies: WRDS and Datastream 3.5 databases.

2. Larry Yost, speech at Management Briefing Seminars, Traverse City, August 2000.

3. G. Lapidus et al., "Ford Motor Company, Equity Research Report," Goldman Sachs, New York, December 2001.

4. In 1991, GM incurred a loss of $4.5 billion. By the end of 1992, the chairman, the president, a vice-chairman, and an executive vice-president had been forced to retire, and the

CFO had been demoted. After reporting continuous losses from the second quarter in 1990, it took GM until the last quarter in 1992 to regain profitability. Source: *Automotive News Yearbook*, 2002, p. 126.

5. R. Lacey, *Ford: The Men and the Machine* (Little, Brown, 1986).

6. R. Sherefkin, "Leuliette jeered, cheered," *Automotive News*, August 19, 2002: 1.

7. Larger first-tier suppliers are now starting to behave very much like their customers and "squeeze" the second-tier suppliers—a behavior they used to criticized harshly when they themselves were subject to "squeezing." Visteon for example, one of the largest component suppliers in the world, recently started demanding annual price reductions of 6% from its suppliers, alongside of advance payments for these cost reductions at the start of the contract. The power-driven adversarial approach to managing supplier relations, pioneered by Henry Ford early last century, hence now extends upstream into the supply chain. See R. Miel, "Visteon demands advance payments," *Automotive News*, February 24, 2003: 1.

8. R. Sherefkin, "Scheele urges Ford to treat suppliers better," *Automotive News*, September 2, 2002: 1.

9. Sean McAliden of Center for Automotive Research, cited in L. Chappell, "Mortgaging the future," *Automotive News*, September 9, 2002.

10. M. Rechtin, "Ford dumps pay-on-production," *Automotive News*, September 30, 2002.

11. Speech by Gretchen Perkins, Management Briefing Seminars, Traverse City, August 2000.

12. L. Chappell, "Toyota: Slash—but we'll help," *Automotive News*, September 16, 2002: 4.

13. Public funding for VW included $50 million in industrial development loans, $20 million for highway improvements, $14.5 million for rail spurs, $3 million for job training programs, $6 million loan from the state employees and teachers' pension fund, and $6.8 million for capital costs. Source: D. Copeland, "Why not here?" *Pittsburgh Tribune-Review*, August 18, 2002.

14. H. Shapiro, "The mechanics of Brazil's auto industry," in NACLA's Report on the Americas, January-February 1996.

15. J. Goodman, "Argentine crisis sparks industry retreat," *Automotive News*, April 8, 2002: 9.

16. G. Lapidus and C. Laporte, "GM-Ford-DaimlerChrysler exchange," Goldman Sachs, New York, 2000.

Chapter 9

1. While the specific updates vary by manufacturer, the more common overnight runs related to the following process steps: order generation, whereby the order entered by the dealer is converted from "dealer codes" into "manufacturing codes," checked for build feasibility and transferred into the order bank as "available for scheduling"; order expansion, whereby the order, i.e., the particular manufacturing codes, are "exploded" into the bill of materials for that order. Order scheduling, transferring the scheduled order from the order bank into the production schedules, which are then made visible to the assembly plants and suppliers through the supplier scheduling system, such as CMMS3 for Ford or MGO for

GM. Order sequencing, converting the weekly or daily schedule into a sequence of orders, which generally requires another over-night transfer. Transfer to traffic control system, whereby the vehicle data post-build is transferred from the plant system into the distributions or "traffic control" systems. This can induce even further delays, as in some cases the vehicle cannot be physically moved, unless the order is electronically visible in the system.

2. The introduction of GM's global material control system, MGO (Material Global Optimization), which replaced the 30-year old AMK and EuroMAIS material control and supplier scheduling systems, can be seen as a good example here. The global implementation had started more than 10 years before it finally came online in the UK in November 1999.

3. Jay Forrester of MIT discovered this effect in 1958. Since then, it has sparked many additional studies and extensions. For more details, see J. Forrester, *Industrial Dynamics* (MIT Press, 1961); H. Lee, V. Padmanabhan, and W. Seungjin, "The bullwhip effect in supply chains," *Sloan Management Review* 38 (1997), no. 3: 93–102.

Chapter 10

1. Estimates of strategic planning staff at Dell.

2. See H. Mather, *Competitive Manufacturing* (Prentice-Hall, 1988).

3. Sony, another electronics firm, is specifically looking to use Sony stores to sell high-end consumer electronics equipment to order under its new Qualia brand. Source: "Sony's new super-clear 36-inch TV costs $11,000," CNN, June 10, 2003.

4. D. Morse, "Fast furniture," *Wall Street Journal*, November 19, 2002.

5. Sources: Alcoa web page; Alcoa annual reports; C. Adams, "Corporate focus: Alcoa profit rises despite slump in aluminum industry," *Wall Street Journal*, May 10, 1999.

6. For another discussion of the transition to such a "capacity-availability" booking system within manufacturing supply chains, see D. Kehoe and N. Boughton, "New paradigms in planning and control across manufacturing supply chains," *International Journal of Operations and Production Management* 21 (2001), no. 5/6: 582–593.

7. Currently, the average delay is 30 days. Assuming a five-day locked assembly sequence to provide suppliers and logistics companies with a reasonable planning horizon, this would mean that 25 days of delay in the order-to-delivery process are eradicated.

8. "Der 50-Milliarden-Euro-Marktplatz von VW," Heise Online News, November 20, 2001; K. Neubauer, "VW setzt auf elektronische Beschaffung," *Informationweek* 26, November 29. 2001.

9. In Europe, Renault and BMW lock their sequences 5 days prior to production. In Japan, Mitsubishi does the same. Nissan operates in similar time frames, locking the sequence 4 days before production in Japan and 6 days before production in Europe. This is also sometimes referred to as "D -4" or "D -6" scheduling.

10. A large majority of specialist and volume brand dealers agreed that the role of the dealer is threatened by the Internet. 196 UK dealers were interviewed. Source: B. Waller, "Internet selling in the UK," presentation at 3DayCar Programme Sponsor Conference, Bath, UK, June 2000.

11. All the experts agree on this, yet we have found very different numbers for expected savings. We will leave this qualitative statement unchallenged here.

12. Bill Ford, speech at *Automotive News* World Congress, January 19, 2000.

13. K. Turnbull, "Autobytel UK and the future of Internet car retailing," Goldman Sachs Automotive Distribution Conference, London, November 1999.

14. Admittedly, we were among the 2,000—sorry, Vauxhall!

15. "Coming soon: Built-to-order cars delivered in 10–15 days," *Atlanta Journal-Constitution*, March 26, 2001.

16. Sources: Gartner survey of 40,000 US households conducted between September 1999 and March 2000; M. Anderson, "Autos in the Networked Economy—the Next Wave," ICDP Sponsors Meeting, Solihull, March 2000. Internet usage estimates by J.D. Power and Associates, 2000.

17. B. Waller, "Internet selling in the UK," presentation at 3DayCar Programme Sponsor Conference, Bath, June 2000.

18. Anderson, "Autos in the Networked Economy."

19. Waller, "Internet selling in the UK.'

20. Other e-commerce dimensions include "E2E" ("engineer to engineer") during product development and telematics (e.g., GM's OnStar technology). These areas are expected to grow tremendously.

21. Source of estimate: COVISINT.

22. Roland Berger, *Automotive e-Commerce* (Roland Berger, 2000).

23. COVISINT is a joint effort of several vehicle manufacturers, and started when Ford and GM merged their Internet exchanges called AutoXchange and TradeXchange. The name COVISINT is an amalgamation of the primary concepts of why the exchange is being formed: COnnectivity, COllaboration and COmmunication, VISibility through the internet, VISion of the future of supply chain management, and INTegrated solutions.

24. "USA: COVISINT spending $12 million a month—report," Reuters, April 3, 2001.

25. Chris Moritz, speech at Management Briefing Seminars, Traverse City, August 2000.

Chapter 11

1. The work system index is the sum of the z scores for each individual items, re-scaled from 0 to 100. For this application, we broke the index into four equal groupings. For more on the index, see J. MacDuffie, "Human resource bundles and manufacturing performance: Organizational logic and flexible production systems in the world auto industry," *Industrial and Labor Relations Review* 48 (1995): 197–221; F. Pil and J. MacDuffie, "The adoption of high-involvement work practices," *Industrial Relations* 35 (1996), no. 3: 423–455.

Chapter 12

1. Value ex factory gate, excluding the cost of raw materials.

2. We have observed a strong trend toward sourcing components from low-labor-cost countries. For the US, this generally means sourcing from Mexico and Asia, and in Europe from Eastern Europe and North Africa. We found that the decision to relocate parts production to such countries is commonly made on the basis of direct labor and transportation cost only, and omits a range of less visible costs. The hidden costs of global sourcing include for example the overhead costs that remain at the main facility, the cost of additional inventory of goods in transit to cover the distance, as well as additional safety stocks to ensure uninterrupted supply, the costs for expedited shipments in case of unforeseen problems, or the cost of stock-outs in the instances where parts cannot be delivered in time. Furthermore, the travel cost for engineers and management to visit the facility abroad can be substantial. This is particularly the case at the early stages of the learning curve at the new facility.

3. T. Jones, "Body block," *Forbes*, March 4, 2000.

4. Several themes within this discussion could be identified. The most widely discussed issue is the shift from adversarial, price-driven to partnership-driven collaborative relationships. A wide range of studies have been undertaken, and evidence has been reported from the UK (P. Turnbull, N. Oliver, and B. Wilkinson, "Buyer-supplier relations in the UK automotive industry," *Strategic Management Journal* 13, 1992: 159–168; F. Ali, G. Smith, and J. Saker, "Developing buyer-supplier relationships in the automobile industry," *European Journal of Purchasing and Supply Management* 3, 1997, no. 1: 33–42), from the US (S. Helper, "How much has really changed between US automakers and their suppliers?" *Sloan Management Review* 32, 1991, no. 4: 15–29), from comparative studies with Japan (M. Cusumano and A. Takeishi, "Supplier relations and management," *Strategic Management Journal* 12, 1991: 563–588; P. Hines, "Benchmarking Toyota's supply chain," *Long Range Planning* 31, 1998, no. 6: 911–918), from Spain (J. Gonzalez-Benito and B. Dale, "Supplier quality and reliability assurance practices in the Spanish auto components industry," *European Journal of Purchasing and Supply Management* 7, 2001: 187–196), from Italy (G. Calabrese, "Small-medium supplier-buyer relationships in the car industry," *European Journal of Purchasing and Supply Management* 6, 2000: 59–65), and from Turkey (H. Gules, T. Burgess, and J. Lynch, "The evolution of buyer-supplier relationships in the automotive industries of emerging European economies," *European Journal of Purchasing and Supply Management* 3, 1997, no. 4: 209–219), and large-scale benchmarking studies have been reported (The Lean Enterprise Benchmarking Report, Andersen Consulting, London, 1993; The Second Lean Enterprise Benchmarking Report, Andersen Consulting, 1994). The overall conclusion highlights the trends toward, and the benefits of, close collaborative relationships, and the positive effect of close integration on performance. Similarly, the positive effect of close integration on new product development has been highlighted (S. Croom, "The dyadic capabilities concept," *European Journal of Purchasing and Supply Management* 7, 2001: 29–37).

5. A. Harrison, "An investigation of the impact of schedule stability on supplier responsiveness," *International Journal of Logistics Management* 7 (1996), no. 1: 83–91; P. Hines, "Benchmarking Toyota's supply chain," *Long Range Planning* 31 (1998), no. 6: 911–918.

6. See M. Sako, R. Lamming, and S. Helper, "Supplier relations in the UK car industry," *European Journal of Purchasing and Supply Management* 1 (1994), no. 4: 237–248; Hines, "Benchmarking Toyota's supply chain"; J. Jayaram, S. Vickery, and C. Droge, "An empirical study of time-based competition in the North American automotive supplier industry," *International Journal of Operations and Production Management* 19 (1999), no. 10: 1010–1033; J. Griffiths and D. Margetts, "Variation in production schedules," *Journal of Materials Processing Technology* 103 (2000): 155–159. Further aspects discussed include product quality

(Turnbull et al., "Buyer-supplier relations in the UK automotive industry") and parts variety (Hines, "Benchmarking Toyota's supply chain").

7. The supplier research was conducted in two phases. The first phase mapped the main processes at five major European component suppliers. The mapping workshops were complemented by 14 semi-structured interviews and 8 plant tours, including three supplier parks. In the second phase, 17 European suppliers were surveyed. For more details, see M. Holweg, The Three-Day Car Challenge, Ph.D. thesis, Cardiff Business School, 2002.

8. MRP is a set of time-phased planning techniques that uses bill of material data, inventory data, and the master production schedule to calculate requirements for materials. It makes recommendations to release replenishment orders for material. Further, because it is time-phased, it makes recommendations to reschedule open orders when due dates and need dates are not in phase. Time-phased MRP begins with the items listed on the Master Production Schedule and determines the quantity of all components and materials required to fabricate those items and the date that the components and materials are required. Time-phased MRP is accomplished by "exploding" the bill of material, adjusting for inventory quantities on hand or on order, and offsetting the net requirements by the appropriate lead times.

9. If one uses a logic similar to that put forth by S. Nakajima as Overall Equipment Effectiveness. See Nakajima's *Introduction to TPM* (Productivity Press, 1988).

10. In other words, if suppliers had to increase capacity, there would be on average 41.6% capacity available (minimum 24.6%; maximum 49.8%) if production hours were extended to the maximum of 24 hours, 7 days a week

11. J. Dyer, "Dedicated assets," *Harvard Business Review*, November-December 1994: 174–178.

12. The suppliers are co-located and deliver systems, components, and modules in sequence. Companies include Delphi, Bosal, TI Bundy, Valeo, VDO. Source: "GM do Brasil inaugurates a new industrial model," GM press release, July 20, 2000. See also R. Kisiel, "Fred and Ginger," Automotive *News*, August 3, 1998.

13. In Japan, supplier quality is generally measured in parts per million, and the best performers are several orders of magnitude better than those in our survey.

14. D. Guilford, "Storm before the calm," *Automotive News*, January 21, 2002: 57.

15. "Mayor Daley, Governor Ryan team with Ford Motor Company to bring North America's first supplier manufacturing campus to South Chicago," press release, Office of the Mayor of Chicago, September 7, 2000.

16. M. Sako and M. Warburton, Modularization and Outsourcing Project—Preliminary Report of European Research Team, International Motor Vehicle Program, 1999.

17. L. Chappell, "TNT takes over more chores for automakers," *Automotive News*, August 5, 2002.

Chapter 13

1. Source: Reuters, September 14, 2001.

2. Renault values this advantage at 1% of the selling price (S. de Saint-Seine, "Renault quits build-to-order quest," *Automotive News Europe*, January 14, 2002: 4).

3. U. Stautner, *Kundenorientierte Lagerfertigung im Automobilvertrieb* (Gabler, 2001), p. 106

4. The logistics research used process mapping, semi-structured interviews and questionnaire-based surveys. This approach proved successful on the outbound side, where two mapping workshops, four additional interviews, and a questionnaire survey of eight major UK players was conducted. The sample covers eight major logistics service providers, covering 1,537 trucks and 3.1 million annual vehicle movements in the UK for a total of 14 vehicle manufacturers. The survey was conducted in 2000, alongside the process mapping and site visits. The survey covers about 3.5 million annual vehicle movements (in 2000) in the UK and a transporter fleet of 1,537. On a European scale, the companies benchmarked account for c. 10% of the total vehicle transportation volume. For more details see M. Holweg and J. Miemczyk, "Logistics in the three-day car age," *International Journal of Physical Distribution and Logistics Management* 32 (2002), no. 10: 829–850.

5. The lack or inaccuracy of forward information provided by the vehicle manufacturer is criticized and blamed for the inability to conduct accurate forward planning. This lack of planning is often quoted as the root cause of the fact that it takes 1–2 days to build loads! Within this time period, the vehicle routing and scheduling takes least time. It is the time required for sufficient vehicles to become available to enable an efficient transporter load and then the organization of a backload that is the key to reducing the delivery time in a cost efficient way. This is particularly so since backloading is generally based on telephone calls to other logistics service providers, who co-operate at a personal, informal level. Monthly forward planning information is the most common frequency for forecast information, with 31% of logistics operations receiving weekly data; a daily forecast is only given in 19% of cases. This means that at least 50% of logistics company contracts do not give planning information on more than a monthly frequency. In terms of firm order information, only 15% of contracts give any information at all before the actual shipping notification attached to the "physical" vehicle arrives with the logistics company. This indicates both the difficulties of providing reliable shipping information and a certain lack of appreciation of logistics company requirements by the manufacturers.

Chapter 14

1. According to the Benson Ford Research Center in Dearborn, no one ever proved that Henry Ford actually said "any color as long as it's black." Contrary to common belief, at first the Model T was available in many different colors. However, in 1910 all were painted Brewster Green, a very dark green. From 1911 to 1913 all were painted blue. From 1914 to 1926 all were indeed painted black. In 1926 Ford reintroduced a range of colors, although all cars still had black fenders. There has been much speculation as to why Ford painted all its cars black for a time, the most common explanation being that black paint dried the quickest, thus increasing efficiency and decreasing variability in the production process. It has also been speculated that black was the most robust color. For more details, see A. Nevis, *Ford* (Scribner, 1954); B. McCalley, *Model T Ford* (Krause, 1994); R. Kowalke, *Standard Catalog of Ford: 1903–1998*, second edition (Krause, 1998).

2. Sport Utility Vehicles (SUV), Multi-Purpose Vehicles (MPV), and Urban Activity Vehicles (UAV).

3. Commonly also referred to as "cross-overs," as they blur the boundaries between segments.

4. UK-built vehicles: Toyota Corolla, Avensis (previously Carina); Nissan Micra, Almera, and Primera (previously Bluebird); Honda Civic, Accord, and CRV (from mid 2000). Production of the Toyota Yaris in France started in 2001.

5. The reason is that not one, but several Pareto relations underlie volume distribution. We found substantial variations for derivatives (powertrain and body styles), option combinations (front fog lamps, spoiler kit, etc.), and the paint and trim combinations (green exterior, beige interior, etc.). This variation is a fundamental part of the strategy to hold high-volume "runner" specifications in a central finished goods inventory and supply those from stock.

6. The Austin 1100 was produced under other brands in the UK: Morris, MG, Riley, Vanden Plas, and Wolseley. These variants added more complexity to the product range, so we did not include them. The Austin 1100's successor, the Allegro, was offered in the UK as a Vanden Plas model, although this was, strictly speaking, a derivative rather than a model.

7. D. Guildford, "Lutz's view of cladding," *Automotive News*, March 25, 2002: 4.

8. According to Jim Bolte (General Manager of Information Systems Toyota Motor Manufacturing North America Inc.), Toyota North America has been working on reducing complex combinations of options since 1998 by eliminating unnecessary restrictions and providing more last-minute change opportunities. The result, according to Bolte, is a significant increase in flexibility. (Bolte spoke at the August 2001 Management Briefing Seminars in Traverse City.)

9. T. Koblinski, at Management Briefing Seminars Meeting, Traverse City, August 2000.

10. D. Winter and D. Zoia, "Rethinking platform engineering," *Ward's Auto World*, March 1, 2001.

11. C. Ghosn, "Nissan Revival Plan" (Nissan, Tokyo, October 18, 1999), slide 30.

12. "BMW introduces new distribution and production system—quantum leap in time-to-delivery and in flexibility for order changes" and "Der Karosserie-Rohbau: Weniger Varianten erhöhen die Prozesssicherheit," BMW press releases, Munich, June 2000.

13. *Kanban*, the Japanese word for 'sign', refers to a material control system that is crucial to just-in-time production. Taiichi Ohno, its originator, was actually inspired by the supermarkets in the US (Japan had none at that time), and he converted this principle into the *kanban* material control, which uses supermarket storage areas, and signs/cards to trigger replenishment.

14. Valeo, for example, estimates that a modularity project with a vehicle manufacturer has a 10–12-year return. Source: presentation by François Fourcade, IMVP researchers' meeting, Philadelphia, April 2003.

15. E. Chew, "Intier Automotive to develop complete BMW Interiors," *Automotive News*, September 30, 2002.

16. Some manufacturers believe outsourcing will simplify their operations and are even outsourcing some or all of their body shop or paint shop maintenance. In the US, 13% of plants outsource at least some paint shop maintenance. In Japan the percentage is 25, in Europe it is 57, and for new entrants it is 30. In Japan, we found 1 plant outsourcing some body shop maintenance, but 30% of new entrant plants, outsourced some or all of their

body shop maintenance, and in Europe, the percentage was 43. Almost all plants in North American and in new entrant countries had representatives of chemical suppliers on-site. In Europe, a third of plants had such representatives, but virtually none of the Japanese.

17. M. Sako and M. Warburton, Modularization and Outsourcing Project—Preliminary Report of European Research Team, International Motor Vehicle Program, 1999.

18. J. Treece, "Toyota joins march toward modules," *Automotive News*, February 18, 2002: 40.

19. J. Batchelor, "Engineering a vehicle for world-class logistics," in *Human Performance in Planning and Scheduling*, ed. B. MacCarthy and J. Wilson (Taylor and Francis, 2001); D. Kehoe, N. Boughton, and H. Sharifi, "Demand network alignment," UK Symposium on Supply Chain Alignment, Liverpool, July 2001.

20. Unless vehicle manufacturers take the deliberate step to drastically limit external variety to several thousand specifications only. We have observed cases, where very low external variety, paired with a distribution center strategy, allowed 75% of all sales to be sourced from the distribution centers.

Chapter 15

1. G. Lapidus et al., Ford Motor Company, Equity Research Report, Goldman Sachs, New York, December 2001.

2. Many of the Japanese companies spent significantly less. Toyota and Honda spent $528 and $531 respectively. Source: P. Brown, "Incentive wars," *Automotive News*, January 20, 2002.

3. See, e.g., P. Wells and P. Nieuwenhuis, "Why big business should think small," *Automotive World*, July-August 2000: 32–38.

4. This section draws on F. Pil and M. Holweg, "Exploring scale," *Sloan Management Review* 44 (2003), no. 2: 33–40. Please see the article for complete argumentation and a broader range of examples of the ways small scale enhances competitive advantage.

5. Including Audi and Volkswagen convertibles, Mercedes CLK convertibles and coupes, and major components of the Renault Megane, the Jaguar XK8, and the Mercedes SLK.

6. S. Duermeier, Teilzeitarbeit im Kontext Europäischer Kollektivvereinbarungen, European Trade Union Institute, 1999. See also G. Wilke, *Die Zukunft unserer Arbeit* (Campus, 1999): 136.

7. Lately mini-mills have also been expanding into the segments occupied by traditional steel makers. See Pil and Holweg, "Exploring scale."

8. Nor does figure 15.2 show the efforts some airlines make to dispose of unsold seats by tapping more price-sensitive consumers via Internet discounters.

9. P. Rose, "British Airways: Revenue management," presentation at ICDP Forum, St. Paul de Vence, France, October 1999.

10. When Giancarlo Boschetti took charge of Fiat Auto in December 2001, he said that one of the first things Fiat had to do was stop selling vehicles at excessively low prices. Source: "Fiat chief charts a course for calm waters," *Automotive News*, November 18, 2002: 18.

11. G. Williams, "Leaning the new car supply system," in *Case Studies in the Changing Face of Car Distribution*, ed. G. Williams et al. (International Car Distribution Programme, 1998); H. Shioji, "The order-entry system in Japan," International Symposium on Logistics, Morioka, Japan, July 2000. Our recent interviews suggest the Toyota figure may be closer to 50%.

12. Source: Kraftfahrtbundesamt, Flensburg, Germany, 2003.

13. Pre-registration, no longer legal in the UK though still common, still exists in Germany under the name *Tageszulassungen*.

14. In 2002, for example, almost one out of four new cars was registered by manufacturers directly, or by their dealers in Germany. Source: Kraftfahrtbundesamt, Flensburg, Germany, 2003.

Conclusion

1. When we contacted the senior curator at Oberlin College, who specializes in Cage's work, she could not guide us to a source, although she recognized the quote as always attributed to him.

2. P. Drucker, *The Concept of the Corporation* (John Day, 1946).

3. According to the Department of Labor Statistics, the industry now directly employs 675,000 people. In Japan, 10 percent of workers are directly or indirectly employed by the sector, and similar data can be found for Germany and other Western countries. See Japan Automobile Manufacturers Association, "The Motor Industry of Japan—2001"; Bundesministerium für Verkehr (Berlin), "Verkehr in Zahlen 2001."

4. Granted, we have eliminated the need for a separate chassis for most passenger cars, although most SUVs are still built on chassis—much like the Model T.

5. Larry Yost, speech at Management Briefing Seminars, Traverse City, August 2001.

6. John Devine, speech at Management Briefing Seminars, Traverse City, August 2001.

7. Gary Cowger, "Driving in the new manufacturing model," Management Briefing Seminars, Traverse City, August 2001.

8. This is true even for companies that have mastered the traditional forms of lean production. For example, Fujio Cho, Toyota's president, recently argued that "the time had come to apply the company's mastery of 'just-in-time' manufacturing to distribution and marketing." See F. Andrews, "Can car-makers emulate Dell?" *New York Times*, January 25, 2000.

Index